The Sanctuary at Bath in the Roman Empire

The Roman sanctuary at Bath has long been used in scholarship as an example *par excellence* of religious and artistic syncretisms in Roman Britain. With its monumental temple, baths, and hot springs, its status as one of the most significant Roman sites in the province is unquestioned. But our academic narratives about Roman Bath are also rooted in the narratives of our more recent past. This book begins by exploring how Georgian and Victorian antiquaries developed our modern story of a healing sanctuary at Roman Bath. It shows that a curative function for the sanctuary is in fact unsupported by the archaeological evidence. It then re-tells the story of Roman Bath by focusing on three interlinked aspects: the entanglement of the sanctuary with Roman imperialism, the role of the hot springs in the lives of worshipers, and Bath's place within the wider world of the western Roman Empire.

ELERI H. COUSINS is a Lecturer in Roman History at Lancaster University. She works on religion and society in the Roman provinces.

The Sanctuary at Bath in the Roman Empire

ELERI H. COUSINS

Lancaster University

CAMBRIDGE
UNIVERSITY PRESS

CAMBRIDGE
UNIVERSITY PRESS

University Printing House, Cambridge CB2 8BS, United Kingdom

One Liberty Plaza, 20th Floor, New York, NY 10006, USA

477 Williamstown Road, Port Melbourne, VIC 3207, Australia

314–321, 3rd Floor, Plot 3, Splendor Forum, Jasola District Centre, New Delhi – 110025, India

79 Anson Road, #06–04/06, Singapore 079906

Cambridge University Press is part of the University of Cambridge.

It furthers the University's mission by disseminating knowledge in the pursuit of education, learning, and research at the highest international levels of excellence.

www.cambridge.org
Information on this title: www.cambridge.org/9781108493192
DOI: 10.1017/9781108694735

© Faculty of Classics, University of Cambridge 2020

First published 2020

Printed in the United Kingdom by TJ International Ltd. Padstow Cornwall

A catalogue record for this publication is available from the British Library.

ISBN 978-1-108-49319-2 Hardback

Contents

Figures

Acknowledgements

This book has its genesis in my doctoral thesis for the Faculty of Classics at Cambridge, and my thanks go first and foremost to my supervisor, Martin Millett, for his unstinting support before and after my PhD. Second only to Martin stands Caroline Vout, whose clear-sighted and incisive guidance during my doctorate never failed to make me a better scholar. My PhD research was funded by an Arts and Humanities Research Council studentship, and by additional support from the Faculty of Classics and St John's College, Cambridge, and in these days of ever-increasing financial belt-tightening, I am ever more grateful for that. My examiners, Henry Hurst and Ian Haynes, both gave me invaluable advice on the transformation from thesis to book. Ian in particular helped me to find the 'story' hidden (deep) within the thesis, and I am tremendously grateful to him for that, and for his general academic kindness and generosity over the past three years.

Many different people and institutions have helped with the research that went into this book. My thanks go especially to the Roman Baths Museum, and to Susan Fox and Zofia Matyjaszkiewicz in particular, for their support of my research on the site both during my PhD and afterwards. In addition to their academic support, Susan and Zofia also went above and beyond the call of duty by helping to chase spiders away from me while I took photographs on the floor of the temple precinct. I am also particularly grateful to the Bath Central Library and to Anne Buchanan, the Local Studies Librarian at Bath, for all they did to make my research into the Irvine Archive so enjoyable and productive, and to the National Museums Scotland for allowing me to photograph Irvine's papers. At various points during my PhD and afterwards, Barry Cunliffe, Philippa Walton, and Lindsay Allason-Jones have patiently answered my questions and given me information from unpublished research. Finally, I am also extremely grateful to all the museums, authors, and publishers who have given me their kind permission to reproduce photographs and plans.

Several people have generously given over both their time and intellectual energy to reading and critiquing part or all of the manuscript in its various stages. I particularly want to thank here Stephen Harrison, Dawn Hollis,

Kelsey Jackson Williams, Myles Lavan, Rebecca Usherwood, Philippa Walton, and George Watson. The book is so much better for their reading of it, though I apologize to them for the inevitable weaknesses it still contains.

After leaving Cambridge, I found an extraordinarily supportive, if temporary, home in the School of Classics at the University of St Andrews. That this book exists at all is in large part thanks to my wonderful colleagues there, and to the remarkable research environment which they have created on the beautiful windswept coast of Fife. I will be forever grateful to associate it with the time I spent among them.

Finally, and forever, my thanks to George and my family, for everything.

Abbreviations

AE	*Année Epigraphique*
Bossert	Bossert, M. (1998). *Die figürlichen Reliefs von Aventicum.* *CSIR Schweiz I.1.* Cahiers d'archéologie romande 69. Lausanne: Association Pro Aventico.
CIL	*Corpus Inscriptionum Latinarum*
CSIR	*Corpus Signorum Imperii Romani* for Britain
Espérandieu	*Recueil Général des Bas-reliefs, Statues et Bustes de la Gaule Romaine.*
ICLW	Fishwick, D. (1987–2005). *The Imperial Cult in the Latin West: Studies in the Ruler Cult of the Western Provinces of the Roman Empire, Volumes 1–4.* Brill: Leiden.
IGRR	*Inscriptiones Graecae ad Res Romanas Pertinentes*
JTI	James Thomas Irvine
LIMC	*Lexicon Iconographicum Mythologiae Classicae*
RIB	*Roman Inscriptions of Britain*
RIG	*Recueil des Inscriptions Gauloises*
Tab. Sulis	*Tabellae Sulis*
Tab. Vindol.	*Tabulae Vindolandenses*

1 | Discovering Roman Bath

In *A Description of Bath* in 1765, the noted Georgian architect John Wood the Elder related the discovery of the healing powers of the Bath waters by the legendary king Bladud.[1] Bladud, so the story goes, was the only son of King Lud Hudibras, and ninth in descent from the Trojan exile Brute. While still a young man, Bladud had the misfortune of contracting leprosy and was consequently exiled from his father's court. Taking up swine-herding, he eventually found his way, with pigs in tow, to the Avon valley and the place where the hot springs bubbled up from the ground. As Bladud watched his pigs wallow in the mud, he noticed their scabrous skin begin to heal and become smooth. So he tried the waters for himself and to his joy and astonishment they rid him of his leprosy. He returned triumphantly to his father's court and, when he himself at last became king, he established a great city and baths at the springs.

The story of Bladud and his pigs is found in print, in one version or another, from 1672 onwards, and it almost certainly records a local oral tradition which goes back even further.[2] Bladud, minus his pigs, is recorded as the founder of Bath by Geoffrey of Monmouth,[3] who was writing in the first third of the twelfth century, and the hot springs are recorded as a place of healing in the *Gesta Stephani* around the same date. Without a doubt, then, the hot springs of Bath were used for healing by the early Middle Ages, and by the seventeenth century at the latest the curative use of the water had been given an ancient pedigree which was only reinforced by the discoveries of Roman antiquities in the town in the eighteenth and nineteenth centuries. Bladud became supplemented by the Romans, legend – apparently – with hard archaeological fact.

Since that time, the remains of Aquae Sulis (Roman Bath), and in particular the sanctuary to Sulis Minerva at the heart of the site, have been important not only to the town's own heritage and sense of historical identity, but also to archaeological scholarship's understanding of the role of religion in the province of Roman Britain. Over time, however, certain

---

[1] Wood 1765: 71–5.   [2] Clark 1994: 45ff.   [3] Monmouth II.30.

aspects of the narrative of Roman Bath – and in particular the on-going identification of the sanctuary as a curative one – have become too entrenched and unquestioned, especially in light of the extensive excavation in the city in the second half of the twentieth century, which has greatly expanded our understanding of the central monumentalized zone of the site. In this book, then, I seek to re-evaluate the totality of our evidence from Roman Bath – archaeological, epigraphic, and artistic – with the goal of better understanding the complex socio-religious role played by the sanctuary, and in particular its relationship with wider trends in Britain, Gaul, and Germany. This thematic re-evaluation forms the core of this book: Chapter 3 sets the stage by exploring the architectural environment of the Roman-period sanctuary, Chapter 4 then examines how Aquae Sulis was used in the construction of Roman imperialism, and Chapter 5 focuses on the ritual role of the thermal water at the heart of the sanctuary. In Chapter 6, I discuss ways of understanding Aquae Sulis as both distinct from, and related to, the wider world of the western Roman empire. These chapters as a whole present a locally grounded yet geographically and conceptually contextualized narrative for the sanctuary's position and purpose. Before this re-contextualization can begin, however, it is equally important to excavate our current understanding of Aquae Sulis: an understanding which is ultimately rooted in interpretations of the site going back to the antiquarian period. Eighteenth and nineteenth century perceptions of the Roman town and sanctuary were, in their own turn, moulded both by the intellectual culture of the day and by antiquaries' experiences of their own Georgian and Victorian Bath. In this chapter, therefore, I focus on the men (and they were all men) who developed the story of Aquae Sulis from the eighteenth century onwards, and on how the story they developed was the product of their intellectual and social environments, before turning in Chapter 2 to what the implications of this are for those of us trying to understand the site today.

Discovering Bath in the Antiquarian Period

The first major Roman antiquities in Bath started to come to light in the late eighteenth century, a time when antiquarian culture in England was perhaps at its strongest. Consequently, reactions to these finds need to be read in the context of that culture, not least because many of the men responding to these early finds were among the principal antiquarian figures of the day. The attitudes of the antiquaries towards the past were bound up in their perception of, and desires for, their present.[4] English antiquarianism in the eighteenth century focused heavily on county histories, reflecting the importance of history and genealogy in the construction of identity in the period, particularly for the landed country elite.[5] Antiquaries' championing of the value of studying British antiquities was linked to the growth of both national and local identities in the period,[6] while their methodological outlook was perhaps more closely intertwined with natural history than with history.[7] Antiquaries were linked to each other first and foremost through networks of correspondence which served as a vital mechanism for both knowledge-exchange and debate. As the eighteenth and nineteenth centuries progressed, the nascent national and regional antiquarian societies were added to these informal networks. At the national level, the most socially prominent was the Society of Antiquaries, founded in 1707. The Society's success, however, at fostering both discourse and the growth of a vibrant antiquarian community was mixed.[8] Its membership was notably more socially exclusive than the Royal Society, often seemingly prioritizing social rank over antiquarian knowledge.[9] Meanwhile, by the mid nineteenth century, its journal *Archaeologia* was viewed as an intellectual backwater. Far more important for nineteenth century antiquarian life at the national level were the British Archaeological Association and the Archaeological Institute (both founded in 1845 after the splitting in two of the 1843 Archaeological Association), not so much because they succeeded in establishing a nationwide network of scholars (more than half the membership of each stemmed from London and the south-east),[10] but because they served as an impetus and encouragement for the growth of county- and regional-level societies.[11] It was these societies which would do the most to push forward the study of British antiquities in the nineteenth century, through locally driven research agendas which should be seen as the intellectual successors to early antiquarianism's passion for place-specific knowledge and the primacy of the county history.

The decade following the foundation of the Archaeological Association in 1843, therefore, can to some degree be seen as the transition point between one period and the next, from the hey-day of the antiquaries to the mixed antiquarian-archaeological culture of the second half of the nineteenth

---

[4] Jackson Williams 2017: 84–6.　　[5] Sweet 2004: 36–42.　　[6] Sweet 2004: 36.

[7] Hanson 2009: 8–13; Sweet 2004: 8ff, although see Herklotz 2007 for the opposing argument that antiquarianism should be understood as linked most closely with philology.

[8] Sweet 2004: 102ff.　　[9] Sweet 2004: 106–7.　　[10] Levine 1986: 50, fig. 1.　　[11] Levine 1986: 49.

century. This periodization holds true not only for the national level, but also for the intellectual environment at Bath itself. The early 1860s saw the first serious attempts at archaeological and stratigraphic recording in the city, and a generational shift in the men writing about Aquae Sulis occurs around the same time. In what follows, I use two 'biographies', the first of an object and the second of a man, to explore the worlds of these two eras.

The object is, inevitably, the Bath Gorgon, the central image of the pediment of the temple of Sulis Minerva and the quintessential symbol of Roman Bath, seen here through the eyes of four writers in particular: H. C. Englefield, Thomas Pownall, Richard Warner, and George Scharf. The ways these men wrote about the Gorgon, and the discourse surrounding its discovery, provide a particularly fruitful way into how the outlook of the antiquaries writing on Bath could reflect both local concerns and the broader intellectual community of the time. The man is J. T. Irvine, a Scottish architect active in the antiquarian networks of Bath from the 1860s onwards, whose manuscripts and correspondence paint a vivid picture of both the intellectual and interpersonal dynamics of those networks in the second half of the nineteenth century.

Writing the Gorgon

The Gorgon from the pediment of the temple of Sulis Minerva was discovered in 1790 during the construction of the new Pump Room at the centre of Bath, east of Stall Street. It emerged from the ground alongside around fifty or sixty other pieces of architectural stonework, including other portions of the pediment, as well as fragments of the so-called Façade of the Four Seasons.[12] This substantial amount of stonework represented by far the most significant discovery up to that period relating to the Roman town, and quickly drew attention from the wider antiquarian community. While it seems from both Englefield and Pownall's accounts that news of the discoveries spread quickly beyond Bath, and that antiquaries soon sought to visit the town to see the stones for themselves in the months after their emergence from the ground, the first published account was a letter by Englefield which was read to the Society of Antiquaries on 3 March 1791, and printed in *Archaeologia* the following year.[13]

Englefield, the seventh baronet of that name, had been elected to the Royal Society in 1778 and the Society of Antiquaries in 1779; he joined the

---

[12] Cunliffe 1969: 39.   [13] Englefield 1792.

Society of Dilettanti in 1781 and subsequently became its secretary from 1808 until his death in 1822.[14] In addition to his antiquarian interests, he also belonged to the Linnaean Society, the Geological Society, and the Astronomical Society, and made several contributions to the development of portable scientific instruments.[15] Notwithstanding his Catholicism, Englefield's social status, as well as his active participation in both antiquarian and scientific societies, is a fairly common profile for antiquaries at this period. The famed botanist Sir Joseph Banks, for example, was both president of the Royal Society and an increasingly influential member of the Society of Antiquaries in the later decades of the eighteenth century.[16]

Englefield begins his report with a brief description of the circumstances of the stonework's discovery, before moving on to an attempt to reconstruct the elevation of the temple based partly on Vitruvian principles, and partly on what Englefield himself judged to be 'most graceful'.[17] He then turns to the pediment, and in particular to the central head, mixing throughout straightforward description with aesthetic judgment, with particular focus on the relative 'gracefulness' or 'coarseness' of the workmanship.

Both the content and the mode of publication of Englefield's account are typical of antiquarian knowledge-production and knowledge-exchange at the time. A letter read out to the Society, usually recounting personal investigation of the finds, was becoming the standard format for the dissemination and discussion of new discoveries. Englefield's description of the stonework, along with his attempts at reconstructing the elevation of the temple in particular, is the result of personal autopsy during a three-day journey he himself made to Bath in order to examine the finds after their discovery.[18] There it would appear he was in at least some degree of contact with Thomas Baldwin, the City Architect under whose aegis the Pump Room was being expanded, and thus under whose authority the stonework had been excavated, demonstrating the importance of social connections in access to antiquarian materials.[19] Baldwin, according to Englefield, seemingly had intended to publish the discoveries himself,[20] but this account never materialized – perhaps because in 1792 he was dismissed from his post as city architect for embezzlement, and swiftly sank into bankruptcy.[21] The ex officio involvement in the investigation of Roman

---

[14] Nurse 2004.   [15] Nurse 2004.   [16] Sweet 2004: 103–4.   [17] Englefield 1792: 323.
[18] Englefield 1792: 333.   [19] Englefield 1792: 333.   [20] Englefield 1792: 333.
[21] For Baldwin's career and downfall, see Root 1994.

Bath by architects employed by the city for new building projects is a recurring motif in the site's history from this point on.

The classical prejudices implied by Englefield's membership in the Society of Dilettanti also seem to be on display in his less-than-enthusiastic aesthetic response to this piece of provincial art. While the Gorgon would eventually be considered one of the most powerful pieces of Roman art from the Western provinces, the assessment of its artistic merit in this, its first published outing, is muted to say the least: Englefield declared that 'The execution of the whole [pediment] is very indifferent; but the head is as bad as possible, flat, hard, and without taste or expression'.[22] For his sketch of the head and its roundel, he claims faithful accuracy, 'except [for] the head in the centre, into the eyes of which, I fear, I have put a degree of expression which the original wants'. Indeed, the sketch seems to express an irresistible desire on Englefield's part to classicize and three-dimensionalize the face, and bears little resemblance to the original (Figure 1.1); whether it is in fact more expressive is also perhaps debatable.

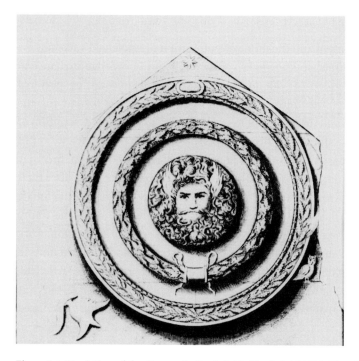

Figure 1.1: Depiction of the Gorgon by Englefield. (Englefield 1792, Plate XXXII.)

---

[22] Englefield 1792: 333.

As for the face's identity – a debate that in some respects continues to this day – Englefield declared:

> The ornament itself admits of many conjectures. Some have thought it the Aegis of Minerva, but the Gorgon's head in that field is I believe invariably female. A gentleman whose knowledge in antiquity is unrivalled, called it a patera with the head of the Sun in the centre; and informed me, that on many medals of temples a large patera fills the tympanum. The head of the Sun, or rather of the great creating and destroying power, is often found with the serpents and wings, and the beard.[23]

I shall have considerably more to say about the identity and consequent symbolic weight of the Gorgon (and I do take it to be such) in Chapter 4; here I am concerned only with the processes by and benchmarks against which the figure was identified in this early period. The general resistance, on account of his maleness, to calling him a Gorgon in this period, and the search for other classical parallels, is perhaps in some way like a lingering echo of the seventeenth century 'Battle of the Books' between the Ancients and the Moderns, centring as it does on a philosophy which seems highly invested in making interpretations of material antiquities align with the written classical canon – this in spite of a general tendency on the part of antiquaries to align with the Moderns in their basic 'assumption that the collection of antiquities could yield up new truths'.[24] At the same time, we can see in Englefield's brief account the influence of other types of material culture on the interpretation: the (unfortunately un-identified) 'gentleman whose knowledge in antiquity is unrivalled' whom Englefield cites is relying primarily on numismatic parallels in drawing his conclusions, which reflects the long-standing importance of coins as primary source material for antiquaries.[25] The references to other scholars, and in particular the unnamed gentleman, meanwhile, encapsulate the ad hoc networks of discussion and debate which defined scholarly production in the period; this is a world in which personal communication, rather than published articles, is still the primary means of knowledge transfer, even as the Society's published transactions in *Archaeologia* began to herald the shift to the now-familiar format of the academic journal.

Similar processes are at play in Governor Thomas Pownall's discussion of the head published a few years later, in 1795. Pownall had also seen the Stall Street sculpture cache soon after its discovery, and indeed had sent a paper on the Gorgon, along with some sketches, which was read to the Society of

---

[23] Englefied 1792: 332.   [24] Sweet 2004: 3.   [25] Crawford *et al.* 1990.

Antiquaries on 1 February 1791, a month before Englefield's paper.[26] He was much more scrupulous, however, concerning Baldwin's right to first publication than Englefield, for, as he explains in the printed version, his paper was read 'under express stipulation (to avoid interfering with Mr. Baldwin's intention of publishing) that it should not be copied in their minutes or published in their Archaeologia'.[27] Pownall continues:

I have withheld this now four years, in hopes that Mr. Baldwin would have come forward with the publication of the engravings. During this period I have applied repeatedly, and by various friends and some relations of this gentleman, requesting that he would either make his publication, or return to me this paper; but that, if from any unfortunate circumstances he was neither in a situation or inclination to do this, I would undertake the work, and would annex descriptions to the engravings, in a way that every merit and every profit, if any such accrued, should be his ... I should not, however, now (as I really meant this paper for Mr. Baldwin's use) have published it, would he have published; and he was previously applied to, before I gave it to the Printer, but neither any answer or the paper has been returned. I have therefore come to a resolution to print that copy of it which was read before the Society of Antiquaries, and I annex to it an engraving of the symbolic ornament, drawn by a scale of half an inch to a foot, on an exact measurement of the parts, taken by myself. I recommend it to any gentleman who is curious in matters of antiquity, and who has an opportunity by being at Bath, to compare this, and every other drawing in this plate, with the originals, before he gives any decided credit to, or forms his opinion on them.[28]

It is hard to tell whether Pownall was truly unacquainted with Baldwin's financial and legal difficulties, which surely were at the root of Baldwin's protracted silence, or whether he was merely being discreet, although the reference to hypothetical 'unfortunate circumstances' perhaps indicates the latter. Meanwhile, Pownall's insistence that other scholars not take his sketches for granted contrasts greatly with the rather self-satisfied claims for accuracy present in Englefield – despite Pownall's etching being notably more similar to the original (Fig. 1.2)! Indeed, Pownall later on in the text rather brutally lays out the inaccuracies of Englefield's sketch point by point.[29] However, this championing of autopsy and accuracy in recording is

---

[26] Pownall 1795: v.   [27] Pownall 1795: v.   [28] Pownall 1795: v–vi.

[29] Pownall 1795: 19–20. ('Sir Henry Englefield, who knows my respect for him and for his literary and scientific abilities, will, I am sure, excuse the liberty I take; he must be sensible that nothing could induce me to make these remarks, but my opinion that, when an object of antiquity is to be represented and exhibited to the public, it is not an elegant picture, but a plain decided portrait that must give it ... ')

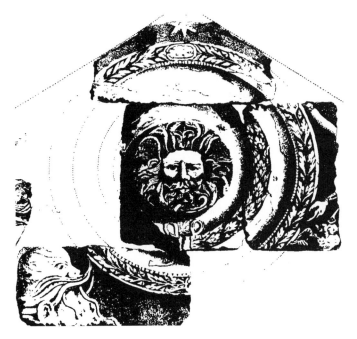

Figure 1.2: Depiction of the Gorgon by Pownall. (Pownall 1795, Plate I.)

to be found consistently in Pownall's work more broadly.[30] Meanwhile, his interpretation of the Gorgon (discussed at greater length below), which he saw as the 'Cherubic Emblem of Sol',[31] although convoluted in the extreme, nonetheless thoroughly reflects Pownall's position as one of the more philosophically and methodologically complex antiquaries of the period.

Pownall, born in 1722 to a family of modest landed means in Lincolnshire, is best known for his time in colonial government in America, beginning in 1753 as private secretary to the governor of New York and culminating as governor of Massachusetts from 1757 to 1759. After his return from the colonies, he entered parliament, but never succeeded in rising very far through the political ranks at home.[32] Pownall's antiquarian writings, particularly his receptiveness to using anthropological accounts of the 'primitive societies' of his own day to elucidate the past, were no doubt to some degree influenced by his American experiences.[33] From his work, two key characteristics of his outlook stand out: first, that human societies are stadial in their development, with civilizations progressing through comparable stages at different points in their history. Following on from this, he believed that by building a model of particular societies through the

[30] Orme 1974: 117.   [31] Pownall 1795: 9.   [32] Gould 2004.   [33] Sweet 2004: 23.

use both of their extant remains and of comparative evidence, even highly fragmentary antiquities could be explained and analysed.[34] As Rosemary Sweet puts it: 'Just as an artist who was well acquainted with architecture could identify any building from a fragment, a "philosophic" antiquary who had studied the different systems of society would be able to tell precisely what kind of society any piece of antiquity belonged to.'[35]

Understanding this philosophical stance of Pownall's concerning the reconstruction of the past is key to contextualizing his analysis of the pediment head from Bath. Like Englefield, Pownall dismissed the possibility of a Gorgon, declaring: 'Whoever examines this symbolic ornament with deliberate and distinct ideas, formed on the fact, will discover that this head is no head of Medusa.'[36] Using a remarkable amalgamation of ancient sources ranging from Ovid to the Chaldean Oracles and the Bible, he endeavoured to prove that the head was instead the Sun crowned by 'the *Serpentine or Cherubic Diadem*, which the Egyptians, Rhodians, and some other nations in the East, placed upon the head of the divine symbol of their God'.[37] The following representative extract gives a flavour of his discussion:

Thus far then we are got in our investigation of the ideas of ancient theology, that the circle or sphere, with wings annexed to it, was the emblematic representation of the sun, when considered as the visible corporeal manifestation of the invisible immaterial Cause. This emblem represented the Universal Intelligible in its Deity whilst the serpent became the emblem or personified *local presence of the numen*. From the combination of these ideas, of the universal circumscribing circle or sphere, of the wings annexed as expressive of intellectual motion, and of the Sar-Oub, or Sar-Oph, the Basilise, as the personified *local presence* of the *numen*, the Egyptians, and after them the Rhodians, formed the notion of the *cherubic or seraphic diadem* which they placed on the head of their gods; and finally, the *caput pinnatum*, as Macrobius expresses it, crowned with this sacred serpentine diadem, became the cherubic symbol of the deity. (Italics Pownall's.)[38]

While the argument today – and, as we shall see shortly, even to some of his contemporaries – seems baffling, Pownall's extensive use of sources from elsewhere in Greco-Roman antiquity illustrates his commitment to the belief that any antiquity was capable of detailed, evidence-based (as he saw

[34] Orme 1974: 122–3; Sweet 2004: 23–4.   [35] Sweet 2004: 24.   [36] Pownall 1795: 2.
[37] Pownall 1795: 3.
[38] Pownall 1795: 7. It is perhaps worth noting here that one of Pownall's contemporaries described his writing as capable of producing a 'most excruciating head-ach', and that John Adams saw fit to publish a *translation* (into plain English) of one of Pownall's pamphlets on the War of Independence (Gould 2004).

it) exposition, as well as his faith in the value of comparative material: for, in his view, the connection between the Sun and serpents in particular was based on 'ideas uniform and almost universal in different parts of the world, although such parts never had any communication of opinions with each other'.[39] In this particular case, however, his methods drew him into dubious waters, as one of his contemporaries, Richard Warner, soon noticed.

Warner, born in 1763 in Middlesex, was a clergyman who came to Bath in 1794 to take up the curacy of All Saints Church, before moving the following year to be curate at St James's, Bath, where he stayed until 1817.[40] As such, he is representative of the importance of the clergy in eighteenth century antiquarianism, particularly outside of urban centres.[41] His antiquarian activities and publications predated his arrival in Bath, but he soon took an active interest in the town's history and antiquities, publishing *Illustrations of the Roman Antiquities at Bath* in 1797, and a *History of Bath* in 1801.

Warner's antiquarian writings on the whole are rather derivative and shallow; however, he is of interest here because, as an inhabitant of Bath, he is the first major local voice to write on the pediment head, and he is the first to espouse in print the view that it is a Gorgon. Furthermore, in so doing he necessarily confronts Pownall, and his approach to his critique of Pownall's theory is a remarkable illustration of the ways in which antiquarian discourse was embedded in the social class structure of the day. The bulk of Warner's discussion of the Gorgon consists of a point-by-point rebuttal of Pownall, concluding, first, that both the ancient literary and iconographic evidence did indeed support the identification of the head as a Gorgon, and second, crucially, that the temple was a temple to Minerva, not to Sol, as Pownall had argued. Warner's own discussion is by no means perfect: for instance, he misreads the outer oak wreath of the pediment as an olive wreath (mistaking the acorns for olives), and his explanation for the 'beard and whiskers' rather smacks of special pleading:

That she [Medusa] is ever represented indeed with a beard or whiskers, I do not find. But these appendages may, I think, be very well accounted for, by taking into consideration that as the sculpture was intended for an elevation of thirty or forty feet, the architect might have added them (improperly enough) for the purposes of giving more character to the countenance, and conveying into it that *masculine ferocity*, which the poets attributed to it. (Italics Warner's.)[42]

---

[39] Pownall 1795: 5.   [40] Hicks 2004.

[41] Sweet 2004: 49 reports that from 1770 to 1796 one third of the papers in *Archaeologia* were written by clergymen. For their role more broadly see Sweet 2004: 49–56.

[42] Warner 1797: 80.

Even so, his demolishment of Pownall is comprehensive. But while to some degree the antiquarian community enabled the blurring of conventional social boundaries, facilitating correspondence between men who, without their shared interest in antiquities, would never have come into sustained contact,[43] Warner was nevertheless clearly aware that he was a humble curate critiquing a former colonial governor and Member of Parliament, and felt the need to open his criticism with an extensive apology:

> It is with considerable diffidence that I enter on the consideration of this piece of antique masonry; being so unfortunate as to differ in opinion respecting it, with a gentleman whose deep erudition and intimate acquaintance with antiquarian subjects, render him so much better than myself, for the investigation, and illustration of whatever is doubtful or obscure in that line of research. But as no Hypothesis, however happy it may be, can amount to absolute demonstration; further conjectures on the subject, not withstanding the ingenious remarks of Governor Pownal [sic], are by no means precluded; and that liberality of sentiment which usually accompanies intellectual excellence, will, I trust, require no apology, when I offer such as have arisen in my mind after an attentive consideration of this curious remain of antiquity.[44]

The context of Warner's discussion of the Gorgon is also affected by his position as a local man. Unlike Englefield's and Pownall's, whose papers were focused only on a discussion of the stones found in 1790, Warner's Gorgon is embedded into the broader history of Roman Bath as Warner understood it. His *Illustrations* is dedicated to the 'Right worshipful the Mayor, Aldermen, and Chief Citizens of Bath', and opens with a lengthy (twenty-five pages) if occasionally highly fanciful introduction to the city in Roman times, before moving on to discuss in turn the individual inscriptions and reliefs which had so far come to light. The '*Aquae Solis*' [sic][45] that Warner describes is a town characterized by luxurious bathing for both health and pleasure, i.e. a town much like that of his own day:

> The new colony being thus furnished with magnificent baths, which were found to be not only pleasurable but (from the quality of their springs) extremely healthy also to those who used them, soon became a place of resort. The Roman enervated by luxury, or worn out with toil, sought strength and renovation in those very streams which give health and energy to the disabled of the present day; and our British ancestors themselves, quitting, by degrees, the wild recesses of the neighbouring forests, and the rudenesses of savage life, would at length be brought to admire the elegancies, and participate in the delights of Aquae Solis.[46]

---

[43] Sweet 2004: 60–1.   [44] Warner 1797: 73.

[45] Even into the twentieth century there was debate over whether the correct name for the town was Aquae Solis or Aquae Sulis; this was part of the justification for Pownall's interpretation of the temple as dedicated to Sol.

[46] Warner 1797: xi.

Warner's elucidation of the individual antiquities, therefore, is part of a broader attempt to connect the present day with the past, creating not only a sympathy of motivation between the Georgians who 'took the waters' and the Romans who did likewise, but also weaving the Romans into an origin story for the beginnings of a British civilization which Warner and his own contemporaries would inherit. The dedication of the book to the town worthies is a further indication that Warner's discussion of 'Aquae Solis' is primarily rooted in the construction of local identity.

The final response to the Gorgon that I wish to examine here takes us forward in time, to 1855, and back to the halls of the Society of Antiquaries in London. There, on 8 February, George Scharf read a paper inspired by a visit he had taken to Bath the previous autumn, during which he had been exposed, seemingly for the first time, to the sculpture from the pediment.

Scharf (1820–95) was an artist who by the 1850s was known for his illustrations of antiquities; he had participated in two antiquarian expeditions to the Near East, and had been elected to the Society of Antiquaries in 1852.[47] In addition to antiquities, he also made lithographs, both original and of the works of others, of scientific subjects, including reconstructions of prehistoric dinosaur scenes.

Scharf's background as an artist and illustrator is representative of yet another strand in the membership of the Society of Antiquaries, a strand which by this point had a long lineage.[48] Some of these men became, like Scharf, relatively engaged in the life of the society, while others belonged primarily to gain access to the Society's publications of subscription-funded prints. Scharf's artistic focus is visible in his paper, which contains a long digression on the history of the depiction of Medusa through the Renaissance, including a lengthy encomium on the Uffizi painting of the head of Medusa, then attributed to Leonardo.[49] This rather immaterial discussion is also perhaps indicative of the changed nature of the Society of Antiquaries by the middle of the nineteenth century – a place no longer on the cutting edge of the discipline, whose members in their meetings flirted with irrelevancy and long-windedness. When Scharf does finally get to the Bath pediment, however, his conclusions are both novel and thought-provoking, even now, and foreshadow the consensus which emerged in the twentieth century that the head is best understood as a careful conflation of Minerva's attribute of the Gorgon with a water god's face symbolizing the sacred waters of the nearby spring.[50]

'I cannot believe this head to be Medusa; nor the Sun, as a friend of Sir Henry Englefield suggested … ', he wrote. 'We shall probably find that this

---

[47] Jackson 2004.   [48] Sweet 2004: 58.   [49] Scharf 1885: 193–4.
[50] Toynbee 1964: 137; Henig 1999: 422.

head is the symbol of the Hot Spring, and that the double wreath refers to oak-groves, which may have surrounded the locality, thus in some degree perpetuating the old Celtic places of veneration.'[51] He went on: 'I must confess myself strongly impressed with the belief that this central head, instead of being a Gorgon, is a personification of the celebrated Hot Spring itself, that the abundant curls pertain to the flowing streams, and that the wings relate to the fleeting nature of the Bath waters, which, from their intense heat, evaporate rapidly.'[52]

Scharf seemed either unaware of or uninterested in the oak wreaths' connection to the *corona civica*; he is, instead, one of the first scholars to incorporate themes of syncretism and continuity of Celtic tradition into his interpretation of the pediment. In fact, Scharf is remarkable for his desire to understand the pediment through its geographical location and British context as much as through its classical connections: he even goes so far as to suggest that the head is placed, not on a shield, but in a *basin*, symbolizing not only the shape of the spring but also the deep valley in which Bath is located.[53] The suggestion was later picked up by the Reverend Prebendary H. M. Scarth, a prominent local antiquary in Bath in the middle decades of the century.[54] Scharf's turning-away from the classical tradition may perhaps be the result of his largely non-antiquarian background – or might be indicative of the increased interest in native British archaeology by this point in the nineteenth century.

Through these four visions of the Gorgon – Englefield's, Pownall's, Warner's, and Scharf's – a picture has been built up of the social and intellectual world of the antiquaries who first set about understanding Roman Bath. The men who followed them in the second half of the nineteenth century continued to engage with and build on the accumulated wisdom of their predecessors, but also increasingly were able to incorporate fresh evidence from new archaeological excavations into their narratives of the Roman town. It is this mid-to-late-Victorian world that I turn to next, examining it through the eyes of one particular man: the antiquary J. T. Irvine.

Irvine and the Mid Nineteenth Century at Bath

James Thomas Irvine has largely fallen out of the annals of nineteenth century architecture – a somewhat surprising fact, considering that he was closely linked to George Gilbert Scott, one of the greatest architects of the

---

[51] Scharf 1855: 194.   [52] Scharf 1855: 196.   [53] Scharf 1855: 197.   [54] Scarth 1864: 22–3.

age, and played an important role in at least two major Victorian restorations of Gothic architecture, Bath Abbey and Peterborough Cathedral. His archaeological and antiquarian legacy has also largely been obscured, although some of his contributions to our understanding of Roman Bath were finally given their due by Barry Cunliffe in the 1960s. Beyond this, however, the most in-depth investigation of Irvine to date is a slim 2011 volume written by Ann Ritchie for the Shetland Amenity Trust, which focuses in particular on his Scottish connections. My goal here is therefore in part to further illuminate the role Irvine played in the investigation of Roman Bath, both during his employment in Bath and through his network of correspondents afterwards. I also seek to use Irvine to reconstruct some of the intellectual networks of nineteenth century Bath, and the impact those networks had on the excavation and interpretation of the Roman city. In so doing, I will be relying almost entirely on Irvine's own papers, which are owned by National Museums of Scotland and held in the Bath Central Library; this archival material includes Irvine's own manuscript plans drawn on the spot in Bath during his time there, his collation of evidence for Roman and medieval Bath (including extensive newspaper clippings reporting finds), which seems to have been an ongoing project throughout his life, and abundant correspondence from figures in the Bath antiquarian community from the 1860s to the 1890s, which paint a vivid picture of that community and its internecine politics (although unfortunately very few of Irvine's own letters survive).[55] In particular, I will explore in depth the relationship between Irvine and two other men, Richard Mann and Charles Davis. The three between them, and Mann and Davis in particular, were responsible for the vast majority of our knowledge of the archaeology of Bath until the second half of the twentieth century. It is therefore particularly important to understand how their personal relationships and intellectual backgrounds shaped their exploration of the city, since in some ways we are still feeling the academic ramifications of both their collaborations and their rivalries.

Irvine was born on Yell, Shetland, in 1826, and was apprenticed to Scott around 1840. He stayed in Scott's employ as a clerk of works until 1877, shortly before the latter's death, and Irvine's writings, along with his obituaries, bear witness to his loyalty and devotion to his employer.[56] Irvine himself never worked independently as an architect, and after his employment with Scott ended, the latter part of his career is marked by

---

[55] Irvine's papers generally are scattered in several different locations, with only those pertaining to Bath held at the Bath Central Library. See Ritchie 2011: 38 for a list of those held elsewhere.

[56] Ritchie 2011: 8.

hints of financial uncertainty and stress. He spent much of the final sixteen years of his life, from 1884 to 1900, as the clerk of works for the restoration of Peterborough cathedral; however, this time was shadowed by conflict with the architect, John Loughborough Pearson, and by a five-year gap in the project which forced him to take a lesser position in Leeds, away from his family in Peterborough.[57] Irvine's published work, manuscript records, and correspondence all bear testimony to his diligence as a clerk of works and architectural draftsman; as Ritchie has put, 'the picture that emerges from … Irvine's work in England is one of an outstandingly competent and admired clerk of works, whose work was always in the best interests of the character and history of the building, and a natural draftsman keen to share his drawings and willing to adopt new methods to do so.'[58]

His skill in his profession both shaped and in turn was shaped by his antiquarian interests. These interests seem to have been sparked originally by his experiences growing up on Yell, and his interest in Shetland archaeology persisted throughout his life.[59] However, much of his antiquarian work stemmed from his professional interest in the above- and below-ground history of the buildings upon which he worked. To this end he contributed frequently to antiquarian journals on Anglo-Saxon and Medieval architecture in particular; the expertise he acquired in turn informed his role in the restoration of medieval buildings. However, he also took careful note of the archaeology which appeared in the course of building works. As the Bath Irvine Papers demonstrate, through the application of his meticulous architectural draftsmanship skills to stratigraphic remains he became part of a brave new world of precision in archaeological recording, adhering to standards of accuracy and clarity which remain exemplary even today. His sighting of the podium of the temple of Sulis Minerva is a key example. When the White Hart Inn in central Bath was demolished in the late 1860s, Irvine in effect assigned himself a 'watching brief', recording the remains he saw through detailed notes and sketch plans and sections.[60] In so doing, he saw and recorded with detailed and accurate stratigraphy the podium of the temple (Figures 1.3 and 1.4). The close-up view seen in Figure 1.4 in particular shows the care with which Irvine recorded stratigraphic layers, depicting them to scale with annotated measurements, and noting the composition of each layer; the inclusion of organic material at the bottom of the section is an especially compelling visual touch. However, he never published this work; in one of

[57] Ritchie 2011: 10–11.   [58] Ritchie 2011: 14.
[59] For more on Irvine's work on Shetland, see Ritchie 2011: 25–35.   [60] Irvine Papers.

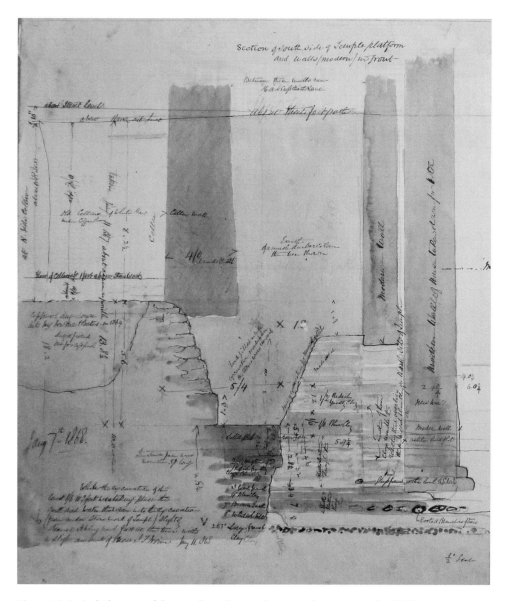

Figure 1.3: Irvine's drawing of the temple podium and surrounding stratigraphy. (Held in Bath Central Library. Reproduced by kind permission of National Museums Scotland.)

his few published writings on Roman Bath, an 1873 synthesis of knowledge concerning the temple, presented to the British Archaeological Association and noteworthy for its erudition and clarity, he passes over his own discoveries in a few words: 'This evidence [for the podium platform] is both too long and loaded with careful plans and sections (all to scale) to detain

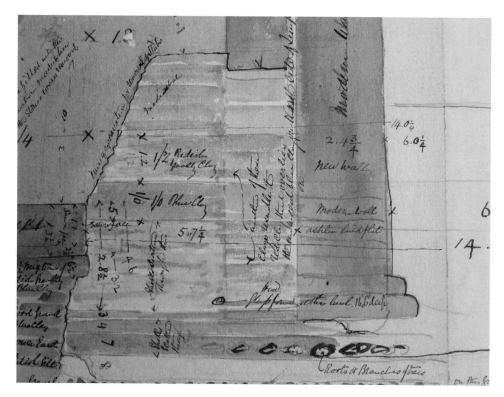

Figure 1.4: Detail of the stratigraphy by the podium. (Held in Bath Central Library. Reproduced by kind permission of National Museums Scotland.)

the Association with at present.'[61] Partly for this reason, and partly because Francis Haverfield, in an unusual lapse of judgement, harshly dismissed Irvine's findings in the 1906 *Victoria County History of Somerset*,[62] Irvine's contributions to our knowledge of the ancient town were not fully appreciated until his papers were re-examined by Cunliffe in the 1960s.[63] This put back our understanding of the layout of the centre of Aquae Sulis by almost a century, since, with Irvine's observations unfairly dismissed, the location of the temple became the subject of (usually inaccurate) debate.[64]

To his contemporaries, however, Irvine was clearly a valued and important authority on ancient Bath, whose relationship with the town and those interested in its history spanned a crucial period from the 1860s to the 1890s, during which time antiquarian investigation of Roman Bath shifted from the reconstructions by Warner and his contemporaries, which relied

[61] Irvine 1873: 381.   [62] Haverfield 1906: 232.   [63] Cunliffe 1969: 8.
[64] e.g. Richmond and Toynbee 1955: 97.

largely on individual epigraphic and iconographic objects which had emerged piecemeal from the ground, to large-scale excavations funded by the city for express archaeological purposes.

When Irvine arrived in Bath in 1864, he had been both a member of the British Archaeological Association and a corresponding member of the Society of Antiquaries of Scotland since the previous year. He seems to have almost immediately taken an active interest in the antiquarian history of the town. A manuscript account by Irvine included in his papers tells of visiting the King's Bath in 1864 in the company of its superintendent and engaging in a close examination of its architectural fabric in order to understand the medieval and post-medieval development of the Bath. By January 1867 he was well-established enough to deliver a paper on the 'Remains of Roman Baths found in Bath' to the Bath Literary and Philosophical Association.[65] The newspaper records of the paper and of the discussion which followed bear witness to the ways in which the association's meetings brought together the local antiquaries of the day, and serve as a useful way into Irvine's connections and position in Bath's antiquarian community.[66] The Reverend Prebendary J. M. Scarth was in the chair, and opened the discussion. Scarth's *Aquae Solis*, the first full-length monograph on the ancient town, had appeared in 1864, the year Irvine arrived in Bath. By this point Scarth was in his fifties, and had been living in Bath for over twenty years; his position as chair of Irvine's lecture reflects his situation at this point as rather the *doyen* of Bath antiquaries. This is also marked by the respect shown to him by Irvine in letters surviving from the 1870s. The clergyman H. H. Winwood spoke next. Winwood was highly active in the Bath Natural History and Antiquarian Field Club through at least the 1890s, and published extensively on geological topics as well as having antiquarian interests. His position in the antiquarian networks of the nineteenth century is demonstrated in his 1886 publication of a carved block found in the Cross Bath (discussed in Chapter 2), where he served as a conduit for several different opinions on the block's iconography, including those of Scarth and of A. H. Sayce, professor of comparative philology (and later of Assyriology) at Oxford, who had accompanied Winwood to see the block in person. With the third respondent to Irvine's paper, we encounter the most controversial and problematic figure of nineteenth century Bath: Major Charles Davis, the city engineer, whose clashes with other antiquaries in the town, but

---

[65] Copy of the November 1866 to April 1867 lecture rota included in the Irvine Papers.
[66] *Bath Chronicle*, 31 January 1867.

particularly with his own project manager, Richard Mann, would severely impact the intellectual environment and harmony of Bath in the later decades of the nineteenth century. The feud between Mann and Davis, and the ways in which the mild-mannered Irvine was caught between the two men, are explored extensively in the pages that follow.

During his residency in Bath, Irvine was actively involved in the excavation and recording of Roman remains in the town, engaging in multiple watching briefs as Victorian construction continued apace. By 1872, however, he had moved on from Bath to another project of Scott's at Rochester Cathedral, and thence in 1874 to Lichfield, where he remained in Scott's employ, as discussed above, until 1877. From the 1870s onwards, therefore, his involvement in Bath archaeology was largely one step removed, taking place through ongoing written correspondence and knowledge-exchange with men on the spot, although he made at least one visit back to the town in 1881. The resulting written record allows us to examine the world of both nineteenth century Bath and nineteenth century antiquarianism through Irvine's eyes. In what follows, I use Irvine's correspondence to tease out several themes concerning the development of archaeological investigation in the town. I turn first to the tragicomedy of Davis and Mann.

A Reluctant Diplomat: Irvine between Davis and Mann

Between them, Charles Davis, as city engineer, and Richard Mann, as his builder, were responsible for the large-scale excavations from the 1870s onwards which produced much of our knowledge of Roman Bath until Barry Cunliffe's projects one hundred years later. These excavations focused on two areas in particular: the reservoir of the King's Spring, and the great bathing complex adjacent to it. Irvine and Davis had begun to take an interest in the bath complex in the 1860s; the discoveries of this period are principally recorded by Irvine's manuscript plans.[67] A major series of excavations were carried out by Mann and Davis throughout the 1880s, ultimately exposing most of the complex; the most complete records of this work are to be found in Mann's manuscript papers, held in the Library of the Society of Antiquaries in London.[68] From 1878 to 1880, they undertook an examination, under difficult conditions, of the Roman reservoir surrounding the spring at the King's Bath. They then continued to excavate sporadically in the temple precinct throughout the 1880s and 1890s.

---

[67] Cunliffe 1969: 90; Irvine Papers.   [68] Cunliffe 1969: 91–3; Mann Papers.

The activities of Davis and Mann transformed the nineteenth century perception of Roman Bath, with the excavation and subsequent reconstruction of the baths in particular demonstrating the potential scale of the Roman remains, and marking the beginning of tourist interest in the town's Roman past. Their activities sparked a new phase of scholarly debate, which has naturally continued to the present day: one focused on describing and interpreting the excavated structural remains of the site. Davis and Mann formed an unlikely partnership, however – the one bombastic, power-hungry, and careless in his excavation habits, the other cautious, careful, and clearly frustrated by the slapdash approach of his supervisor.[69] Indeed, by the 1880s there was open war between them, with acrimonious letters appearing in the *Bath Chronicle*, some anonymous and some not, but all of them attacking their respective scholarly credentials.[70] It is not my intention here to write a detailed account of how their feud developed over the decades. Rather, I want to attempt to see the feud from Irvine's eyes, and examine his engagement with both men.

Mann, Davis, and Irvine were all acquainted by the mid-1860s. We have already seen Davis at Irvine's paper in 1867, but in their correspondence the three men reminisce about encounters dating back to 1865 at least. One anecdote in particular stuck in Irvine's mind: the story of Davis and Mann heading down into a Roman drain leading from the Baths, which Irvine had uncovered by accident in the Kingston buildings in October 1865. In an undated copy of a letter to Mann, almost certainly from 1895, he tells the evocative story:

The discovery of the Roman drain by us was made through merely an attempt of ours to discover the cause of the sinking of part of the Abbey Ch[urch] west end. This could be more readily made in the closed cellars to south of nave. In them tryals [sic] were made at several points one of which happened to be at the east end of the long cellar and on the very top of the Roman drain. This was unknown to Mr C.E. Davis until after drain was opened, and it you ought to know well; for through that very hole you, Mr C.E. Davis and Mr Walker went down; and reemerged (thank God), when I doubted if we would not have to transport your almost inanimate forms through all the horrors of this "middle passage" and as C.E.D. Esq. had gone down from what the men told him I had unfortunately said and did not reappear for an hour and more, and Mrs C.E. Davis came to me to ask, where her husband was. I doubt if I ever passed such a miserable time. Thankful was I when you all appeared and Mr. C.E.D. said "he could not understand where the bottle of brandy came from."

---

[69] Cunliffe 2000: 30.   [70] Cuttings of this correspondence are to be found in the Irvine Papers.

Mann elaborates in a letter from 14 May 1895, which seems to be a reply to Irvine's:

> The horrors of the "middle passage" you mention I well remember, the wading through the cold water; the vapourous heat and stench beyond; and the length of time "below". I went with the mason the whole length to the mouth of the mill tail, C.E.D. and Mr. Walker remained beneath the corner of the Literary Institution and did not essay the part beyond, through which, being lower we were crouching quadrupeds. I remember too the sip of brandy as a very cordial thought, though I knew not you were the sender, and so omitted thanking you, but the delay renders them not the less deep.

Mann's memory in 1895 had failed him, however, for in 1878, when he had been re-exploring the same area, he certainly knew Irvine had been the source of the brandy:

> The Gothic drain crossing the middle passage I have not yet made a finish of clearing just above your opening … The dry drain I have not yet taken any measurement of … The height of it I think would be about 2–9 or 3 ft. and it seemed to take a curved course toward the Chronicle Office.
>
> When I went up it on that eventful day that you as bottleholder came to the rescue of the lost ones, both Mr. Davis and myself heard the thud of the printing machine distinctly.[71]

The obviously long-standing "Middle Passage" joke – not, perhaps, in the best of taste – had been made by Mann earlier in May 1878 as well, where he declared that 'the horrors of [it] are to be "sung or said" by all appreciative travellers'; that Irvine paid special, perhaps chuckling, attention to the reference is evident from a rare annotation on the letter, in which he added 'who have passed through it' to the end of Mann's sentence.[72] The discomfort and excitement of the initial experience, along with its re-telling over the years, was thus clearly a friendship-consolidating story for Irvine and Mann, in a way which will seem familiar to any veteran of archaeological fieldwork even now. For Irvine, however, the associations of the story with regard to Davis were considerably more irksome. He was annoyed for decades that Davis casually claimed joint credit for the discovery of the drain, which Irvine had happened upon in the course of his own work and only subsequently invited Davis to visit. Around the same time as the May 1878 letters from Mann, Davis gave a brief paper to the Society of Antiquaries on some of the finds from the drains that he and Mann were re-opening. The paper opens with these words: 'Some few years ago since I, in

---

[71] Letter from Mann to JTI, 10 May 1878.   [72] Letter from Mann to JTI, 4 May 1878.

conjunction with Mr. Irvine, discovered a portion of the ancient Roman sewer … ' Upon receiving a copy of the paper, Irvine immediately made a note of its topic, and continued 'In which he curiously describes that He and Irvine found Roman drain. <u>He</u> did no such thing.' The same complaint reappears in his 1895 letter to Mann quoted above, where one gets a sense of the exasperation years of hearing the claim had produced in the usually mild-mannered Irvine:

He still, I believe, says He and I discovered the drain. But in my Abbey Bath collections [included in the Irvine Papers held at Bath] you can see the bill I paid to Ambrose for his men's work and the <u>date</u>.

It is mainly through his few surviving letters to Mann, along with one or two annotations on letters or notes, that we get a sense of Irvine's negative attitudes towards Davis. In the May 1895 letter, for instance, he remarks bitterly on Davis's inability to follow through on his public promise to produce plans of all the known Roman remains in the city: 'Mr C.E. Davis will never have proper notes of <u>all parts</u> made however much he may talk about it. To those in future who inquire into the matter it will be just as it was in 1790. In this age the fault is doubly disgraceful.' In his correspondence with Davis himself, however, Irvine seems to have attempted to avoid any firm break with him, or to take an active side in the feud which developed between Mann and Davis.

This ambivalent attitude towards Davis is on display in the fallout to a visit Irvine made to Bath at the end of 1881, in order to visit the excavations then taking place at the King's Spring. The visit was short – only three days – and Irvine seems to have been suffering from ill health during most of it. However, he seems to have at least dined, and possibly stayed, with Mann,[73] and Scarth, too, knew of Irvine's coming enough in advance to have invited him to stay with him and his family, although Irvine did not take him up on the offer.[74] Although ill, he also spent enough time at the site to be able to write two lengthy letters on the finds in December 1881 to Scarth and another unknown correspondent. Davis, on the other hand, received no word from Irvine that he intended to visit, and Irvine did not

---

[73] Letter from Mann to JTI, 3 December 1881: 'The only feature of your visit unpleasant to me was that you did not eat so much as one wished, but I am glad you feel better, and I hope that when you may again favor us with a visit, (and I shall always be pleased for you to do so) you may be <u>very much</u> more destructive.'

[74] Letter from JTI to Scarth, 16 December 1881: 'I was indeed grieved to return without being able to avail myself of your kind invitation to stay at Wrington, and especially so from thus being unable to see Mr. W. Long.'

encounter him during his stay. This seems to have caused some tension when, after the trip, Mann let slip to Davis the news that Irvine had been in town.[75] Considering that by this point relations between Mann and Davis were already quite tense, one wonders whether Mann's 'casual mention' was in fact intended to score points against his nominal superior. Be that as it may, in July of 1882, Davis wrote a brief note to Irvine which concludes, 'I never heard from you in reply to my last. I was very disappointed at finding you have been in Bath without my seeing you. Let me have reply soon.'[76]

It seems fairly clear that Irvine's neglect of Davis during his visit was entirely intentional, especially since he was there to see the excavations that Davis was supposedly overseeing (even if Mann was doing all the day-to-day work). However, from the contents of his rapid reply to Davis's letter, it is also clear that while he may have sought to avoid Davis originally, he was not eager for Davis to realize the snub was deliberate – or to allow Mann, regardless of their friendship, to use him as a tool in his power struggle. In the letter, in light of the contents of his other correspondence on the visit, he seems to downplay the extent to which he had been able to visit Bath itself, and almost certainly exaggerates his illness:

I am grieved that through some blunder of mine your [original] note has not been answered. If it can be found the mistake shall be corrected. I do assure you, Sir, it was not intentional on my part.

My visit to Bath and Wells last year was extremely short and made under severe illness so that I was obliged to be very quiet unless for 3 or 4 days towards the end at Wells. I was <u>miserably</u> ill the whole time. Old age, hard work, small pay and constant pressure begins to tell, and I can scarcely expect it should be otherwise.[77]

Irvine's reluctance to antagonize Davis, and even his desire to play peacemaker between Davis and Mann, is on display as well in his cautious reactions to both men in 1884, when the feud between Davis and Mann broke out in spectacularly public – and petty – fashion.

Relations between Davis and Mann has been souring since at least 1878, when complaints about Davis's slipshod approach to archaeology, and interference with Mann's work, start appearing in Mann's letters to Irvine.[78]

---

[75] Letter from Mann to JTI, 20 April 1882: 'I mentioned casually to Mr. Davis you had been here, he "wanted to ask you many things."'

[76] Letter from Davis to JTI, 16 July 1881.

[77] Letter from JTI to Davis, 17 July 1882. In archive of Davis's papers, Bath Central Library.

[78] Letter from Mann to JTI, 10 May 1878: 'A little while ago I had a sharp word or two with Mr. Davis over the course he thought proper to take as to the contract for proposed Turkish Baths … today

By Irvine's visit to Bath in 1881, things had reached the point where Irvine wrote to an unknown correspondent, 'I was grieved to find Messrs. Davis and Mann at war; the last considered he was left to take the notes, etc., and Mr. C.E. Davis to appropriate the credit,'[79] and by late 1883 Mann wrote to Irvine that for both archaeological and business reasons 'the rupture between us is now complete'.[80] The events which led to the first public airing of this contention between the two men, as well as Mann's feelings which fanned the flames, are referenced in a letter from Mann a couple weeks later:

You would be rather amused I am sure at the assurance often evidenced by our Archaeological Dictator. Sometimes the Revd. Scarth is "sat upon" and contradicted, notably the 1754 men pooh-poohed, Bishop Clifford in error, and at the Somerset Society Meeting a Mr. Green differed on some points as to the Roman Bath, and he was "showing great ignorance."

None of them with confidence can contradict him, and when I see some of the statements he puts out it makes my fingers itch to go at it. The proposal in your last letter [not now surviving] for getting out the truth would be best, if I was careful not to be offending him, but for reasons which I can explain when I see you, I am gone far past that platform of humility and so would prefer to go at him straight but, of course, courteous.[81]

The public humiliation Mann makes reference to of Emanuel Green, a local antiquary and active member of the Bath Field Club, seems to have been the final straw for – or perhaps simply an opportunity seized by – Davis's adversaries. The issue in question was minor enough: Davis, in his public lectures and writings, was deemed to be taking credit for the discovery of the great Roman bath complex, when its existence had been known to some degree since the mid eighteenth century, when the so-called Lucas Baths were sighted. In August 1883, Green seems to have pointed this out to Davis at the lecture mentioned by Mann, and in January 1884, Green wrote to the *Bath Chronicle* describing Davis's put-down, laying out the evidence for previous knowledge of the Baths, and demanding a clarification

---

a warm message was left for me as to the "vanishment" of things [i.e. artefacts] as they are found before he has seen them.' Letter from Mann to JTI, 28 December 1878: 'The paper read at the Field Club on "Subterranean Bath", and the remarks upon it I daresay you have read. In the latter I noticed that what a little time ago he, Mr. D., described in the Herald as an "Amphora", is now designated a Mediterranean flask! What a big jump! The mask of similar metal, and found no great distance from it … said to be Saxon. Something wants rectifying I fancy.'

[79] Copy of letter from JTI to unknown correspondent, early 1882.
[80] Letter from Mann to JTI, 4 November 1883.
[81] Letter from Mann to JTI, 19 November 1883.

from Davis.[82] When Davis failed to reply, Green, Mann, and others, some by name and some anonymous, all began piling in. The attacks quickly became personal: by February 1884 Mann was writing to Irvine, 'On Thursday [in the *Chronicle*] one may expect a severe rejoinder, on what a Pachyderm CED must be'.[83] A month or so later, both Davis and Mann wrote to Irvine, Davis to declare that 'You have seen Peach, Green and Mann's attack on me – the latter has shown the extreme of ingratitude. I gave him the work and after spending nearly £4,000 on which he had 10 per cent – I got rid of him because of his stubborn inattention,'[84] and Mann to announce:

Major Davis has been somewhat venomous in many ways, and now 'he consults his dignity' by informing his friends that I am too ignorant to write the letters appearing in my name, and that I got someone to write them for me.

To be poohpoohed in this way is a taker down, isn't it?

Whether I shall survive it I cannot say.[85]

In addition to these letters, Irvine's notations on his copies of the *Chronicle* correspondence indicate that both Mann and Davis were sending him clippings. Before the spat began, Mann had already envisioned Irvine as a go-between, writing in November 1883, 'Should the first dose be too mild and bring no reply [from Davis] I can alter it in the next, then when it's ding dong with us, a respected and reliable umpire would be found in yourself, a most enviable position, and one in which the confidence of every one would be yours, and readily accorded I am sure.' Irvine, however, for all that his intellectual sympathies may have lain with Mann, clearly did not view the *Chronicle* feud as productive, and seems to have carefully avoided taking sides. Mann's invitation in April 1884 to 'join in the fray' in the *Chronicle* seems to have been ignored entirely,[86] and instead we find Irvine writing to Davis the following day to emphasize his neutral role:

I assure you that to get into Bath Hot Waters else than to 'take dimensions' which I should gladly do or to cure Rheumatism, which it is excellent for, I have no intention.

---

[82] Letter from Green to *Bath Chronicle*, 16 January 1884. This letter, and the bulk of the correspondence which follow, were reprinted in the pamphlet 'The Roman Baths of Bath: A correspondence relating to the discovery of the Roman Bath, and some facts connected therewith'. The pamphlet, compiled and published at the instigation of Mann and Robert Peach, blazoned on its front cover the following hardly subtle epigram, taken from Horace Walpole: 'It is a special trick of low cunning to squeeze out knowledge from a modest man … and then to use it as legally acquired, and pass the source in total silence.'

[83] Letter from Mann to JTI, 26 February 1884.   [84] Letter from Davis to JTI, 21 March 1884.

[85] Letter from Mann to JTI, 31 March 1884.   [86] Letter from Mann to JTI, 6 April 1884.

Indeed I am grieved to see such good and <u>excellent</u> men as you all are engaged in such 'Bathing', expending an amount of writing thereon amply sufficient to set forth a perfect history of the remains found. It seems to me a sin against Bladud, his Waters and the Public who expect the history instead.[87]

In so writing, he reinforced the position he had taken a week earlier to Davis, at which point he wrote:

I confess to beginning to have belief in Bladud's necromancy and his wild fire, nought else could have kindled such a flame among so good and excellent men. I am tempted to send a copy of my dear old Master, Sir G.G.S.'s [i.e. George Gilbert Scott's] note when in his kindest and gentlest manner he spread oil on the troubled waters that had arisen between Mr. P. White (the restoring Builder of so many Cathedrals) during our joint connection over Rochester, and with him say that with such good men there should be no difficulty in making an end of differences.[88]

Irvine was entirely correct in his belief that the immediate feud in the *Chronicle* was both petty and pointless – it served hardly any purpose in the advancement of archaeological understanding of the Baths, and Davis did, after all, have a reasonably legitimate claim to be the discoverer of the central Great Bath, if not the rest of the complex. Nevertheless, its roots were in a much more serious issue: the increasingly bitter resentment of men such as Mann and Green at what they perceived to be the triumph in Bath antiquarianism of, as Mann put it in a letter to Irvine, the 'inaccurate, the pretty and effective description' over the '<u>sober and solid</u>, and accurate record'.[89] In the private letters from Davis and Mann to Irvine in March 1884, we can see as well the enduring role of social class. Mann was undoubtedly the better and more knowledgeable archaeologist, but his status as merely Davis's builder dogged his efforts to set the archaeological record straight and undermined his standing in the public eye; meanwhile, Davis's social connections continued to give him authority and decision-making power over the town's Roman remains even after the antiquarian community had almost universally rejected him: a few years later, for instance, in 1886, the town council would be trusting Davis's (deeply flawed) judgment on the effect of the construction of new buildings over the site of the Baths, and choosing to snub Mann entirely.[90] The one issue was affected by the other, therefore: expertise was trumped by social standing, and the archaeology suffered as a result.

---

[87] Letter from JTI to Davis, 7 April 1884. In archive of Davis's papers, Bath Central Library.

[88] Letter from JTI to Davis, 1 April 1884. In archive of Davis's papers, Bath Central Library.

[89] Letter from Mann to JTI, 4 November 1883.

[90] The social aspects of this unfortunate episode are on display most clearly in a lengthy, frustrated, and impotent letter from Mann to JTI dating to 24 March 1886.

The Awakening of Archaeology

The contentious relationship between Mann and Davis, Davis's slapdash recording habits, and Mann's lack of the social authority necessary to override Davis's unwillingness or inability to fully publish the finds of the 1870s and 1880s are important for the ramifications they had on both the quality of the excavations themselves and the (lack of) dissemination of their results. Had Mann been in charge of deciding how to proceed with excavation in the 1870s and 1880s, rather than Davis, or had he been able to counter Davis more effectually, we would almost certainly be in possession of much more detailed information concerning the chronological development of the baths in particular, where occupation contexts were removed with virtually no attempt to record them.[91] On a more abstract level, however, Mann and Davis can be seen as archetypes for the growing pains of archaeology as a discipline in the second half of the nineteenth century. Davis owed his role in the uncovering of Roman Bath entirely to his professional standing as city engineer, and to the social influence which accompanied it. However, he lacked the methodical care essential for archaeological investigation, especially at a time when the growth of knowledge depended entirely on the meticulous compilation and organization of manuscript notes, and he was separated, too, from the more vibrant sectors of archaeological society. The former is apparent not only from Mann's complaints, but from Davis's own correspondence with Irvine. Thus in 1876, when Davis sent a tracing of the location of discoveries to Irvine, we hear, in his typically brief and abrupt prose, that first he '[has] not retained a copy; should therefore be obliged if you would let me have one', and then 'I wish you would give me the depths of the sinking you have shown on the tracing. I have mislaid my sketch book.'[92] Indeed, letters from Davis to Irvine were more often than not requests for information which Davis should already have had in hand, or mistaken representations of what he did possess. In 1880, for instance, we see Davis writing to Irvine and sending on plans of what Davis thought to be Irvine's excavations at the White Hart from the 1860s. Irvine annotated the letter with one of his rare bursts of exasperation. After Davis's declaration, 'I enclose your drawings you made of the White Hart,' Irvine wrote emphatically 'No. York Street, his own discovery in 1869' and scribbled at the top of the letter, 'The 2 drawings, a plan and sections sent to me with this was merely the original sketches I did for him of his own discoveries in York Street in 1869.'[93] Irvine sent the papers all right back to Davis the following day.

---

[91] La Trobe-Bateman and Niblett 2016: 12.   [92] Letter from Davis to JTI, 4 February 1876.
[93] Letter from Davis to JTI, 16 June 1880.

But probably more important, and frustrating, in Irvine's eyes was Davis's lack of engagement with the more active archaeological networks of the day. This is on display most clearly in their correspondence leading up to a lecture given by Davis in 1880 to the Society of Antiquaries. As discussed earlier in this chapter, by this point in the nineteenth century the Society of Antiquaries was viewed as a backwater by many of the more active antiquaries and archaeologists of the period, and Irvine was no exception. He repeatedly urged Davis, to no avail, to seek a different venue for his findings on Bath. One of his principal criticisms rested on the Society's extremely slow publication of material given to them. Thus in November 1879, we find Irvine writing to Davis, in response to the publication earlier that year of Davis's short account of finds from the Bath drain, presented to the Society in 1878:

Your notes printed by the Antiquaries are very interesting. I wish they could be got to give all your discoveries. Unfortunately they do so little are heard of so little that I am afraid there is not much hope of it from that quarter. I know that some years ago Mr. J.H. Parker gave them some exquisite drawings of Lincoln, but whether they will ever appear in the time of the present generation is questionable.[94]

This was the same paper in which Davis had taken joint credit for the discovery of the drain, to Irvine's immense private irritation, as we have seen. Given this, Irvine's diplomacy in the letter seems particularly illustrative of his character, and of his willingness to sacrifice point-scoring in pursuit of the archaeology's broader good. This was a lesson Mann never really succeeded in learning; however, we may ask too whether Irvine's softer approach produced anything more in the way of concrete results. Certainly his subtle hints as to the suitability – or lack thereof – of the Society as a venue for publication went unheeded by Davis, who, six months later, wrote to Irvine requesting information to help him bulk out yet another paper to be delivered at the Society's meetings.[95] In his response Irvine rather more forcefully pressed the story of J. H. Parker's drawings:

I am glad you are actually going to give us an account but rather sorry it is where it is for I suppose there is no hope of seeing it printed in <u>our lifetime</u>. When I was in London last year I asked after Mr. J.H. Parker's Paper with the <u>wonderful</u> drawings of Lincoln given to them several years ago; and there was no knowledge then of

---

[94] Letter from JTI to Davis, 24 November 1879. In archive of Davis's papers, Bath Central Library.

[95] 'I am going to read a paper at the Antiquaries on June 10. Kindly let me have your measurements … also what I sent you of the building under the Poor Law Board. Also what you measured under the White Hart … If you have anything else kindly oblige me with it. If you let me have originals you shall have them back again directly … My Paper at the Antiquaries is to be as full as possible. I wish to give credit to all discoveries.' Letter from Davis to JTI, 22 May 1880.

when it would appear. <u>Small</u> notes appear in their Proceedings tolerably well [i.e. like the one Davis had sent in in 1878]; but as to such excellent papers as yours will be it is a wonder how they get anyone to <u>sacrifice</u> themselves for what at earliest will appear to the next generation.[96]

And then, in a final last-ditch attempt the week before the paper:

Alas! I am at present trembling in terror from the circumstance that when 'The Antiquaries' find the to them 'Godsend' of your paper they will inevitably honour it with 'condemnation' to the Archaeologia which practically means to say it may not be seen again for say 70 years or so. Thus no one of the present generation will be likely to benefit by its valuable information, far less your obliged and Humble though Aged servant, Jas. T. Irvine.[97]

Davis's only response to all this urging reveals the degree to which he had become alienated from the more vibrant archaeological circles of the nineteenth century:

As to reading at the Antiquaries, after being for years almost a mainstay of the British Archaeological, they behaved badly to me, refused to refund me money out of pocket when I acted for them here and whether I with annoyance wished them to take my name off or whether I was in arrears I know not, but I am no longer a member as to publication … [98]

In the end Irvine's fears were justified, and Davis's paper was never published – although a manuscript copy can be found in the Library of the Society of Antiquaries.[99] Meanwhile, Davis's separation from the centres of British archaeology only seemed to increase: by July 1890 he was writing to Irvine, 'I wish you could lend me Mr. Scarth's last paper [Scarth had died in April] on the Roman Antiquities he read to the Brit. Arch. Assn. I do not subscribe to the Association and I know no other subscriber except yourself.'[100] What is remarkable here is not so much that Davis was not a member, but that Irvine was his only correspondent who was. For a man who had such authority over the excavation and preservation of one of the most important Roman sites in the country, Davis's isolated position within antiquarian networks is perhaps a more telling indicator of his lack of true archaeological credentials than any of Mann's attacks.

[96] Letter from JTI to Davis, 24 May 1880. In archive of Davis's papers, Bath Central Library.
[97] Letter from JTI to Davis, 17 June 1880. (The paper had been pushed back from the 10th to the 24th). In archive of Davis's papers, Bath Central Library.
[98] Letter from Davis to JTI, 26 May 1880.   [99] La Trobe-Bateman and Niblett 2016: 209.
[100] Letter from Davis to JTI, 30 July 1890.

Mann himself, on the other hand, appears in Irvine's letters as almost a Ghost of Christmas Past for modern archaeology, in particular through his meticulous attention to detail, and his deep commitment to the protection of archaeological heritage. As Irvine himself put it to a correspondent, 'By a very unusual and remarkable piece of good fortune the Builder engaged, a Mr. Richard Mann, is one of those Antiquaries nature produces found blooming all unseen and unknown in its by-lanes but without a kindred spirit near.'[101] In 1878, for instance, in one of the more entertaining and yet at the same time evocative passages from his letters to Irvine, Mann wrote:

In shifting a piece of earth from alongside one [of these stones] I disturbed a frog's last resting place. This could not have been the proverbial frog that lives on after being buried for centuries. To be more natural this poor fellow had died. With great respect to his memory, as he must have been so very much my Senior, I preserved what little I could find of him (though I use the masculine gender I take no oath on the point) and that is one little bone, a miniature thigh bone, a wee thing only half an inch in length, and, that part of him which in his sphere, was the 'means whereby he lived', that means, his mouth. Beside this there is sacred to him a half bucket of the adjacent earth reserved for further search, in hope of finding more of him.[102]

The tone of the passage may be jocular, but the archaeological instincts it betrays are impressive – for in the episode Mann succeeds in foreshadowing not only modern faunal analysis, but also environmental sampling!

Coupled to Mann's archaeological recording of 'the greatest accuracy and astonishingly careful character', as Irvine put it,[103] was a profound love for and desire to protect the archaeological heritage of the city that was his home. From the 1880s onwards, indeed, the primary focus of Mann and Irvine's correspondence shifts from the interpretation of new discoveries to concern for the preservation of what had already been found. In 1886, in the midst of his increasingly frantic desperation at Davis's plans for construction over some of the remains of the Baths, Mann wrote heart-wrenchingly:

I have read again and again [Davis's] baseless stories, until in justice and common honesty to those he was deceiving, & still more the almost reverential regard I feel for these grand and silent Roman works – I could not, but give the truth respecting them, and in doing that personal feeling seemed banished as being too petty for association with such a subject.[104]

---

[101] JTI's copy of letter from JTI to unnamed correspondent, late 1881 or early 1882.
[102] Letter from Mann to JTI, 10 May 1878.
[103] JTI's copy of letter from JTI to unnamed correspondent, late 1881 or early 1882.
[104] Letter from Mann to JTI, 24 March 1886.

Mann tried, ultimately in vain, to muster up enough protest from the antiquarian community to prevent the construction, telling Irvine, 'Kindly give your aid in any way you think best, I shall send similar tracings and request to Brit. Archaeological per E.L. Brock, Esq., another to the Society of Antiquaries and most probably to Mr. Reynolds and get him to submit it to Bishop Clifford.'[105] Irvine himself succeeded in getting the Society to protest to the mayor and Corporation, thanks to the intercession of J. T. Micklethwaite, a fellow former pupil of George Gilbert Scott,[106] but in the end the construction was approved by the Corporation by only one vote.[107]

By the early 1890s, Mann's skills as an archaeologist were sufficiently recognized even outside of Bath to enable him to take a supervisory role in the Society of Antiquaries' excavations at Silchester. Even so, here as well he seems to have run up against the tension between social standing and archaeological expertise which had brought him so much grief in the past. Frederick Vinon, a member of the Society, had openly praised Mann's work at Silchester in the *Bath Chronicle* in February 1891;[108] however, in a letter to Irvine a year later, Mann described his impatience with Society members who turned up at the excavations to 'play Stanley', damaging the remains through their incompetence, and overriding Mann's instructions to workmen without cause – in consequence of which Mann finished by leaving the project.[109]

The overall impression of Mann's life is that he was a man whose natural aptitude for archaeology was honed by rigorous training – but whose ability to contribute to archaeological research was hampered again and again by his status, as a builder, as one rung below the professional class of men who dominated the national archaeological societies, as well as the civic order at Bath. In his story, therefore, we can see the consequences, both social and intellectual, of archaeology's continued standing as an amateur discipline in the late nineteenth century. Work by men such as

---

[105] Letter from Mann to JTI, 24 March 1886.
[106] Letter from Micklethwaite to JTI, 8 April 1886.
[107] F. H. Vinon, Letter to Editor, *Bath Chronicle*, 26 February 1891.
[108] 'Perhaps it would be impossible to find more important testimony to Mr. Mann's ability than his appointment last year, by the President and Council of the Society of Antiquaries of London, to superintend the first work of the Society undertaken out of London, viz. the excavation of what was covered of the Roman remains at Silchester. As a Fellow of this Society I am in a position to say that Mr. Mann's work – nearly 5 months in operation – has given the President and Council unqualified satisfaction.' F. H. Vinon, Letter to Editor, *Bath Chronicle*, 26 February 1891.
[109] Letter from Mann to JTI, 16 February 1892.

Mann and Irvine demonstrates that at a technical level the discipline was becoming highly advanced. At least in Bath, however, the lack of an organized archaeological profession or the existence of archaeology as a full-time vocation meant that the two men most active in excavation in the city, Davis and Mann, were marginalized (albeit for very different reasons) from the core of the field.

Irvine died aged seventy-five in 1900 at Peterborough, and Davis followed two years later in May 1902.[110] Mann, on the other hand, endured for more than a quarter-century further, finally passing away at the age of ninety-three in October 1929. His archaeological activities seemed to have long ceased; however, his obituary notes that 'a generation ago Mr. Mann was a very prominent citizen, having a considerable reputation in the antiquarian world'.[111] He continued to write occasional letters to the *Chronicle* on archaeological and historical issues until a few months before his death,[112] but the last extensive evidence of his involvement in the heritage of the town is in the years after Davis's death, when he offered to sell his plans and papers on the nineteenth century excavations to the town. The offer was weighed for over two years, but despite the urgent support of the antiquarian community for the purchase, and the positive recommendations of several sub-committees, it was ultimately rejected, in large part due to lingering partisanship for Davis by members of the town council: the published council minutes show that several vocal members declared, despite testimony to the contrary, that Mann's papers could give no new information that was not already present in Davis's records.[113] The plans ultimately went to the Society of Antiquaries in London, where they remain an invaluable resource, since, along with Mann's letters to Irvine, they are the only surviving record for much of Mann and Davis's excavations.

Through these narratives of the Gorgon and of Irvine, we have seen how the antiquaries who wrote about Aquae Sulis were embedded not only in the intellectual culture of their day, but also in the society of eighteenth and

---

[110] Irvine's obituary appears in the 7 June 1900 *Peterborough Advertiser*, and Davis's in the 15 May 1902 *Bath Chronicle*.

[111] *Bath Chronicle*, 29 October 1929.

[112] e.g. a note on 15 August 1925, on the modifications to the baths in the 1890s. His final letter, on the flooding of the Avon, appeared on 20 April 1929.

[113] See extensive discussion in the *Bath Chronicle*, 1905 to 1907. Key points: 27 April 1905: Mann's initial offer. Editorial in favour: 27 September 1906. Record of letter to council from antiquaries in favour: 4 October 1906. Sub-committee's report in favour, with subsequent discussion by Davis partisans: 1 August 1907. Final decision against: 31 October 1907.

nineteenth century Bath itself. This had a profound effect in particular on their understanding of the Roman use of the hot springs as curative. By looking at the development of the spa town, and the way in which antiquarian interests intersected with the town's position as a centre for healing in the eighteenth and nineteenth centuries, we can see how Bath's modern identity has informed archaeologists' understanding of Roman Bath. It is to this that I turn in Chapter 2.

2 | From Bath to Aquae Sulis

The Development of the Healing Spa

Bath's identity during the Middle Ages was primarily as a cathedral city and as a centre for the wool and cloth trade, not as a spa town.[1] Nonetheless, the waters were both known and used for bathing in the medieval period. The renovation of the King's Bath in the early twelfth century is likely to be attributed to John of Tours (d. 1122), a priest and physician who was also responsible for moving the see of the bishopric from Wells to Bath.[2] Certainly, as discussed at the opening of Chapter 1, the baths were known as a place of healing by the first half of the twelfth century; the *Gesta Stephani*, c. 1138, mentions that the town is called Bath, because 'sick persons from all England go there in order to bathe in the healing waters, and the healthy as well in order to see these miraculous outpourings of hot water and to bathe in them'.[3]

When the priory foundation was dissolved in the wake of the Reformation, and as the cloth trade waned, the town began to reinvent itself as the pre-eminent healing spa.[4] More extensive interest in the use of the waters for curative purposes had started to take off in the late sixteenth century, as physicians began to write about the health benefits of bathing, and of mineral water in particular.[5] This interest only increased during the seventeenth century, as physicians based in Bath began extolling in both books and pamphlets the ability of the springs to cure virtually every ailment. One physician at the baths, Dr Thomas Venner, proclaimed in 1628 that

They be of excellent efficacy against all diseases of the head and sinews, proceeding from a cold and moist cause, as rheums, palsies, lethargies, apoplexia, cramps, deafness, forgetfulness, trembling or weakness of any member, aches and swellings of the joints.[6]

---

[1] Davis and Bonsall 2006: 38ff.   [2] Davis and Bonsall 2006: 38; Cunliffe 1986: 64; 72–4.
[3] *Quae civitas Batta vocatur, quod ex Anglicae linguae proprietate trahens vocabulum, Balneum interpretaur, eo quod ad illam ex omni Anglia infirmi causa in salubribus aquis diluendi, sani vero gratia mirabiles calidae aquae eruptiones videndi, et in eis balneandi, concurrere solent* (*Gesta Stephani* 28). My translation.
[4] Hembry 1990: 26–7.   [5] Hembry 1990: 6ff; Davis and Bonsall 2006: 67.
[6] Quoted in Davis and Bonsall 2006: 73.

The tireless efforts of these Bath-based physicians contributed a great deal to the rise of Bath as a resort. Physicians promoted tourism to the spa through their writings, through their positions on the town's governing board, and, many of them, through their status as landlords of lodging houses.[7] Thus by the mid eighteenth century, when Bath reached the peak of its social cachet as a resort for the elite of the kingdom, extolling the healthful qualities of the water was as ubiquitous as it was necessary for the continued life of the spa and all of the urban infrastructure and development which had accompanied Bath's rise to fame.

At the same time that the curative powers of the water became gospel, Bath's image as a 'valley of pleasure', as one writer put it,[8] was becoming entrenched both in literature and in the popular imagination. The picture of Georgian Bath, the social whirl of theatres, assembly rooms, card parties, the promenades up and down the pavement, all set against a backdrop of both the truly invalid and the merely fashionably so, remains an alluring one.

The glory days of Bath, at least from the point of view of social exclusivity, were fading, however, by the end of the eighteenth century. Bath, in essence, had become too popular for its own good; the most fashionable ranks of society deemed the town passé and moved on to the new seaside resorts, and a more middle-class clientele took their place.[9] Bath's story in the nineteenth century, at least as it was perceived at the time by the city's burghers, was one of social and economic stagnation and slow decline.[10] By the end of the nineteenth century, Bath, with its inexpensive living conditions,[11] was seen as a place for retirees or impoverished spinsters: its cachet as a destination had faded.[12] Healthfulness, however, was still central to its identity – Bath was a salubrious place to be.

---

[7] Davis and Bonsall 2006: 73. Davis and Bonsall, however, slander Dr William Oliver (bap. 1658, d. 1716), author of *A Practical Dissertation on Bath-Waters* (1707), in which he opined that there was no reason not to drink the waters year round. They confuse him with a later William Oliver (1695–1764), town councillor and inventor of the Oliver biscuit medical diet, and imply that his motivations for so writing were more economic than medical, seeking to keep his patients in Bath for longer than the then-short tourist season. While the earlier Dr Oliver did live in Bath for a period, there is no evidence that he practised medicine while he was there (Courtney 2004). Meanwhile, the later Dr Oliver, despite being a pre-eminent medical figure in the town, did little writing on the waters, his most important literary contribution being a pamphlet on the treatment of gout. Nevertheless, he was an important public face of the Bath medical community, particularly through his activities on behalf of the Bath General Hospital (later the Royal Mineral Water Hospital), and tangled on at least two occasions with physicians who doubted the waters' efficacy (Borsay 2004).

[8] Quoted in Neale 1981: 12.   [9] Davis and Bonsall 2006: 151.   [10] Hembry 1997: 54ff.

[11] Hembry 1997: 62–3.   [12] Davis and Bonsall 2006: 154–5.

This backdrop of social rise and fall centred on curative springs, then, is essential to understanding how antiquaries and, later, archaeologists wrote about the discoveries of the remains of Roman Aquae Sulis. We have already seen in Chapter 1 how deeply early writers were affected by the society of the town and the intellectual climate of their day in terms of their general approach to the Roman remains; I turn now to charting one particular aspect of this discourse: Aquae Sulis's perceived nature as a curative spa. I begin once again in the eighteenth century, when, as we have seen, antiquarian interest started to ramp up in response to the first major archaeological finds; like the Gorgon, many of these early objects came to light during the re-building of the town centre which took place in the Georgian period.

An Antiquarian Vision: Aquae Sulis as a Healing Sanctuary

In June 1753 an inscription was found which recorded the restoration of a sacred place, a *locus religiosus*, by a centurion named Severius Emeritus.[13] A few months after the discovery, John Ward, then Gresham Professor of Rhetoric and vice-president of the Society of Antiquaries, put forward the suggestion that the *locus* in question might have been a public cemetery.[14] As I will discuss in Chapter 6, he was almost certainly incorrect, but his justification reveals his preconceptions about the nature of Roman Bath:

[T]here was no town, to which this could be more suitable than Bath, on account of the great number of strangers, who resorted thither for the benefit of the salutiferous springs. For as some of those, who came from distant parts, may be supposed from time to time to have died there; a public cemetery for the burial of them was highly requisite.[15]

In a similar vein forty years later, in response to the discovery of the pediment of the temple of Sulis Minerva and one of the *pro salute* inscriptions discussed in the next section, Governor Pownall suggested that 'there might have been erected at the Roman town Aquae Solis an *Aedes Salutis* – the very sort of place whereat to erect and dedicate such a temple'.[16]

Ward and Pownall were writing at a time when knowledge of Roman Bath was extremely limited, confined to the few contextless inscriptions and reliefs which had been found by the eighteenth century. We can, therefore,

---

[13] *RIB* 152, discussed at much greater length in Chapter 4.   [14] Ward 1753–4: 334.
[15] Ward 1753–4: 337.   [16] Pownall 1795: 16.

easily see the influence of Georgian Bath's status as the pre-eminent place of healing in Ward's and Pownall's writings and in the propositions they made about the ancient town; it was all they had to draw on when envisioning the Roman site. Their assumptions that Bath was 'the very place' for healing, that nowhere 'could be more suitable' than there, are rooted only in the unshakeable eighteenth century belief in the curative nature of the Bath waters. Yet, even as archaeological evidence increased, the antiquaries' conceptual links between the Bath of their own days and Aquae Solis were not weakened: on the contrary, they became more explicit. By the mid nineteenth century, Scarth in *Aquae Solis*, the first full-length work on the Roman town, was overtly comparing the modern and ancient: 'The natural features of the country remain unchanged, the Springs pour forth their healing as they did of old, but a free, active, enlightened, united, and strong people, governed by just laws, and encouraged to active endeavours, have taken the place of an enslaved and degenerate race, the victims of oppression and cruelty.'[17] The Victorian morality inherent in the rhetoric is compelling. However, this assumption that the nature of Bath was the same in antiquity and in the modern period quickly led scholars to dismiss the lack of evidence for a healing sanctuary – even when they consciously knew the lack was there. Scarth himself, for example, declared that

It is most probable that a School of Medicine existed in Bath at an early period. The Mineral Springs being visited by many patients for their healing benefits, would naturally cause the residence of eminent Physicians in the neighbourhood. *No record, however, has been found of any patients, nor have we any Votive Altar put up by a Physician, as at Chester, or any memorial to a Physician, as on the line of the Roman Wall in Northumberland*' (emphasis mine).[18]

It is hard, reading Scarth's postulations about physicians, not to be reminded of the crowd of doctors who made their living by promoting the baths; Scarth's School of Medicine clearly comes more from the medical culture of his own day than from anything to do with Roman Britain.

The central importance of the curative nature of the water for Bathonian identity is also on display in response to Irvine's 1867 paper to the Bath Literary and Philosophical Association. Amongst his broader observations, Irvine remarked in passing that analysing the Bath waters could potentially pose difficulties 'from the fact that the hot water probably percolated through the Roman debris before reaching the surface'.[19] Umbrage was

---

[17] Scarth 1864: viii.   [18] Scarth 1864: 32.

[19] This quote, and the discussion which followed, is reported in the *Bath Chronicle*, 31 January 1867.

taken by several of those present, with Winwood defending the legitimacy of previous analyses of the water, and a Mr Moore declaring point blank that 'with regard to the analysis of the Bath waters he could not admit that any impurities could at any time find their way into the systems of the Baths; it could not be correct that the waters at any time washed away any of the debris, or dirt, or refuse of the Roman times, and even if they did, all the impurities would have been removed before this'.[20] To argue that the waters could possibly be tainted was clearly an affront to a central component of some of Irvine's listeners' worldview.

As the nineteenth century came to a close, writers continued to see Roman Bath mirrored in their own contemporary experiences of the town. Emanuel Green (last seen in Chapter 1 sparring with Davis in the *Chronicle*) wrote in 1890 that

Some accommodation there must have been [for strangers and invalids] as the place, with such magnificent baths, must be judged to have been much what it has been and may be still, a place of ease and idleness; a mixture of groans, music, and flippancy; a resting place for humanity, old, infirm and in ruins; a comfortable thoroughfare from this world to the next.[21]

In Green's words we can easily recognize the haven for retirees which Bath had become by the late Victorian period. In the early twentieth century, Haverfield continued the equation of modern and ancient, writing that 'No doubt a population of others than invalids dwelt round the springs, as it does to-day. But, first and foremost, Bath was a bathing place.'[22] He also shared the assumption that the springs were undoubtedly curative, declaring that 'The reason for the occupation of the site is simple. In the level space within the fold of the river rise mineral springs, hot, medicinal, abundant; and their waters, suitable alike for drinking and for bathing, have power over gout and rheumatism and serious skin diseases.'[23]

By the late twentieth century, these long-standing assumptions concerning the curative nature of the Bath waters and Aquae Sulis's status as a healing sanctuary continued to be unconditionally and unquestioningly accepted by modern archaeologists. In 1971, Barry Cunliffe, the principal modern excavator, would open his book *Roman Bath Discovered* with the words, 'Throughout its two thousand years of life, the town of Bath has always been famous as a great religious centre and for its thermal springs with their

---

[20] Given his attitude to the waters, this is possibly the same Moore who, as city alderman, served at some point as Chairman of the Baths Committee for the Town Council, and who in 1906–7 was strongly opposed to purchasing Mann's plans for the town (*Bath Chronicle*, 1 August 1907).
[21] Green 1890: 126.   [22] Haverfield 1906: 216.   [23] Haverfield 1906: 219.

curative associations,'[24] and in his seminal report on the tablets from the reservoir Roger Tomlin would write the blunt sentence that 'the waters of Bath can cure disease'.[25] In Peter Salway's words, 'In Roman times the spa was middle class, respectable, and seriously dedicated to healing and recreation,' we can still see the effect of Bath's modern past: such words could as easily have been written about the town Jane Austen depicts in *Persuasion*.[26] Most recently, Eberhard Sauer has argued at length for the place of the Bath goddess as a variant of Minerva Medica,[27] and Miranda Aldhouse-Green for an understanding of the 'curse' tablets as an inversion of Sulis's healing function.[28]

The automatic acceptance of the spa as a healing site, even in the second half of the twentieth century, is unsurprising. How could anyone think otherwise, when up until as recently as 1976 a doctor's prescription was apparently required in order to use the spa?[29] But is this premise factually necessary? Do the waters of Bath in fact possess special curative properties? The discovery of the deadly amoeba *Naegleria Fowleri* in the King's Spring, which led to the 1979–80 excavations by Cunliffe of the spring, also provided the impetus for multiple chemical and geological analyses of the water. The conclusions concerning Bath's claim to fame were ultimately ambiguous. On the one hand, the reports concluded that 'No evidence has yet been found to show that the chemistry of the water has any particular quality which is of outstanding medicinal value.'[30] On the other hand, studies did show that immersion in hot water (of any origin) could indeed produce positive physiological changes, and both historical evidence and modern trials seemed to indicate that the Bath waters had some effect on paralysis brought on by lead poisoning.[31] The idea, however, that the waters are effective at healing a wide range of conditions, and consequently that any use of the hot springs must have healing in mind, is a cultural construct. It is a construct that for us today has behind it the weight of centuries, but there is nonetheless no reason to assume the Romano-British who venerated the spring shared this construct, or that it was the primary impetus for the worship of Sulis and the construction of her sanctuary.

The Evidence from the Roman Period

By now, it should be clear where my argument is heading: a straightforward examination of the archaeological evidence from the Roman period of Bath reveals no proof that the sanctuary was curative. Of the eighteen known

---

[24] Cunliffe 1971: 1.   [25] Tomlin 1988b: 102.   [26] Salway 1981: 688.   [27] Sauer 1996.
[28] Aldhouse-Green 2006.   [29] Rolls 1991: 57–8.   [30] Kellaway 1991b: 22.
[31] O'Hare *et al.* 1991; Heyward 1991.

altars and dedications set up to the principal goddess Sulis and other gods, none were explicitly given in thanks for healing, nor are any dedicated to other healing deities such as Aesculapius or Hygeia. We also do not find requests for healing anywhere in the site's large corpus of so-called curse tablets, the pewter petitions for justice or vengeance thrown by worshipers of Sulis into the reservoir of the town's largest hot spring. Most instead are concerned with the theft of small items and with dedicating lost objects to the goddess: they do not even ask that Sulis strike the thief down with illness. Similarly, the ex-voto objects recovered from the spring evince no connection to either sickness or healing. By far the most common offerings were coins, over twelve thousand of which have been found. The more than one hundred other objects from the reservoir, ranging from a catapult washer to gemstones to pewter pans, are principally characterized by eclecticism. Finally, the sculptural corpus from Bath contains no scenes of healing or depictions of healing deities.

The overall assemblage from the sanctuary, then, shows no clear interest in or connection to healing or curative rituals. Is there any archaeological material at all from Bath that can be associated with healing?

The only ex-voto from the reservoir possibly associated with healing is a pair of ivory breasts. I am willing to accept that this anatomical ex-voto may well have been deposited for or after a cure.[32] But as John Scheid has pointed out for Gaul, one anatomical ex-voto does not make a healing site.[33] To pluck this object out of the ex-voto corpus and focus on it alone is to miss the point: the very variety of objects from the spring challenges our idea of Sulis Minerva as a goddess with a single primary purpose.

Meanwhile, three altars have occasionally been casually cited as part of healing cult.[34] All three were set up by freedmen to Sulis, for the welfare, *salus,* of their legionary former masters. Two (*RIB* 143 and 144) are dedicated *pro salute et incolumitate* – for the welfare and safety – of the same man, Aufidius Maximus, while the third (*RIB* 147) is *ob salutem sacrum* – dedicated on account of the welfare – of Gaius Iavolenus Saturnalis. But the *pro salute et incolumitate* and *ob salutem sacrum* formulae are petitions for general welfare, not just health, and are more about the continuance of well-being and the prevention of harm, than a direct reaction to illness.[35] Indeed

---

[32] Anatomical votives have usually been read as offerings either asking or giving thanks for a cure of the depicted body part (Potter 1985: 34ff). Nonetheless, it is important to note that, at least for some body parts, this interpretation may not be valid; for example, votives of feet may represent a desire for a good journey, or ears a wish to be heard by the god (Scheid 1992: 30; Recke 2013: 1075–7).

[33] Scheid 1992: 35. [34] e.g. by Salway 1981: 688. [35] Le Glay 1982: 427; Marwood 1988: 1.

both phrases were used frequently in routine and regular petitions by citizens and the state on behalf of the emperor, and are encountered on inscriptions at sites throughout the province. I will discuss these three inscriptions and the implications of their language at much greater length in Chapter 4. Here, I note only that, given the lack of other evidence for healing cult at Aquae Sulis, nothing about their texts indicates that we must read them as set up in response to a cure. *Pro salute* language elsewhere in the province has never been read as indicating a locus of healing cult; to do so at Bath is therefore a circular argument predicated on the assumption that the site was curative.

An oculist's stamp (*RIB* 2446.10; now lost), found in 1731 in the Abbey Yard, has also been cited as proof of medicinal activity at the sanctuary.[36] However, over thirty oculists' stamps have been found in Britain, from a wide range of (predominantly urban) sites.[37] They are a normal and relatively frequent part of the material culture of the north-west provinces in general.[38] As with the *pro salute* altars, we would not choose to read oculists' stamps at, for instance, London or Colchester as indicative of ritual healing: why then should we do so at Bath?[39]

A final object, *CSIR* I.2, 3, deserves extended attention, since it is often casually cited as proof of the worship of Aesculapius in Bath (Figure 2.1).[40] This smallish block (0.76 × 0.46 × 0.25 m) was found in 1885 in the Cross Bath hot spring, some 6 meters below the surface. It is extremely worn, and none of the scenes on its three carved sides (the fourth side is broken) can be identified with absolute confidence. Its size and shape, particularly its corniced top, are most in keeping with its having been an altar. One of the two larger faces depicts two figures. The right-hand figure, reclining with torso turned to face the viewer, has been identified as female, mostly nude except for drapery across the lower legs; the left-hand nude figure, standing and facing the first, is probably male. A bowl, sometimes identified as a tripod (although the legs cannot be seen), is placed in the space between the two figures, and an extremely worn animal is above them. The other wide face is blank on the lower half, while the upper half contains a carving, in slightly lower relief, of a tree and a quadruped, often

---

[36] Scarth 1862: 32ff; Sauer 1996: 73.   [37] Frere and Tomlin 1992: 46.

[38] Boon 1983: 3; Jackson 1990: 275.

[39] Scheid 1992: 28 makes the more general point that oculists' stamps, scalpels, and other medical equipment should not be taken to be indicative of a healing sanctuary, since they are found in a wide variety of public spaces.

[40] e.g. Cunliffe 1969: 4; Davenport 2000: 21; Davis and Bonsall 2006: 24. It is currently labelled as Aesculapian in nature in the Roman Baths Museum.

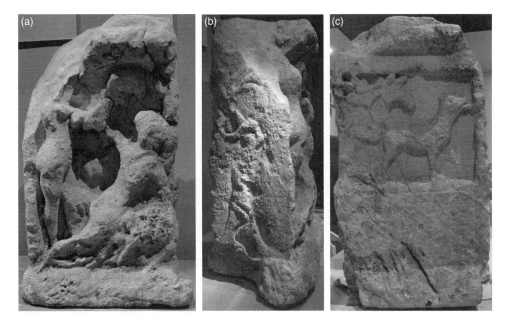

Figure 2.1: Sculptured block with unidentified figures (*CSIR* I.2, 3). (a) Front; (b) Left side; (c) Back. (Photos by author.)

identified as a dog. The one narrow face which remains shows a tree (much more satisfactorily proportioned than the tree on the quadruped face), around which a snake is entwined; the snake's upper body and head emerge from the left side of the tree-trunk about half way up the stone. This relief is very shallow – 'little more than incisive work' as the letter recording its discovery put it[41] – but nonetheless both more delicate and more detailed than those on the other faces. The relief with the two figures has always been identified as the front face, due to its deeper carving and the fact that it takes up the whole of the space on the stone; however, if the object is indeed an altar, perhaps we should take the scene with the quadruped as the front, on the grounds that the uncarved lower half may have contained a painted inscription, which could easily have been destroyed by the block's long sojourn in the Cross Bath. In support of this are the traces of a rectangle carved around this lower section, which could have provided a border for an inscription.

Without an inscription, our only clue to the deity/deities which inspired the stone's commissioning lies in the iconography. The flurry of scholarly epistolary debate, recorded by H. H. Winwood, which followed the altar's

---

[41] Winwood 1886: 79.

discovery established an Aesculapian link, due to the snake and the supposed dog. To date, this theory has been rejected only by Toynbee, who deemed it – and the consequent identification of the main two figures as Apollo and Coronis, Aesculapius's mother – as unsatisfactory.[42] Toynbee saw instead Bacchus waking Ariadne; in this interpretation, the animal above the two figures would be a panther – albeit a very inexpertly carved one.

The two deities in question – Bacchus and Aesculapius – are both rarely depicted in stone in Britain.[43] Aesculapius is hardly encountered at all, either in inscriptions or imagery, outside of military sites. The rarity of Aesculapius's appearances in Britain also makes it perhaps more unlikely that a worshiper would choose to depict an obscure mythological scene connected to him, rather than simply the deity himself, which would have had a better chance of being recognizable and familiar both to the dedicator and to potential viewers. (Indeed, mythological scenes of Aesculapius are extremely rare across the ancient world, even in places where his worship was very well-established.[44]) For Bacchus, the nearest geographical parallel is in fact another block from Bath, discussed in Chapter 6. A marble statuette from a grave near Winchcombe shows Bacchus in a similar pose to the male figure from the Cross Bath block, standing with the left knee bent, and the panther by his side shares the squat proportions of the unidentified animal above the two figures.[45] Bacchus and Bacchic imagery are more frequently found in mosaics and metal objects from the later Roman period. On balance, given these distributions, Toynbee's identification of the scene seems more likely, if one or the other has to be chosen, although the lack of any vine or grape imagery, otherwise common to all secure depictions of Bacchus in Britain, is suspicious, especially given the two excellent opportunities for such decoration provided by the trees. The stronger possibility remains, however, that the altar depicts an unknown and unrecoverable local myth. A secure Aesculapian meaning for

---

[42] Winwood 1886: 80ff; Toynbee 1964: 160, n. 4.

[43] For Bacchus: *CSIR* I.8, 2 is unconvincing, and *CSIR* I.8, 38 and 39 are even more so. *CSIR* I.7, 17, a head from Cirencester identified by Henig as either Bacchus or Apollo, lacks any attributes and could well be neither. *CSIR* I.5, 7, though highly fragmentary, is more likely, though little enough remains that it is not useful here for comparative purposes. *CSIR* I.7, 18, a Corinthian capital, is a good example of the vegetal décor often found with Bacchic imagery. Aesculapius appears in a relief from Chesters (*CSIR* I.6, 1) and possibly in one from Carrawburgh, with Minerva (*CSIR* I.6, 85), and alongside Telesphorus, Hygiea, and a Dioscurus in a relief from Risingham (*CSIR* I.1, 220) but these examples lack scenes similar to the Bath piece, and since it has never been argued that the male figure on *CSIR* I.2, 3 is Aesculapius himself, the Hadrian's Wall comparanda are of limited utility.

[44] *LIMC* II.1: 865.   [45] *CSIR* I.7, 1; Toynbee 1964: 69. Now in the British Museum.

the snake on the tree is undermined by the presence of almost identical imagery on stones dedicated to the Matronae Aufaniae in the Rhineland, where the snakes entwined on trees must relate to indigenous myth (Fig. 2.2).[46] Meanwhile, the possible dog is, to mix zoological metaphors, quite simply a red herring. Aesculapian meanings for dog iconography are often assumed in Romano-British scholarship; this association was the basis for endowing a healing aspect to Lydney Park,[47] and, as noted above, the apparent dog on the Bath block has been used as a support for an Aesculapian reading. It is unclear, however, how this association came about for archaeologists working on Roman Britain, for it has almost no basis in either Roman or Greek iconography or mythology concerning the deity. Dogs do seem to be an aspect of Asklepios's cult at Epidauros: Pausanias (2.27.2) reports that the cult statue included a dog as well as a serpent, and some of the epigraphy from the site reports cures effected by dogs (presumably via licking).[48] This aspect seems to be unique to Epidauros, however, and the material collated in the *LIMC* makes clear that dogs are virtually, or indeed entirely, absent from Greek and Roman Aesculapian iconography, with the exception of Epidauros and Athens (where they are still extremely rare).[49] For this particular block, then, even if the quadruped is identified as a dog, this should not be taken as indicative of an Aesculapian meaning, and Romano-British scholars generally should discard the conception that dogs symbolize healing. (We can probably lay the blame for the initial equation on the antiquarian tendency to seek classical explanations, however strained, for British material – after which the link between dogs and Aesculapius seems to have slowly taken on the status of received wisdom.) In conclusion, since either traditional identification – Bacchus and Ariadne or an Aesculapian scene – would be almost unique in Britain, the testimony provided by this stone about deities honoured in Bath is too tenuous and too potentially overemphasized (especially in the case of Aesculapius) to be blithely accepted.

Thus the material evidence offers no support for the idea that Roman Bath's principal function was that of a healing sanctuary. Is there any reason to think, even in the absence of archaeological evidence from the site, that the hot springs of Bath would have been perceived as curative by the Romans? That is, did the Romans view all hot springs as water with healing

---

[46] Espérandieu XI, 7768, 7772, 7777; Lehner 1930: 6–17, 37. See also Bauchhenß 2013 for further examples of trees, not always with snakes, on the side of Rhineland altars.
[47] Wheeler and Wheeler 1932: 41.   [48] Reinach 1884: 130–1; Dillon 1997: 78.
[49] *LIMC* I.2: 865 and *passim*.

Figure 2.2: Side of altar (Espérandieu XI, 7777) to the Matronae Aufaniae from the Rhineland, depicting a snake entwined around a tree. (© LVR-LandesMuseum, Bonn.)

power, and thus do we necessarily have to view Roman use of the Bath springs as having a healing intent?

Turning first to the literary evidence, there are two particularly lengthy descriptions in ancient texts of the effects of mineral water. The first comes from Vitruvius, who discusses the nature of hot springs in chapter 3 of Book VIII of the *De Architectura*. Vitruvius does claim that all warm springs are curative.[50] His reasoning stems from his understanding of the nature of hot springs: in his geology, they occur through water's encounter with subterranean fires ignited by the presence of minerals, specifically alum, bitumen, and sulphur.[51] All hot springs therefore are imbued with the power of these minerals, each of which is seen to be efficacious in curing different types of ailments.[52]

The Elder Pliny's discussion of the properties of water in Book XXXI of the Natural History is similar to Vitruvius's. It is clear, however, that Pliny the Elder only considered some hot springs – not all – to be of medicinal value. As he puts it, 'Everywhere in many lands gush forth beneficent waters, here cold, there hot, there both … in some places tepid and lukewarm, promising relief to the sick and bursting forth to help only men of all the animals.'[53] Pliny's description makes it clear that it is not the temperature of the water which is key, but rather its mineral properties, factors which for him are not correlated: of the springs at Baiae, which according to Pliny have the most varied medical effects, 'some have the *vis* of sulphur, some of alum, some of salt, some of soda, some of bitumen, some are even acid and salt in combination'.[54] Indeed, he later explicitly states that not all hot springs are medicinal.[55] It is also clear from Pliny's discussion of individual springs that, like Vitruvius, he believes each water source to be particularly effective at healing one specific ailment; most waters will not act as a universal remedy.

The difference of opinion between Pliny and Vitruvius casts enough doubt on the matter of the healing power of hot springs, so that we are not able to assume, as casually as some have done, that because Bath has hot springs, it must be a healing site. That some waters were held to be curative in the ancient world is clearly beyond question. But there was also clearly debate even among the learned over what constituted healthy or curative

---

[50] '*Omnis autem aqua calida ideo [quod] est medicamentosa … '* (But all hot waters are on that account medicinal … ') Vitr. VIII.3.4.

[51] Vitr. VIII.3.1.   [52] Vitr. VIII.3.4.

[53] '*Emicant benigne passimque in plurimis terris alibi frigidae, alibi calidae, alibi iunctae … alibi tepidae egelidaeque, auxilia morborum profitentes et e cunctis animalibus hominum tantum causa erumpentes.*' *Nat. His.* XXXI.4. Loeb translation.

[54] '*aliae sulpuris vi, aliae aluminis, aliae salis, aliae nitri, aliae bituminis, nonnullae etiam acida salsave mixture.*' *Nat. His.* XXXI.5. Translation after Loeb.

[55] '*nec vero omnes quae sint calidae medicatas esse credendum … '*: 'nor indeed should all waters which are hot be thought of as medicinal.' *Nat. His.* XXXI.61.

water.[56] Pliny the Elder's opinions demonstrate that we cannot assume that in the first centuries BC and AD there was consensus on the matter even in Rome, let alone in the provinces; we therefore have no real literary support for assuming that Aquae Sulis must have functioned as a health spa.

The archaeological evidence on the subject is trickier to approach, since assumptions about the curative nature of excavated water sanctuaries very often depend on the acceptance of the very postulates I am rejecting with respect to Aquae Sulis, in particular that mineral waters by their very nature should be assumed to be the *locus* of healing cult. It is not enough, in other words, to examine whether a given sanctuary site at a hot spring is presented as curative in the literature, and to identify further spring sites as curative based on analogy with others so identified; what we are dealing with here is in fact a fundamental difference of opinion over whether the presence of mineral springs in itself is enough to label a sacred site as curative.

The first approach – the assumption that mineral springs are curative as a starting point – is the outlook which lies behind much recent work by European scholars, for example Gonzàlez Soutelo for Spain, and Bassani for Italy.[57] For Gonzàlez Soutelo, the connection is so fundamental that she refers not simply to mineral waters, but exclusively to 'aguas mineromedicinales', 'mineromedicinal waters'. For this branch of scholarship, consideration of the use of the waters for healing in antiquity, and in particular the use of specific waters for specific cures, then frequently proceeds along two lines: (a) using medieval and post-medieval associations with Christian saints to postulate about the water's significance in antiquity,[58] and (b) basing arguments concerning use on chemical analysis of the waters.[59] This scholarship is usually thorough in its knowledge of the archaeological evidence of the sites it discusses, and coherent within its theoretical framework. However, it is inevitably and unavoidably at cross-purposes with those, like myself, who do not share the assumption that mineral = mineromedicinal, to use Gonzàlez Soutelo's terminology. My starting point is entirely the opposite: the connection to healing cult can never be assumed simply by the nature of the water, but must always be proved by the ritual context as a whole. The approach I subscribe to was neatly summed up by

---

[56] Vitruvius and Pliny the Elder also differ over the quality of rain water, with Vitruvius holding it to be the best water, because it is the 'lightest', and Pliny the Elder finding rain-derived cistern water to be unquestionably the most revolting.

[57] e.g. Gonzàlez Soutelo 2011 and 2014; Bassani 2014a and 2014b; Carneiro 2016. See also the session 'Rethinking the concept of "Healing Settlements": Cults, Constructions and Contexts in the Western Roman Empire' at the 2016 Roman Archaeology Conference, held in Rome.

[58] e.g. Piboule and Piboule 1985.   [59] e.g. Gonzàlez Soutelo 2011: 383–4.

Scheid in 1992: 'on ne saurait considérer comme sanctuaire guérisseur (dont la fonction première est de guérir) qu'un sanctuaire qui livre des témoignages parfaitement explicites de guérisons, inscriptions univoques et/ou nombreux ex-voto de toutes sortes d'organes' ('We should consider as a healing sanctuary (whose primary function is to heal) only a sanctuary which produces perfectly explicit evidence of healings, unequivocal inscriptions, and/or numerous ex-votos of all sorts of organs).[60] As we have seen, Bath does not meet these criteria, and, in my opinion, nor do many mineral water sites in Spain, Gaul, and Italy which have been casually cited as curative.[61]

Nonetheless, it is not my purpose here to present a full counter-argument to this scholarship: we begin from such entirely different postulates that this is, indeed, impossible. Those who subscribe to the view that spring sanctuaries must have a curative purpose will likely never agree with my argument that Bath was no healing sanctuary. However, I nonetheless hope that they will still find value in the analysis which lies in the rest of this book. If a cache of unequivocal ex-votos related to cures from Bath came to light tomorrow, the arguments in the chapters which follow concerning Aquae Sulis's broader place in the north-west provinces, and the general ritual characteristics of the site, would I think nonetheless still hold true. In other words, even for healing sites (and even if Aquae Sulis were one), healing is only one aspect of the story.

---

[60] Scheid 1992: 35.

[61] That said, many clearly are, and some of these will be discussed in Chapter 5. The general impression from the evidence is that Gaul has produced more firm indications of healing cult on the whole than the other western provinces. In my opinion, there is no clear-cut case of a curative sanctuary at all from Britain.

3 | Experiencing Aquae Sulis

The previous two chapters have explored our modern understanding of Roman Bath and how it has been shaped by the site's post-Roman history. I turn now in this chapter to Aquae Sulis proper, and in particular to the ways in which Roman-period visitors would have experienced the sanctuary and its architecture. I begin by presenting a picture of how the sanctuary environment would have appeared to visitors, taking as a primary vantage point its appearance towards the end of the second century (which, as far as we can tell, represents roughly the peak of its monumentalization), but also clarifying the ways in which the fabric of the sanctuary developed from the first century AD onwards. The account which I present here in the main body of the text is deliberately impressionistic, qualitative, and relatively brief, although supported throughout by concrete archaeological evidence. I have confined that evidence here to lengthy footnotes, which should be understood as a commentary – perhaps even *scholia* – on the main narrative. My reasons for this are two-fold. The appearance in 2016 of a detailed archaeological assessment of Bath by La Trobe-Bateman and Niblett, commissioned by English Heritage, has filled a previously urgent need for an up-to-date and comprehensive synthesis of our archaeological understanding of the site. It is therefore neither necessary nor useful to reduplicate their work here. However, a qualitative description of the site, which takes into account both our current knowledge and the substantial remaining archaeological *lacunae*, does remain a necessary thing. It is useful in and of itself, as a clear and accessible presentation of an important site for scholars who do not work closely on material from Bath, and thus for whom detailed engagement with La Trobe-Bateman and Niblett's work is unnecessary, and of course it is also necessary within the broader context of this book, in order to set the physical scene into which the religious rituals, mentalities, and connections which are the focus of subsequent chapters must be placed.

This chapter begins, then, as stated, with a description of what a visitor to Aquae Sulis around AD 200 would have seen as they approached the site and moved through it. I then use this description as a springboard to discuss two different key aspects of the background to visitor experience at the sanctuary. The first is the way in which classicizing monumentalization would have shaped every aspect of the sanctuary's environment. The second emphasizes the importance of understanding the sanctuary as a space outside the bounds of normal lived experience, using pilgrimage as a tentative framework within which to conceptualize this aspect. Both of these elements – the classicizing nature of the sanctuary's monumental architecture, and Aquae Sulis's inherent nature as a set-apart place in the landscape which must be travelled to – should then be understood as underlying and shaping the sanctuary's other functions which I discuss in the chapters which follow.

Envisioning Aquae Sulis

Visitors approaching Aquae Sulis in AD 200 would have approached the heart of the sanctuary from the north, along a road which branched off from a main east-west artery. That artery stretched in one direction all the way to the provincial capital at London and in the other to the port at Sea Mills, Abonae, and after that by sea to Wales. From this junction, a little to the east of where the London road met the Fosse Way heading north to Cirencester, a visitor could have looked down onto the route that led through a moderate-sized settlement to the sanctuary, whose *temenos* embankments would have been visible in the shallow valley below (Figure 3.1).[1]

They would have then headed down the line of what is now Walcot Street, passed through a thriving community of shops and houses and industry, centred on this main crossroads and spreading south from it.[2] As they continued down the road towards the sanctuary, these buildings thinned a little, before they passed through the earthen rampart which marked the edge of the sacred zone.[3] Due to these defences, from the outside Aquae

---

[1] The settlement and sanctuary lie in the Avon valley at the southern end of the Cotswolds, with limestone uplands rising to some 230 m to the north and south of the site; the walled zone is surrounded on three sides by a loop of the river Avon, although the precise course of the river's meandering has changed somewhat since Roman times.

[2] Urban archaeology in recent decades has added greatly to our understanding of this extramural settlement, particularly along modern Walcot Street, which was an area of mixed use, with evidence for burials, domestic contexts, and industrial activity found in the same areas, seemingly throughout the Roman period (Davenport 2000: 14–15; La Trobe-Bateman and Niblett 2016: 84–8). Davenport argues that we should see the development along Walcot St not as a straggling settlement spreading from the monumentalized zone around the springs, but rather originating at the major road crossing at Cleveland Bridge; the Walcot St settlement as it spread south and sanctuary area together, then, formed 'what might be described as a dumb-bell plan' (Davenport 2000: 17).

[3] Evidence for the settlement walls is surprisingly limited. The polygonal shape reproduced on all maps of the Roman settlement is based on the assumption that the course of the Roman walls was the same as those of the medieval town (Wedlake 1966: 85). Excavation at various points, most notably at the Upper Borough Walls in the northern part of the town, implies that the Roman town

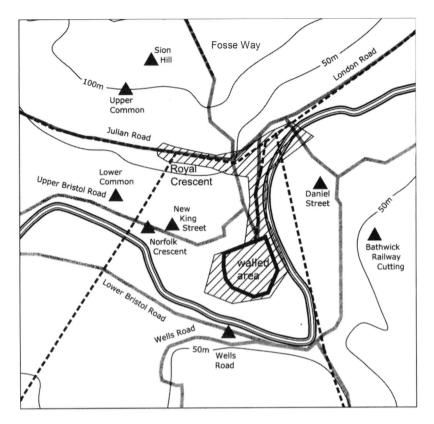

Figure 3.1: Area around Bath, showing roads (both ancient and modern) and villas (triangles). (After Davenport 2007, Figure 22.8. © Oxford University Press; reproduced with permission of the Licensor through PLSclear.)

Sulis looked like many small towns. But within, the atmosphere was different. Big buildings rose up in the spaces in front of them, and the clamour of everyday life was gone – there were no ordinary houses and shopfronts, no yards for blacksmiths or carpenters (Figure 3.2).[4] Buildings

---

was originally surrounded by an earthen rampart (La Trobe-Bateman and Niblett 2016: 77–81). The limited pottery evidence suggests a construction date in the late second century (Cunliffe 1969: 166; Cunliffe 1971: 77); La Trobe-Bateman and Niblett place it 'some time after the early to mid-second century' (La Trobe-Bateman and Niblett 2016: 80). This rampart appears to have been a substantial feature, at least 2 m high and 9 m wide (Cunliffe 1971: 77). The later wall, 3 m thick, was built against it. The date of the wall is difficult to determine. Portions of the wall visible in other parts of the city do look like Roman masonry, rather than medieval work (Cunliffe 1971: 78; Plate XXXb), but as yet no date can be attached to its construction (La Trobe-Bateman and Niblett 2016: 81).

[4] The walled area is notably lacking in 'ordinary' urban fabric – in particular evidence of domestic, commercial, or industrial contexts – until the second half of the fourth century, when the temple precinct began to be abandoned (Davenport 2000: 11–14; La Trobe-Bateman and Niblett 2016: 100–3). This strongly supports an understanding of the area around the springs as a sacred, or

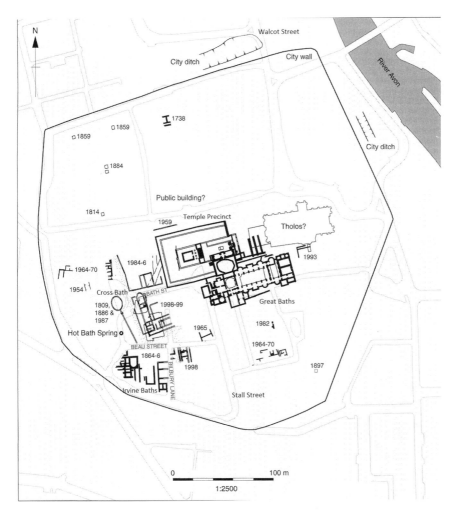

Figure 3.2: Map of the walled area of Aquae Sulis and excavated areas within it. (After Davenport, Poole, and Jordan 2007: fig. 1.3. Reproduced with permission of Oxford Archaeology.)

immediately after entering the ramparted area were sparse.[5] But a couple hundred meters away was a cluster of monumental buildings. To the right side of this cluster, rising above a low colonnade, visitors would see the roof and column capitals of a temple; beyond this, barrel-shaped rooftops

---

even *temenos*, zone, with the second century earthworks functioning as a marker of the boundaries of sacred space (Dark 1993).

[5] There is limited evidence for the Roman occupation of the north-east quarter of the walled zone; however, what there is implies that there was little occupation until the later Roman period, when high-status buildings, indicated by rich mosaic finds, began to appear (La Trobe-Bateman and Niblett 2016: 77).

implied a great building.[6] On the left was the second precinct of elaborate buildings.[7] Somewhere in this view they could also spot an elegant round columned structure, a *tholos*.[8] From here they could make their way towards the gateway which would have been visible in the eastern wall of the temple's precinct (Figure 3.3).

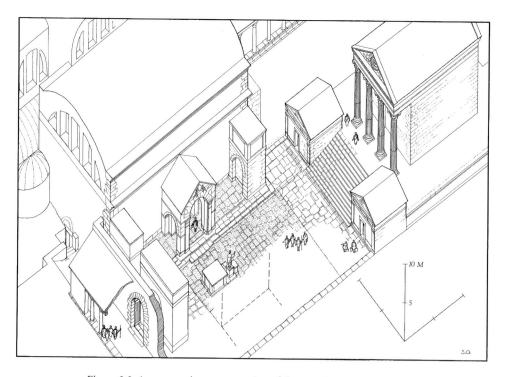

Figure 3.3: Axonometric reconstruction of the temple precinct roughly as it would have appeared at the start of the third century. (Cunliffe and Davenport 1985, Figure 112. Reproduced by permission of the School of Archaeology, University of Oxford.)

[6] Within the walled zone rise up three hot springs, known today as the Hot Bath, Cross Bath, and King's Spring. The King's Spring has by far the largest flow, with the Hot and Cross Baths springs providing together only about 10 per cent of the total flow from the three (Kellaway 1985: 8). The reservoir enclosing the King's Spring seems to have been the ritual heart of the site, with the temple to Sulis Minerva and the large bathing complex adjacent to it.

[7] It is clear that there was another monumental precinct or platform under what is now the west end of the Abbey, sighted occasionally from the nineteenth century onwards, with our main evidence coming from Mann's papers (Mann Papers, plan no. 2); due to its location, however, archaeological investigations have been limited (La Trobe-Bateman and Niblett 2016: 55–7).

[8] We possess parts of the ornately decorated frieze and architrave from this building, which was around 9 m in diameter (Cunliffe 1989: 63–4). Its location remains a matter of speculation. It is too large to fit in any of the unexcavated spaces of the precinct of the temple of Sulis Minerva (Cunliffe 1989: 67). The suggestion that it was placed in the precinct under the abbey (Cunliffe

As they turned into the precinct, they would see before them a stone monument decorated with images of the gods.[9] Behind this, some way further back, was the temple. Through its open doors a hint of bronze might have been visible glinting in the dark, while outside its four Corinthian columns rose to an elaborately carved pediment.[10] Its tall steps were flanked by two small chambers, and it was surrounded on three sides by a walkway raised above the precinct floor.[11]

There would have been an abundance of imagery everywhere visitors looked, both within this precinct and outside it. One building had an elegant façade with seated women, above whom the Four Seasons flitted in the shape of cupids. The *tholos* was decorated with more images of the gods, and small stone votive reliefs were scattered throughout the space, showing Minerva, Mercury, and other, perhaps local, deities whose iconography might have been recognizable only to a few.

1989: 68; La Trobe-Bateman and Niblett 2016: 57), while appealing, has no archaeological foundation as yet. As for its date, the ornamentation has been dated stylistically to the early second century (Cunliffe 1989: 67; Blagg 2002: 104); Cunliffe has suggested it might coincide with Hadrian's visit to the province (Cunliffe 1989: 69). This too is unprovable.

[9] This monument, traditionally interpreted as an altar, is discussed at length in Chapter 6.

[10] The glint of bronze represents the likely cult statue of Sulis Minerva, whose surviving gilt bronze head is discussed in Chapter 6. The architectural decoration on the temple of Sulis Minerva indicates that it was constructed in the first century AD, most likely in the late Neronian or early Flavian period; the closest stylistic parallels are found in north-eastern Gaul, and it is likely that artisans from this region were brought to Bath to help in the temple's construction. Blagg 1979 and Blagg 2002: 101–2 lay out the stylistic arguments for the temple's date and closest parallels.

[11] The temple in its first phase was a tetrastyle building in the Corinthian order, with the columns rising to a height of about 8 m, based on the diameter of the bases. (The reconstruction of the elevation drawn by Lysons in 1813 is still regarded as generally correct; some elements of his reconstruction of the pediment were modified by Richmond and Toynbee 1955. The carved pediment is so far unique in the north-western provinces.) The temple was about 9 m wide (as shown by the width of the tympanum), and probably no more than 14 m long (Cunliffe and Davenport 1985: 27, 33). It stood on a thick podium at least 1.2 m, but possibly up to 2 m high (Cunliffe and Davenport 1985: 29); the facing from this podium has not survived, but its core was of oolitic limestone rubble set in mortar (Wedlake 1979: 81). A flight of steps descended from the top of the podium to the paved surface of the precinct (Cunliffe and Davenport 1985: 33). The temple seems to have remained largely unchanged for around one hundred years after its construction, until widespread modifications occurred at some point after the third quarter of the second century (Cunliffe and Davenport 1985: 34; fragments of *terra sigillata* dating to AD 160–80 found in this period's make-up layers provide a rough *terminus post quem*). The flight of steps was probably re-treaded at this point, and a pair of rooms was added, which flanked the steps and extended from them to the edge of the podium on either side (Cunliffe and Davenport 1985: 33). The steps and these rooms formed a straight line fronting the inner precinct. Around the same time, a paved ambulatory seems to have been placed around the remaining sides of the temple, bringing the raised area around the temple into line with the respective north and south walls of the north and south rooms. This ambulatory seems to have been lower than the original podium, but still higher than the surrounding precinct (Cunliffe and Davenport 1985: 30–2).

As one stood on the threshold to the temple precinct, to the left was a four-sided archway surmounted with a relief of two nymphs on either side of a spring gushing from a rock.[12] Its imagery hinted at what the great vaulted building behind it contained, and the steam issuing from the archway itself would have confirmed it: here was the heart of the site, the hot spring sacred to the goddess Sulis Minerva.

Visitors arriving a century earlier would not have needed these hints: they would have seen the surface of the spring's reservoir as soon as they entered the precinct, and been able to lean over an iron balustrade to get even closer to it.[13] A few decades before that, they could have witnessed the reservoir's construction: the ring of wooden piles driven into the water-sodden ground, the labour to remove the mud within this ring, the construction of the reservoir walls in stone and lead, Roman engineering fighting – and winning – against a quarter of a million gallons of hot water each day.[14] But this struggle against nature, the way the land was turned from a muddy, hot swamp overflowing with steaming water into a controlled

---

[12] Cunliffe and Davenport 1985: 57ff. It is clear from the foundations that the spring was accessed in this period by a monumental doorway in the shape of a quadrifrons. The attribution of the fragmentary relief of the nymphs with the spring to this monument is unproven but attractive; Cunliffe's addition of a relief of Sol, reconstructed as a roundel held aloft by the nymphs, has in my opinion little to recommend it, especially since the Sol fragment is considerably thinner than the others (33 cm vs c. 60 cm).

[13] The reservoir in its earliest phase was unenclosed, but stone blocks with sockets for a metal grille were found by Davis in the rubble of the spring (Cunliffe and Davenport 1985: 42). At some point, probably in the second century, the reservoir was then enclosed in a massive stone structure with ashlar walls, measuring 23.4 × 15.3 m (Cunliffe and Davenport 1985: 49). This structure, considerably larger than the temple, would have dominated the precinct.

[14] Today the King's Spring produces 250,000 gallons a day, at a temperature of 46.5°C; geologists working on the appearance of the springs in prehistory and the Roman period have assumed that there has been no significant change in the flow since then (Cunliffe and Davenport 1985: 37; Kellaway 1985: 7–8). A quarter of a million gallons a day is an extraordinarily large volume to control, and the design of the reservoir demonstrates both the detailed Roman knowledge of the workings of the spring, and Roman determination to render its output tameable. The waterlogged mud which surrounded and clogged the spring on the east, west, and possibly north sides was first consolidated by a wide ring of wooden piles (Cunliffe and Davenport 1985: 39). Probably after construction of the permanent main drain, which led out water through a gap in the pile ring, mud was dug out from the spring head between the wooden piles. This involved a considerable amount of earth-moving, to a level at least 1.5 m below the tops of the piles (Cunliffe and Davenport 1985: 39). The building of the massive bathstone wall of the reservoir was the next stage, with a sluice slot for the draining of the reservoir placed on the west side, and an outlet leading to the box drain of the Great Bath on the south side (Cunliffe and Davenport 1985: 39–40). (The sluice seems to have been more for occasionally draining accumulated sand, with seemingly all the spring water sent to the baths (Cunliffe and Davenport 1985: 42).) Finally, the interior was lined with lead sheeting 10–20 mm thick, and the tops of the piles closed over with waterproof mortar, ensuring that the whole remained watertight (Cunliffe and Davenport 1985: 40).

human space of stone buildings, was in the past by this point. A hint of the water's natural origins remained only in the way the coins which worshipers dropped soon disappeared into the sandy, silty murk, as if vanishing into the depths of the earth.

Back in the bright sunlight of the precinct, huge barrel roofs visible above the reservoir and the colonnaded portico on the southern side of the precinct would have indicated the presence of a great building, but there seems to have been no way into this massive complex from the temple's courtyard.[15] To investigate, visitors would have had to head out the eastern gate and circle round until they found the entrance to what would soon be evident to them as a massive bathing complex.

Where exactly they would have entered we are still not sure (Figure 3.4). Inside, they would have made their way through open-plan courts and smaller bath suites[16] to a central hall with a circular bath. In earlier times, before this pool was added, they could have looked out from the hall into the reservoir of the spring. But by the late second century, this vista was closed off, and the spring was no longer visible from within the bath complex.[17] From this room they could enter the Great Bath, with the largest pool of the complex, fed directly by the spring's thermal waters.[18] Beyond this great room was a second suite of bathing rooms, heated by hypocausts rather than by the spring.[19]

If this mighty bathing complex did not suit the needs of visitors, there were smaller, more intimate bathing complexes elsewhere in the city, most

---

[15] While it is usually assumed that the bath complex, reservoir, and temple are all roughly contemporaneous, there seems to be no direct point of access between the two – and the orthodoxy that they were laid out as a coherent unit (La Trobe-Bateman and Niblett 2016: 52) should be approached with a degree of caution. The complex went through several phases of expansion and reconfiguration over the centuries, and the full extent of the building, including where and how it was entered, is still not fully known. However, thanks to careful survey in the twentieth century first by I. A. Richmond and then by Barry Cunliffe, the basic sequence of the baths' development, through five major periods, may be delineated, although the dating of these periods is obscure.

[16] The southern part of the complex is still not completely understood. First-period small bathing rooms were replaced in the second period by an open court immediately to the south of the circular bath, and somewhat larger baths to the court's east (Cunliffe 1969: 106–8). This area was further expanded to the east in Periods 3 and 4, although the easternmost limit has yet to be traced, and the purpose of this later expansion is unknown (Cunliffe 1969: 108).

[17] Richmond in Cunliffe 1969: 103–5. The changing access points to the reservoir are discussed in greater detail in Chapter 5.

[18] Richmond in Cunliffe 1969: 95.

[19] To begin with, this suite, now known as the Lucas bath, was heated with thermal waters (Richmond in Cunliffe 1969: 95). In subsequent periods, it underwent multiple transformations, with the addition of various heated rooms and pools, in essence becoming a more 'traditional' bath suite, rather than a thermal suite (Richmond in Cunliffe 1969: 113–14).

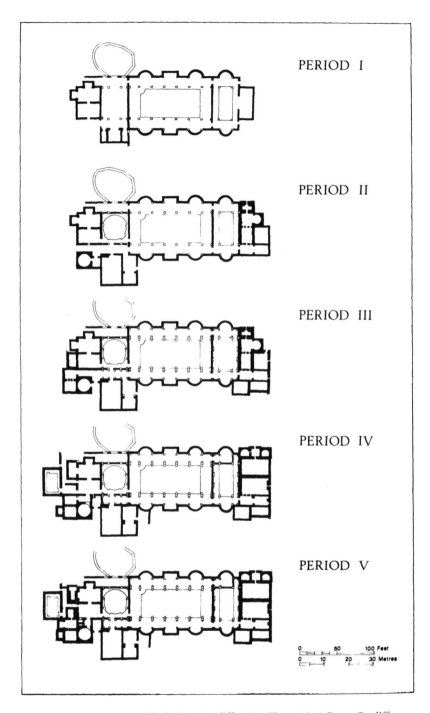

Figure 3.4: Development of the baths. (Cunliffe 1976, Figure 12. © Barry Cunliffe 1976. Exclusive Licence to Publish: The Society for the Promotion of Roman Studies, published by Cambridge University Press.)

notably in the south-west corner of the walled zone, where a substantial suite was fed by water from the Cross and Hot Baths.[20] At both of these smaller springs, people would have seen evidence that other worshipers had stopped to venerate these waters, too: altars were placed around the Cross Bath, and perhaps they would have watched someone drop in an offering in the form of a coin at the Hot Bath, or indeed made such a gift themselves.[21]

Visitors' overall impression of the sacred space within the earthwork boundaries would have been of monumentality, and classicizing monumentality at that. They would never have seen such a quantity of architectural elaboration outside of the provincial capital, and certainly never so densely crowded in such a small place. I now wish to turn to examine the elements of this architectural environment in a little more depth.

Classicizing Monumentality at Aquae Sulis

The architectural environment at Aquae Sulis needs to be understood in part in light of both the sanctuary's and Britain's incorporation into the Roman empire. This aspect of the story is explored further in subsequent chapters: in Chapter 4 we shall see how the construction of the temple, reservoir, and baths in the first century AD may have been part of a self-conscious

---

[20] This complex is known primarily from J. T. Irvine's manuscript plans, drawn during the 1864–6 construction of the Royal United Hospital (Irvine Papers); he recorded a series of rooms, some with hypocausts, and the remains of at least two pools, extending at least 18 m east-west and 20 m north-south. Observations by Taylor in 1908 suggest that the baths in fact continued for some way to the east, to the west side of Hot Bath Street (Cunliffe 1969: 152). This, combined with the direction of the northernmost wall seen by Irvine, would suggest that the edges of this complex came very close to the Hot Bath, and it seems reasonable that they were fed at least in part by the thermal waters of the spring. Furthermore, a pipe has been traced from the Cross Bath almost all the way to Beau Street (Davenport 1999: 39); given the considerably smaller outflow of both Hot and Cross Baths compared to the King's Spring, it would not be surprising if the Irvine Baths were fed by both. The date of the complex is unknown.

[21] Examination of the archaeology of the Hot Bath has been limited to sieving the material from a borehole sample (230 mm in diameter) during the New Royal Bath excavations (Davenport, Poole, and Jordan 2007: 9). This sieving produced 330 coins, of which 218 are identifiable as Roman (Corney in Davenport, Poole, and Jordan 2007: 149). There is no evidence that the spring was contained in a reservoir like that of the King's Spring; it has been suggested that in the Roman period water was carried away from the spring in stone culverts, probably towards the Irvine Baths to the south (Davenport, Poole, and Jordan 2007: 145). At the Cross Bath, an elliptical tank and drain heading southeast from the spring are Roman but cannot be dated more precisely than that. In the Cross Bath spring itself, two altars (one uninscribed, the other to Sulis Minerva and the Numina Augustorum), as well as the carved block with mythological scenes discussed in Chapter 2, were found at various points in the nineteenth century.

and imperialism-laden expression of ownership of the site by the new Roman establishment, while Chapters 5 and 6 will discuss the ways in which Aquae Sulis became more organically integrated into the iconographic and religious networks of the north-west province as time went on. Throughout and despite these changes in the site's role and context, its ongoing architectural development nevertheless remains a continuous drumbeat grounded above all in an aesthetic of classicizing monumentalism. Indeed, the evidence as a whole from Aquae Sulis indicates that the sanctuary possessed, from an early date, some of the most elaborate architectural ornamentation in the province.

The temple of Sulis Minerva sets a Mediterranean architectural tone at the heart of the site, although it is not the most ornate structure in the sanctuary. The temple broadly is in the Corinthian order, although there is (as yet) no evidence for a frieze.[22] While the acanthus leaves of the column capitals are strong rather than delicate, which slightly lessens the effect of the elaboration, the fluted column shafts, meanwhile, are unique in Bath (Fig. 3.5); all other shafts found so far are plain.[23] The cornice, although carved in the same 'strong' style as the capital, is more ornate in terms of its elements, incorporating not only acanthus leaves on its cyma, but 'scrolls, sprigs, flowers, and bunches of fruit' on the soffit as well (Fig. 3.6).[24]

Figure 3.5: Column capital from the temple of Sulis Minerva.
(Photo by author.)

[22] Blagg 2002: 99.   [23] Cunliffe 1989: 62.   [24] Cunliffe and Davenport 1985: 116.

Figure 3.6: Soffit of the cornice from the temple of Sulis Minerva. (Photo by author.)

Furthermore, the sheer presence of a sculptured pediment, unique so far amongst temples in not only Britain but the rest of the north-west provinces, also serves to mark the temple out as an elaborately decorated monument.

The surrounding area of the temple precinct also contained several other monuments with classical architectural elements. As we have seen, from probably the mid second century onwards, the entrance to the spring was a quadrifrons, with pilasters on the front and a sculptured pediment depicting nymphs and water gushing from a rock.[25] The reservoir seems to have possessed an undecorated cornice and a plain frieze.[26] The most ornamental element apart from the temple, however, was likely the so-called Façade of the Four Seasons. Although extremely fragmentary, enough remains to show that this monument, with its series of elegant pilasters, between which were set cupids and seated figures in shell-shaped canopies, must have created a highly decorative – and delicate – façade for a substantial section of the precinct, although its precise location is unknown (Fig. 3.7).[27] Outside of the temple of Sulis Minerva and its precinct, there is evidence for at least one other major building with elaborate architecture from the first or early second century. Architectural fragments of a large, early building have been found in the foundations of a later (second century) building (so-called "Building D") uncovered during excavations at the New Royal Spa, to the southwest of the precinct around the King's Spring, between the King's

---

[25] Cunliffe and Davenport 1985: 120.   [26] Cunliffe and Davenport 1985: 122–3.
[27] Cunliffe and Davenport 1985: fig. 70.

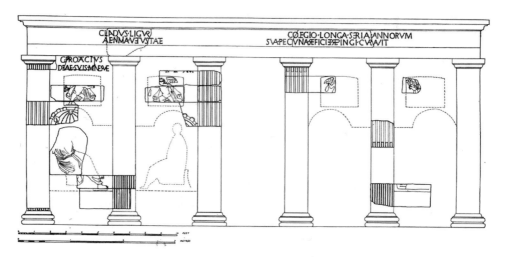

Figure 3.7: Façade of the Four Seasons. (Cunliffe and Davenport 1985, Figure 70. Reproduced by permission of the School of Archaeology, University of Oxford.)

Spring and the Hot Bath.[28] The location of the building these fragments came from is unknown – it was certainly not on the site of the later structure – but it was clearly a public building of some degree of grandeur.[29] Fragments of columns, column capitals, attached columns, and possible evidence for a cornice and an arched opening have been found.[30] Nonetheless, these fragments, although indicating a certain architectural magnificence, do not possess the elaborate decorative elements seen on other structures from the town: the capitals, for instance, are in a plain, more 'Doric', style, without any vegetal decoration, as is the cornice fragment (although it is not certain the cornice fragment comes from the same structure). On the other hand, a large amount of painted plaster was mixed in with the stone in the foundations, which would indicate that the interior of the building may have made up for the relative plainness of the exterior.[31] ('Relative' is the key word here.) The function of this structure is unknown. Davenport has posited that it may belong to a 'military administration headquarters or regional office, built in the mid-to-late first century to a suitably high standard, and demolished when the administrative structures became fully civilianized in the middle years of the second century'.[32] However, since there is no evidence that Aquae Sulis was ever under direct military control, and no such

[28] Davenport, Poole, and Jordan 2007: 58–63.   [29] Davenport, Poole, and Jordan 2007: 31–2; 68–9.
[30] Davenport, Poole, and Jordan 2007: 58–63.   [31] Davenport, Poole, and Jordan 2007: 32.
[32] Davenport, Poole, and Jordan 2007: 69.

administrative building is known from elsewhere in the province, this seems an unlikely theory.

Another very large and elaborate building – larger than the temple of Sulis Minerva – is known only from four remnants of its cornice, which was decorated with foliage and also heads with holes for rainwater.[33] The location of this structure is unknown, although the cornice fragments were found around thirty-five meters north of the temple.[34]

The most ornate building in Aquae Sulis appears to have been the circular monument, deemed a *tholos* by Cunliffe, which was located somewhere outside the precinct of the temple of Sulis Minerva.[35] We possess parts of the frieze and architrave from this monument; it has been suggested that a piece of cornice and some unassigned Corinthian columns could also come from it, but there is no firm proof for this.[36] The building was around nine meters in diameter, a considerable size, and given the proportions probably had columns at least seven meters high.[37] The pieces of frieze are decorated on both the outside and inside faces; both have elaborate vegetal decoration and the outer face also possessed panels with sculpted figures, although these are all now too damaged to allow for identification of the figures.[38] The architrave also has foliated decoration.

Both frieze and architrave are noteworthy features. Architraves in general, let alone elaborately decorated ones, are rare in Britain (although a plurality of the known examples come from Bath); the only other two architraves with 'enriched mouldings' from the province both come from arches.[39] Friezes in entablatures are equally rare.[40] The *tholos*, then, was remarkable not only in its circular shape but also in the richness of its decoration: this was probably one of the most architecturally elaborate buildings in Britain, let alone Aquae Sulis.

The high level of architectural ornament in Aquae Sulis would have served to create a general atmosphere of elaboration and classical sophistication at the site, particularly compared with elsewhere in the province, and particularly from the second century onwards. Thus by the time they entered the temple precinct, visitors to the sanctuary would have been primed to feel that they were, overall, in a sophisticated – and, more importantly, Romanly

---

[33] Blagg 2002: 93; 100.   [34] Cunliffe 1969: 149.   [35] Cunliffe 1989; Blagg 2002: 102–3.

[36] Cunliffe 1989: 62–3. The study of this building and the architectural elements we possess from it had long been hampered by Haverfield's mistakenly stating its radius as its diameter, leading later scholars to think the structure was half the size it actually was; this mistake was not rectified until Cunliffe re-measured it in the late 1980s (Cunliffe 1989: 70, note 7).

[37] Cunliffe 1989: 63–4.   [38] Cunliffe 1989: 60–1.   [39] Blagg 2002: 88.   [40] Blagg 2002: 91.

sophisticated – built environment. As Blagg has put it, 'A stone column with capital and base mouldings is not just a means of support. It is a statement of the adoption of classical values, an architectural mode of expression, cognate with the adoption of the Latin language.'[41] The sheer density of classical architecture within the bounds of the ten hectare area delineated by the later walls would have turned Aquae Sulis into one of the most emphatically Roman architectural spaces in the province.

Coming to Aquae Sulis

In the opening section of this chapter, our hypothetical visitors turn down a minor road at a crossroads to come to the sanctuary, rather than continuing on the main east-west road. What would have motivated such a visit in the first place? And how might sacred travel have contributed to worshipers' experience of the sanctuary? The construction of a sanctuary at Aquae Sulis in the first place was due to the sacrality endowed to the landscape by the presence of the hot springs. For many outside visitors, the sanctuary was therefore, from the beginning, a destination in its own right, regardless of its positioning within other networks. This marks it out from, for example, shrines which sprang up on major travel routes (e.g. the sanctuary of Jupiter Poeninus on the Grand-Saint-Bernard pass in the Alps), or temples and sanctuaries which developed within already established urban contexts.

In addition, however, Aquae Sulis was positioned on major road networks and would have been experienced by travellers passing through on their way to other destinations. It is listed in both Ptolemy's *Geography* and Itinerary XIV of the Antonine Itinerary.[42] Itinerary XIV places Aquae Sulis on the journey from Caerleon to Silchester, and by extension to London.[43] This means that anyone travelling from the provincial capital to the legionary fortress by this route would have passed by the sanctuary. The Fosse Way, another very important artery, also passed Aquae Sulis on its way northward to Cirencester.[44] A significant number of people may have passed through Aquae Sulis in this way; recent isotopic analyses of cemetery populations in Winchester, York, and Gloucester have suggested that mobility within Roman Britain, both by people born in the province and by immigrants from the continent, may have been quite high.[45]

---

[41] Blagg 1996: 9.   [42] *Geog.* II.3.13; *AI* 486₃.   [43] Rivet and Smith 1979: 176–7.
[44] Margary 1967: 130.
[45] Eckardt *et al.* 2009: 2820–4; Leach *et al.* 2009: 555; Chenery *et al.* 2010: 158–9.

We can, then, posit two principal categories of visitors to the sanctuary: (1) purposeful visitors, for whom Aquae Sulis was the final destination and whose trip there was the result of deliberate choice, and (2) incidental visitors, who stopped out of interest or curiosity on their way to other places. Given the sanctuary's probable stature and uniqueness, these incidental visitors are still likely to have known already about Aquae Sulis's hot springs and religious centre; this assumption is bolstered by the evidence of the third century author Solinus, whose writings (discussed further in Chapter 5) demonstrate that the temple of Minerva and the hot springs were known even outside the island. For these visitors, Aquae Sulis may therefore have been one of the 'sights to see' if given the opportunity: 'worth a detour', in the words of the Michelin guides.

Where were visitors staying? Despite a few suggestions to the contrary,[46] we have no archaeological evidence of housing provision for either long- or short-term visitors. This is not to say that it did not exist. Since Aquae Sulis appears in the Antonine Itinerary, there almost certainly must have been hostels or *mansiones* for travellers passing through, whether in the sanctuary zone or (perhaps more likely) in the 'normal' town which developed around the crossroads.

We cannot know how many visitors Aquae Sulis would have received in a year. Furthermore, visitor levels may not have remained constant throughout the year; peak periods for purposeful visitors in particular may have corresponded with seasonality or festivals. There is no faunal evidence of sacrifice or ritual feasting; occupation debris in the precinct only begins to build up after the temple fell into disuse. However, faunal remains from several other major Romano-British sanctuaries show evidence both of seasonality (e.g. a preponderance of very young animals, indicating a peak in springtime rituals) and the sort of large-scale feasting which would be appropriate in a festival context.[47] Uley, where sacrifice seems to have peaked during the autumn,[48] is noteworthy in this respect, since it is geographically close to Bath, and resembles it in some key aspects of ritual practice, most notably the large-scale deposition of lead-alloy 'curse' tablets. Festivals do play a pivotal role in Roman religion as portrayed in our literary sources and surviving calendars; however, (*pace* Henig) there is little evidence, apart from some of the Vindolanda tablets, of specific Roman festivals being celebrated in Britain.[49] Of course, this is potentially simply a deficiency in

---

[46] It has been suggested that the second century 'Building D', near the Hot Bath, may have been a *mansio*, but the evidence is not entirely convincing (Davenport, Poole, and Jordan 2007: 87).

[47] King 2005: 357.   [48] Levitan 1993: 300.   [49] Henig 1984: 26–32.

our source material: festivals are ephemeral events unlikely to be highly visible, or even visible at all, in the archaeological record, and apart from texts like the Vindolanda tablets, written sources from Roman Britain which might mention festivals are rare indeed. They are not usually an epigraphic concern, and we have no insular literature from the classical period. The Vindolanda tablets do imply that the first century AD military community, at any rate, was highly festival-oriented. Most references are to festivals celebrated empire-wide, like the Saturnalia[50] or the Matronalia,[51] and to preparations for festivals, in particular accounts of the purchase of food.[52] One requests that a priest be sent to the prefect about a festival.[53] However, the religious atmosphere of a military fort is not necessarily the religious atmosphere of any specific sanctuary. In particular, we should be wary of assuming that any festivals celebrated in provincial sanctuaries aligned with the ritual calendar as we know it from Italy. Nonetheless, communal gatherings at specific and special times for the worship of Sulis seems like a reasonable possibility, especially given the size of the precinct around the temple, a space which could accommodate a fair-sized crowd. The size of the baths, moreover, implies either high levels of visitors in actuality or at the least a desire to have (or display the capacity for) such high levels.

Another possible comparative model for understanding the motivations of purposeful visitors in coming to Aquae Sulis is that of religious pilgrimage. The phenomenon of pilgrimage outside of more well-known Christian contexts has been the object of considerable study by anthropologists, with Morinis defining the term as one which 'can be put to use wherever journeying and some embodiment of an ideal intersect … the pilgrimage is a journey undertaken by a person in quest of a place or a state that he or she believes to embody a valued ideal'.[54] He goes on to divide pilgrimages or sacred journeys into six categories, '(1) devotional; (2) instrumental; (3) normative; (4) obligatory; (5) wandering; and (6) initiatory', though each pilgrimage may have elements from more than one category.[55]

Meanwhile, the place and function of pilgrimage in society as a whole has been heavily debated by anthropologists. For many years the prevailing model was that put forward by Victor and Edith Turner in *Image and Pilgrimage in Christian Culture*.[56] The Turners argued for pilgrimage as a conduit for *communitas*, i.e. 'the individual pilgrim's temporary transition away from mundane structures and social interdependence into a looser

---

[50] *Tab. Vindol.* II, 301; *Tab. Vindol.* III, 622.   [51] *Tab. Vindol.* III, 581.
[52] *Tab. Vindol.* II, 190c; *Tab. Vindol.* II, 180.   [53] *Tab. Vindol.* II, 313.   [54]Morinis 1992: 3–4.
[55] Morinis 1992: 10ff.   [56] Turner and Turner 1978.

communality of feeling with fellow visitors';[57] in other words, they saw pilgrimage as a place/journey which created a temporary reprieve from the normal bounds of societal rules and hierarchy. On the other hand, Eade and Sallnow argued in the introduction to their influential volume on Christian pilgrimage that pilgrimage should rather be seen as a '*realm of competing discourses*' (emphasis theirs).[58] As such, 'it is the meaning and ideas which officials, pilgrims, and locals invest in the shrine – meanings and ideas which are determinately shaped by their political, religious, national and regional, ethnic and class backgrounds – which help to give the shrine its religious capital, though this investment might well be in a variety of theological currencies'.[59] More recently, Coleman has called for a happier medium between Eade and Sallnow's model of pilgrimage as a place of social contestation and the Turnerian model of *communitas*.[60]

Pilgrimage has historically not often been a model for religious behaviour in antiquity, at least before the Christian period. In the past twenty-five years, however, there have been increasing attempts to view ancient activity through this lens, particularly with regard to the eastern Mediterranean;[61] Petsalis-Diomidis, for example, has applied conceptions of pilgrimage to great effect in her work on the cult of Asklepios.[62] Most recently, Kristensen and Friese have brought together a volume of papers by scholars attempting to bring archaeological approaches to the study of ancient pilgrimage, though with varying degrees of success.[63] While Elsner has rightly pointed out some of the methodological hazards in trying to ascribe pilgrimage motivations to visitors to ancient sanctuaries, especially in the absence of corroborating literary testimony,[64] I would argue that there is nonetheless some worth in thinking of Bath as a site with similarities to a pilgrimage destination. Aquae Sulis, we know, was emphatically not a 'small town' in the traditional sense, with its walled area containing few if any elements of normal urban fabric, and with its grand architecture and massive public buildings unjustified by the size of the settlement; it is accepted that we should understand the walls more as a delimiter of sacred space – even a *temenos* boundary, as Dark has suggested.[65] Thus by its very layout, Aquae

---

[57] Coleman 2002: 356.   [58] Eade and Sallnow 1991b: 5.   [59]Eade and Sallnow 1991b: 15.

[60] Coleman 2002: 359ff.

[61] e.g. Coleman and Elsner 1995: 10–29; Elsner and Rutherford, eds. 2005. In the latter volume, all contributors bar one (Fear 2005, who deals with the shrine of Hercules at Cadiz) are concerned with the eastern Mediterranean (both pre- and post-Roman conquest).

[62] Petsalis-Diomidis 2010.   [63] Kristensen and Friese 2017.   [64] Elsner 2017: 267–9.

[65] Cunliffe and Davenport 1985: 10; Dark 1993; Davenport 2000.

Sulis indicates that we must think of it as perpetually a destination, something outside the normal bounds of lived environments, and which must be travelled to from those environments, via the journey to a sacred place which is the marker of pilgrimage. Meanwhile, of Morinis's categories, Aquae Sulis potentially fits well into three: the devotional, instrumental, and normative. As he puts it, 'devotional pilgrimages have as their goal encounter with, and honouring of, the shrine divinity, personage, or symbol … instrumental pilgrimages are undertaken to accomplish finite, worldly goals [e.g. a cure for illness]', while the normative type of pilgrimage 'occurs as part of a ritual cycle, relating to either the life cycle or annual calendrical celebrations'.[66] Devotional behaviour is witnessed by ex-votos to Sulis, particularly from soldiers or other individuals we can be reasonably confident were not resident in Bath. Instrumental behaviour is seen, potentially, in some of the curse tablets, particularly in one like *Tab. Sulis* 31, referencing the theft of a ploughshare, which seems unlikely to have occurred within the city walls; therefore the victim must have been driven to travel to the goddess's sanctuary from elsewhere, in search of retribution. Instrumental pilgrimage is obviously at the core of the worship of Asklepios as examined by Petsalis-Diomidis, and of the worship of Sulis as traditionally understood, but as I have laid out in Chapter 2, healing was very likely not central to Sulis's cult. Normative pilgrimage may have taken place in the context of seasonal festivality.

Ultimately, keeping anthropological models of pilgrimage in our mind when thinking about visitor patterns at Aquae Sulis is useful, because it draws us back to an understanding of the sanctuary which is based on the special qualities of it as a place embedded in the landscape, a place not only with remarkable natural features which formed the basis for its sacredness, but also a place which was simultaneously 'other' and separated from the rest of the communities of Roman Britain, and yet also was linked, through its very uniqueness, to those communities, and indeed served as a point of convergence for them. As such, it becomes an environment which enables both Turnerian construction of *communitas* and Eade and Sallnow's competing discourses, in particular through its role as a locus in which worshipers could both confront and construct their social and religious identities as inhabitants of the Roman empire. This role played by the sanctuary in the expression and resolution of social tensions is an underlying theme of the rest of this book.

---

[66] Morinis 1992: 10–11.

A particularly thought-provoking parallel for Aquae Sulis is provided by Sallnow's work on Christian shrines in the Andes.[67] He shows that Andean Christian pilgrimage sites were placed at or near earlier indigenous sacred sites[68] and argues that contemporary forms of Andean pilgrimage owe as much to the retention, and indeed reclamation, of earlier traditions (often focused on the sacrality of the landscape) as they do to imported European Christian practices.[69] Thus, for example:

When Christ and the Virgin Mary began to manifest themselves in the Andes through apparitions and miracles, their devotees vested the prodigious occurrences with radically different interpretations. For the Spaniards, they provided incontrovertible proof that their conquest had been divinely vindicated, and that the Christian God was finally wrestling the New World from the hands of Satan … For the native Andeans, however, the phenomena conveyed an altogether different meaning. To them, they signified that the innate sacred powers of the landscape were now working not just through the familiar spirits of mountains, crags, and springs, but through the medium of these imported *wak'as* as well.[70]

The Christian context notwithstanding, the Andean situation provides a potential parallel for the processes of syncretism and the creation of site-specific practices within a broader provincial cultural frame that we can trace at Aquae Sulis. As will be discussed in Chapter 5, several modes of ritual practice at Aquae Sulis, particularly the deposition of coins and watery deposition generally, can be understood as acting simultaneously as continuations of both insular Iron Age traditions and imported Mediterranean ones. Meanwhile, the later Andean shrines' adoption not only of earlier shrines' locations, but also their continued acknowledgement of the landscape characteristics which rendered those locations sacred, echoes the Roman appropriation of the hot springs, a theme which I have broached in this chapter, and will continue to explore in Chapter 4.

This chapter, then, has set the scene, both physical and conceptual, for visitors' engagement with the site. In the following chapters, I explore in depth the nature of that engagement, starting with the site's role as a locus for the expression and construction of Roman imperialism.

---

[67] Sallnow 1987; Sallnow 1991.   [68] Sallnow 1991: 141.   [69] Sallnow 1991: 149ff.
[70] Sallnow 1991: 149.

4 | Aquae Sulis and Empire

Religion and Empire

The role played by religion and ritual action in the construction and conceptualization of empire in the Roman provinces is a crucial theme in this chapter. It is in turn wrapped up in a broader, reciprocal problem of how to approach and understand the incursion – or influence, to use a less loaded term – of Roman imperialism into both individuals' and communities' engagement with the divine, and the ways in which all activity, including religious activity, in the Roman provinces is affected by provincial peoples' conquest by, and integration into, the entity we call the Roman empire. The transformations brought about by these processes vary, of course, in terms of both degree and overtness. Nor should my placement of the word 'conquest' before 'integration' be seen as championing a linear progression from one to the other. With respect to conquest, for Britain it should now be taken as axiomatic that the societies of the island, in particular its southern half, were reacting to and transforming continental and Mediterranean cultural forms long before Claudius crossed the channel to join Plautius's army in triumph.[1] As for integration, the most damning indictment of Romanization, in my view, has always been that it is both an inherently teleological and a static concept, assuming at its core that provinces, when conquered, begin a gradual and measurable journey to a particular, definable, state of Roman-ness, rather than acknowledging that the definition of 'Roman' was under constant renegotiation across both the hundreds of years and the hundreds of thousands of square miles which composed the empire, and that the provinces themselves were active creators of the definition of 'Roman' towards which they were supposedly journeying. Integration into empire is undoubtedly a key theme of this book, but by it I mean the ways in which provincial communities, and Aquae Sulis in particular, linked themselves to each other, how those links waxed and waned over both time and space, and how local, regional, and empire-wide networks and relationships were enmeshed in the creation of provincial society.

[1] Creighton 2006.

To this end, in this chapter I focus on the position of Sulis Minerva and her sanctuary within the wider networks of empire, and in particular on the different ways in which Roman imperialism was negotiated at the site throughout its history. I will begin by arguing that the foundation of the sanctuary in the Flavian period, and in particular the construction of the spring reservoir and the monumentalization of the zone around it, should be read primarily as an imperialist act designed to proclaim ownership of an indigenous sacred site. While this emphasis on imperial domination faded in later periods, Aquae Sulis then continued to be a place where individuals, especially soldiers, used the worship of Sulis, and in particular epigraphy linking the deity to the imperial cult, to structure their identity and relationship to the emperor specifically and to broader conceptions of empire more generally. The second half of this chapter will explore these dynamics, focusing on the inscriptions at the site which were set up by members of the military community and their dependents.

The Foundation of Aquae Sulis[2]

We have seen in Chapter 3 that the monumentalization of the sanctuary in the Roman period almost certainly began in the early Flavian or possibly the late Neronian period. What has not yet been addressed is why and how this came about, and what individuals or groups may have been the driving force behind the first century construction of the temple, reservoir, and baths. In the absence of any dedicatory inscriptions, this becomes a controversial topic.

Martin Henig has come to think that the 'patron' behind the construction was Togidubnus, the client king of Rome known to us from Tacitus and from epigraphy, commissioning a new sanctuary at the end of his reign at the edge of his expanded kingdom.[3] Cunliffe and Davenport, on the other hand, saw the provincial government as the likely instigator. They speculated that the decision might have been made 'in the aftermath of the Boudiccan rebellion. To lavish such care and expense on one of the great shrines of the western Celtic fringe might have been designed to be an act of reconciliation, the careful conflation of the native deity with the Roman Minerva representing the new spirit of partnership'.[4]

An unusually powerful and wealthy local figure (whether or not Togidubnus), or a man or men connected to the provincial government

---

[2] Parts of what follows have appeared as Cousins 2016.
[3] Henig 1999; Henig 2000: 126; Henig 2002: 48.   [4] Cunliffe and Davenport 1985: 179.

(whether or not acting in their official capacity), are by far the most likely possibilities for the patrons of the sanctuary. Aquae Sulis at this early period was not – and indeed would never become – an urban environment with a sufficiently large population to provide enough wealthy men of ordinary rank to fund an undertaking as large as the sanctuary. The suggestion of Togidubnus, however, should be treated with caution. Henig's conviction that Togidubnus's kingdom was expanded to encompass the area around Bath – a considerable distance from his centre of power at Chichester – is not truly supported by Tacitus, whose sentence 'quaedam civitates Cogidumno regi donatae' (Agricola 14), appearing as it does immediately after Tacitus's discussion of the conquest of Britain, is much more naturally interpreted as the sole and original bestowal of client-kingship on Togidubnus by the Romans,[5] rather than a later expansion as a result of continued loyalty, as Henig would have it.[6] Ptolemy does list Bath as part of the territory of the Belgae;[7] however, Ptolemy's tribal attributions generally seem suspect and possibly arbitrary, and the coin evidence more likely places the site amongst the Dobunni.[8] Meanwhile, the temple of Neptune and Minerva at Chichester, known from *RIB* 91 and built by the local guild of smiths with the sanction of Togidubnus, is sometimes cited as a demonstration of Togidubnus's interest in Minerva and a parallel in support of his involvement at Bath.[9] Apart from the fact that it is not a true parallel – there is no evidence that Togidubnus supported the Chichester temple financially, and a group like a guild is very unlikely to have been the driving force behind Bath – we should be careful to read too much into what is likely to be a coincidence. Togidubnus's involvement in a temple to Minerva at his known power base does not prove his involvement at another temple to the goddess outside his likeliest sphere of influence.

In some respects, the Togidubnus theory should be approached carefully precisely because it is tempting. Since he is one of the few powerful Britons at this period known to us by name, it is easy and often convenient to suggest him as the force behind major monuments found through archaeology, from Fishbourne Palace to Bath, and to forget how little we actually know about him and his actions; in doing so, however, we run the risk of inadvertently ascribing to him a greater role in the province's early history than he may have had. It is important to remember how thin our written sources for the period are. If the sanctuary's patron was a member of the British elite, it is not impossible that Togidubnus was that person, but

---

[5] Barrett 1979: 231–4.   [6] Henig 1999: 419.   [7] *Geog.* II.3.13
[8] Rivet and Smith 1979: 121, 256.   [9] e.g. Henig 1999: 422

likewise the mere fact that we know his name and no other does not rule out the existence and involvement of a local figure, closer to Bath, who is unrecorded in our sources.

Whoever it was who funded the sanctuary, they were well connected enough to harness the significant resources and organizational capabilities necessary for such an undertaking at such an early date. The impetus to build the Great Bath in particular must have come from people thoroughly immersed in Roman ways of life; the engineering requirements of the reservoir are extremely high and likely to be beyond the capabilities of local groups at this date; and the use of craftsmen from Gaul for the temple would indicate the patron(s) were connected to inter-provincial networks as well as intra-provincial ones. If the patron held official rank, a man such as Gaius Julius Alpinus Classicianus, procurator of the province immediately after the Boudiccan revolt, offers a potential model (although Classicianus himself is too early to be a valid possibility): a member of the Gallic nobility, presumably wealthy and well-connected in the north-west provinces, yet whose family history and own career both demonstrate commitment to Rome.[10]

Both Henig and Cunliffe and Davenport, although they differ on the identity of the patron, agree on the general principles behind the sanctuary. It is an olive branch, a sign of peaceful Romanization and an attempt to portray the incorporation of Britain into the empire in a positive light, through the joining of separate British and Roman goddesses and religious traditions into a syncretic whole. I do not wish to assume automatically that Roman rule in the provinces is always a negative thing to be met with resistance by the 'natives'. The complex negotiations of identity by men such as Togidubnus and Classicianus are proof enough against such a simplistic response. Nonetheless, it must be noted that if the site of the hot springs was considered sacred by the local population before the Romans arrived, as it almost certainly was, then the transformations made in the first century would have rendered the valley unrecognizable to those who knew it before. The harnessing of the water of the King's Spring alone involved a massive engineering project, encasing a formerly wild spot with lead and concrete and moving so much earth that, if there was ever any secure archaeologically visible Iron Age activity at the spring, the Roman period activity has destroyed every trace of it.[11] When this is combined

---

[10] For Classicianus's career in Britain, see Birley 2005: 303–4. Classicianus's name indicates a Gallic background (Birley 2005: 304), and Trier has been suggested as a likely possibility (Grasby and Tomlin 2002: 65–7). His wife was the daughter of Julius Indus, a member of the Treveran nobility who helped quell the rebellion of Florus in AD 21 (Birley 2005: 304).

[11] Cunliffe and Davenport 1985: 38–9.

with the construction of the massive bathhouses, temple, and many other monumental structures of decidedly Roman architectural form, it seems more likely that we have here an imperial power placing beyond question or challenge its appropriation of an indigenous sacred spot, rather than coming to a harmonious understanding with earlier tradition.

I have said in the preceding paragraph that the hot springs were almost certainly a sacred place in the pre-Roman period. As with the healing sanctuary hypothesis, this is a proposition which has generally been accepted, but for which there is in fact very little direct evidence. It is therefore right for us to approach this assumption with a critical eye. The underlying logic for it is usually that Sulis is a name with Celtic origins, and therefore surely a deity with pre-Roman roots. So far, so unconvincing: names can be very problematic sources of religious evidence, and there is no guarantee that local-looking names do genuinely reflect the continuity of indigenous pantheons. But, as was *not* the case for healing cult, other circumstantial supports for Iron Age veneration of the springs are quite strong, and there are also legitimate archaeological reasons, beyond actual lack of Iron Age activity, which can explain the general lack of Iron Age material at the site. We can rest the circumstantial argument on two foundations: first, what we know about general attitudes to watery places in LPRIA Britain, and second, what happened at the springs in the early Roman period. As Chapter 5 will discuss in detail, we have abundant evidence that the sacrality of water and watery places played a central role in Iron Age engagements with the divine. In both the volume and temperature of their waters, the hot springs at Bath constitute a watery landscape unique in Britain; it seems not only beyond the bounds of reasonable scepticism, but almost a non sequitur to argue that Iron Age ritualization of water in Britain would have excluded the most extraordinary watery site in the island. (Precisely what form religious engagement with the waters at the site would have taken is another question, and one which *is* unanswerable without more evidence.) Meanwhile, the first century Roman interventions at the spring, especially the iconography of the temple pediment, to which I will turn in the next section, are without question making an emphatic statement about imperial conquest and ownership. Whoever was responsible for this statement must have considered the hot springs a suitable venue for it, which strongly suggests that they were already laden with socio-religious significance, ripe to be harnessed for new purposes in the post-conquest period. As for the lack of firm evidence of Iron Age activity at the springs, several historical and site formation considerations mean that this is almost to be expected. Iron Age religious sites are usually quite ephemeral, with relatively few examples so far that have clear architectural evidence for shrines.[12] This means that it is not unusual that there is no evidence for Iron Age built structures at Bath. Meanwhile the swampy nature of the landscape before the Roman controlling of the spring would have meant that the demarcation of space through ditched enclosures, a common Iron Age strategy elsewhere, would have been hard to accomplish, and probably impossible to maintain. The site's subsequent history, both ancient and modern, may also be reasonably expected to have affected the survival of Iron Age material. As discussed above, the first century AD activity at the site, particularly the construction of the King's Spring reservoir, would have been more than substantial enough to disturb Iron Age stratigraphy. Furthermore, the site's location under a modern city means that our archaeological windows, even for the Roman period, are extremely patchy. In particular, the Georgian predilection for deep cellars has done considerable damage to the ancient stratigraphy. Taken all together, then, and given the broader social circumstances, the lack of firm Iron Age activity is not in itself proof that the site was not ritually significant in the Iron Age. Indeed, these site formation points make the possible *hints* of Iron Age activity – the presence of eighteen Celtic coins in the spring, and the possibility of a gravel causeway leading to it[13] – more compelling than they might otherwise be, since any evidence at all, however ephemeral, can be seen as surprising.

What is most important for my purposes in this chapter, however, is that the people responsible for the first century AD sanctuary were clearly placing the site in dialogue with Roman conceptions of empire and conquest. This is made utterly explicit by the iconography of the temple pediment, to which I now turn.

The Pediment of the Temple of Sulis Minerva

Although the pediment today is fragmentary, enough remains for the general scheme to be reconstructed (Fig. 4.1). The reconstruction now commonly accepted is that of Ian Richmond and Jocelyn Toynbee, which finally superseded Lysons' drawings from the early nineteenth century (Fig. 4.2).[14] At its centre is the head of a male Gorgon, mounted on a large circular shield and surrounded by two concentric oak wreathes. On either

---

[12] Cunliffe 2005: 561–5.   [13] Cunliffe 1988: 1.
[14] Richmond and Toynbee 1955: Plate XXVII.

Figure 4.1: The surviving portions of the temple pediment. (Photo by author.)

side, winged Victories standing on globes support the shield. Below the shield to the left is a strange helmet, with ears attached to its sideguards and a zoomorphic peak, possibly intended to be a dolphin or other marine creature; there are no known exact parallels, either iconographic or archaeological, for this helmet.[15] A star sits in the apex of the pediment.

Richmond and Toynbee conjectured that the owl visible to the right, on the other side of the shield, may have been standing on a second helmet, to be symmetrical with the zoomorphic helmet on the left. They suggested that a torso draped with seaweed visible beneath the victory in the right-hand corner formed part of a Triton blowing on a conch shell, whose tail would have fit into the pediment's corner; they placed a second triton in the parallel position in the opposite corner.

This reconstruction by Richmond and Toynbee was, in the words of Barry Cunliffe, a 'detailed and reasoned account unlikely to be superseded'.[16] Indeed, it has not been, and I do not intend to do so here, other than to offer a reminder that the Tritons they depict in the corners are mostly conjectural, and the clenched hand visible to the lower left of the owl remains an arguable objection to the reconstruction of a helmet beneath. The owl may

---

[15] Toynbee 1964: 132–3.
[16] Richmond and Toynbee 1955; Cunliffe and Davenport 1985: 116.

Key: existing stones are shaded.

Scale of 0 1 2 3 4 5 6 7 8 9 10 11 12 13 14 15 16 17 18 19 20 Feet.

F.A.C.

Figure 4.2: Reconstruction of the pediment by Richmond and Toynbee. (Richmond and Toynbee 1955, Plate XXVII; © I. A. Richmond and J. M. C. Toynbee 1955. Exclusive Licence to Publish: The Society for the Promotion of Roman Studies, published by Cambridge University Press.)

instead have been perched on the wrist of an unknown figure; this was the reconstruction suggested by Lysons in the nineteenth century.[17] Apart from this, I take as accepted the general layout of the pediment, as shown in F. A. Child's illustration accompanying Richmond and Toynbee's article (with the addition of a block uncovered in 1983).

The first thing to stress here is the Roman-ness – even the imperialness – of the majority of the elements on the pediment. The central shield with the Gorgon's head is flanked by two winged Victories standing on globes. Little remains of either Victory, but enough is present to assure us that they are of a standard iconographic type, with drapery flowing out behind them, sandaled feet, and globes criss-crossed with lines marking the paths of the planets. Richmond and Toynbee declared that the 'Victories on globes symbolise Sulis-Minerva's universal conquest of sickness, just as Minerva features as conqueress of death in Roman funerary contexts,'[18] an observation which Cunliffe repeated without criticism.[19] This interpretation, however, can hardly be justified. The image of Victory standing on a globe was introduced to Roman iconography by Augustus after the Battle of Actium, and, more than any other Victoria-type, was inextricably linked to the person of the emperor and to imperial military victory right up until late Antiquity.[20] Indeed, Victories on globes appear frequently in military contexts in Britain. It is surely in the light of this connection that we must see the Bath Victories; there is no reason to ascribe to them a radically different connotation. The Victories on the pediment of the temple of Sulis Minerva are symbols of imperial might.

The Victories are not the only elements on the pediment associated with imperial iconography; the oak wreaths which encircle the Gorgon were also closely linked with the image of the emperor. *Coronae civicae* made of oak leaves were awarded in the Republican period to soldiers who rescued a comrade in battle; however, after one was bestowed on Augustus by the Senate in 27 BC, they increasingly became, in the words of Paul Zanker, 'tokens of monarchical rule'; for later emperors, the oak wreath had turned into simply 'an insigne of power, completely removed from its original meaning [and] oak leaves became widely understood as synonyms for "Augustus"'.[21] Henig also points out that *coronae civicae* are frequently found on coins struck under Vespasian, roughly contemporary with the Bath pediment.[22]

The final element of the pediment which is possibly linked to imperial iconography is the star at its apex. Henig has argued that the star references either the deified Julius Caesar or a deified emperor, in his view most likely

---

[17] Lysons 1813, Plate V.   [18] Richmond and Toynbee 1955: 99.
[19] Cunliffe and Davenport 1985: 115.   [20] Hölscher 1967: 6–17 and 22–34.
[21] Zanker 1988: 93–4.   [22] Henig 1999: 422.

Claudius.[23] Stars in general by the end of the Republic were 'a well-recognized, though not standard, attribute of divinity', particularly on coinage.[24] Meanwhile, in the Hellenistic East, stars had become symbols not only of gods but of deified kings.[25] Early in Octavian's reign, the star became an emblem attached to statues of Julius Caesar and on coinage depicting not only Caesar but Octavian as well.[26] As time went on, however, Caesar seems to have become more closely linked with the image of the comet (shown with a tail) which supposedly appeared shortly after his death, not a star simply indicating divinity.[27] Overall, it does not seem proven to me that stars became inevitably linked with the imperial cult, despite Weinstock's attempts to link the Julian star with later radiate crowns and the connection between Sol and the emperor.[28] The pediment star (and another one like it from the sanctuary precinct, *CSIR* I.2, 66) seem likely to be linked to divinity, but cannot be proven to be imperial in tone.[29]

Nevertheless, the pediment obviously has Roman imperial power as a central theme. This explanation of the pediment, however, fails to incorporate the central Gorgon, and therefore must be incomplete.

Reading the Gorgon

As we saw in Chapter 1, from the time of its discovery in the late eighteenth century the Bath Gorgon has been both a challenging and a deeply arresting image for scholars of Roman Britain. It is now almost universally described as a variant of the classical image of the Gorgon, with snakes in its hair and wings at the side of its head (Fig. 4.3);[30] in the century following its discovery in 1790, there was often great resistance to this identification, due to the

---

[23] Henig 1999: 419–22.   [24] Gurval 1997: 46.   [25] Weinstock 1971: 375.

[26] Gurval 1997: 61.   [27] Gurval 1997: 59.   [28] Weinstock 1971: 383–4.

[29] *CSIR* I.2, 66 was originally identified as a flower, but I agree with Henig (1999: 419) that it is certainly a star; see, e.g. Gurval 1997: 47, figs. 1–12 for comparanda. *Contra* Henig, there seems to be no reason to assign this second star to the Temple (Cunliffe and Davenport 1985: 131).

[30] The snakes can be difficult for the casual viewer to spot. From the ears of the head upwards, snakes alternate with the hair. The snakes are distinguishable from hair by their lack of incisions, and, in some cases, the hint of an eye and mouth at the head. They interlock with the hair locks; each lock is fat at the base and then narrows, while each snake, narrow at the bottom and fatter at the top, fits into the gaps created by pairs of hair locks. Framing the beard at the bottom of the face are the reared heads and curved necks of the two snakes whose bodies are tied in an elaborate (and slightly confused) knot at the base of the beard. These snakes appear to be crested (the crest is most visible on the right hand snake), and therefore male. As the sculpture stands now, these elements are in fact quite hard to make out; however, they were probably more visible in antiquity. While no paint remains on the pediment, red paint is visible on parts of the temple's cornice (Irvine 1873: 385) and it thus seems likely that the pediment was also painted, which would have made the contrast between snakes and hair much easier to distinguish.

Figure 4.3: The Gorgon from the temple pediment. (Photo by author.)

figure's maleness. In the twentieth century, however, the consensus
emerged that the head is best understood as a careful conflation of Minerva's
attribute of the Gorgon with a water god's face symbolizing the sacred
waters of the nearby spring.[31] This is the general interpretation to which I
subscribe in this book. Objections to the figure's identity as a Gorgon due
to its maleness are not securely founded in classical iconography; although
the Gorgon becomes conflated with the (unquestionably) female Medusa,
it has an iconographic and, seemingly, mythological tradition of its own in
which gender is much more ambiguous.[32] An isolated bearded and
moustachioed head, flanked by wings, like that which appears on the Bath
pediment, is in fact entirely in keeping with Gorgon iconography dating
right back to Archaic Greece. Leaving aside classical antecedents, the
conflation of the snake-haired Gorgon with a male bearded water deity, as
I will discuss below, is also a logical iconographical syncretism for the site
itself, placing it in dialogue not only with the characteristics at the heart of
Aquae Sulis's ritual significance, but with contemporaneous iconographic
trends in the urban spaces of the western provinces.

   More importantly, in the twentieth century the Gorgon became seen
not only as a powerful work of art, but indeed as one of the most – if not
the most – iconic images of Roman Britain. Toynbee saw it as 'the perfect

[31] Toynbee 1964: 137; Henig 1999: 422. Hind 1996 suggests that it is the monster Typhoeus.
    However, Typhoeus's story is known principally from Pindar, and is thus not only obscure but
    also very remote both geographically and chronologically from Bath.
[32] Ogden 2008: 37.

marriage of classical standards and traditions with Celtic taste and native inventiveness'.[33] No praise was too high for its unknown creator. Haverfield declared in the *Victoria County History* for Somerset that 'Here for once we break through the conventionality of the Roman empire, and trace a touch of genius.'[34] Elsewhere he went even further: 'Whatever its precise original, the head is perhaps the most remarkable product of Roman provincial art in western Europe. Its marked individuality and astonishing vigour are hardly less extraordinary than its technical features.'[35] Even R. G. Collingwood, notoriously harsh on Romano-British art in general,[36] was impressed by the Gorgon and saw in its vigour proof of the sophistication of its creator: 'The Bath sculptor was a man of high education, deeply versed in the technique of his art and coolly skilful in the execution of it. His Gorgon is barbaric for the same reason that Caliban is barbaric – because its creator was a skilled artist, and wanted to make it barbaric, and succeeded.'[37]

Yet, in making the Gorgon the iconic image of Roman Britain, scholarship has lost sight of the role it plays as the centrepiece of the pediment. If this is indeed the premier expression of Romano-Celtic art, a piece which epitomizes both the religious and artistic syncretism between native and Roman, how does it fit in with the rest of the pediment, which, as we have seen, is defined primarily by Roman iconography and ideology? To answer this question, we need to put the Gorgon back into the wider context of similar images in Roman art, particularly provincial art. Is the Gorgon in fact a unique image, and if not, what connotations might its category of images convey?

Other instances of Gorgons or Medusa in Romano-British art, for instance on mosaic floors or jet pendants, are all considerably later than the Bath Gorgon, and thus of little use in understanding its original context. When searching for comparative material for the Gorgon, Richmond and Toynbee turned primarily to the heads of Medusa and sea-goddesses from the Severan Forum at Lepcis Magna,[38] possibly because they considered the pediment to date most likely to the third century.[39] In doing so, however,

---

[33] Toynbee 1964: 137.   [34] Haverfield 1906: 236.   [35] Haverfield and Stuart Jones 1912: 135.

[36] 'On any Romano-British site the impression that constantly haunts the archaeologist, like a bad smell or a stickiness on the fingers, is that of an ugliness which pervades the place like a London fog: not merely the common vulgar ugliness of the Roman empire, but a blundering, stupid ugliness that cannot even rise to the level of that vulgarity' (Collingwood and Myres 1937: 250).

[37] Collingwood 1934: 115.   [38] Richmond and Toynbee 1955: 102–3.

[39] Richmond and Toynbee 1955: 99. This was long before Blagg 1979 showed on stylistic grounds that the work belonged to the first century, and, more importantly, before finds from modern excavation showed that cutting on the back of pediment pieces, previously seen as evidence of ancient refacing (and thus a later date for the pediment than for the temple), must in fact have been done in the eighteenth century to lighten the weight of the recently discovered pieces (Cunliffe 1969: 184; Blagg 1979: 104–5; Cunliffe and Davenport 1985: 116).

they neglected an entire series of parallels which are much closer stylistically, geographically, and chronologically: namely, the roundels ultimately derived from the Forum of Augustus which are found in first and early second century contexts at multiple urban sites in the western provinces, in particular Gaul and Spain.

Before examining this provincial material, however, we should take a brief look at the archetype: the Forum of Augustus. The format of the Forum, with the temple of Mars Ultor at one end, and the sides lined by porticoes displaying statues from Roman history (and the Julio-Claudian family), is well-known and does not need extensive reviewing. My focus here is on the attic of the porticoes. Here, shields, or *clipei*, bearing heads of Jupiter Ammon, 'barbarians' wearing torques, and possibly other deities[40] were framed between standing caryatids (Fig. 4.4). Zanker, following Vitruvius, has argued that both the caryatids and the shield-heads are to be related to themes of triumph and victory.[41] It is also possible that the shields in particular are intended to evoke memories of the shields Alexander the Great hung on the Parthenon.[42] Whether we should take Vitruvius's understanding of caryatids as the humiliated women of conquered nations

Figure 4.4: Reconstruction of portico attic from the Forum of Augustus. (Sovrintendenza Capitolina di Roma Capitale, Museo dei Fori Imperiali, Archivio Fotografico.)

[40] Zanker 1968: 8.   [41] Zanker 1968: 12–13. For Vitruvius on caryatids, see *De. Arch.* I, 1.5.
[42] Zanker 1968: 13; Verzàr 1977: 34–5; Fishwick 2004 (*ICLW* III.3): 14.

at face value, it is certainly true that the overall atmosphere and function of the Forum of Augustus was one of triumph and victory, with the temple of Mars Ultor used by the Senate, by imperial decree, as the place for deliberating both wars and claims for triumph.[43]

Apart from the general motif of a head placed inside a shield roundel, the heads of Jupiter Ammon from the Forum do not necessarily bring to mind the Gorgon from Bath. The heads display none of the interest in circularity and patterning which defines the Gorgon: the outline is most certainly that of a head, rather than a circle, and the style, unsurprisingly, is marked by high-quality classical realism. However, as we move to adaptations of the Forum of Augustus in the western provinces, the stylistic parallels become clearer.

There are several examples of urban centres in Gaul and Hispania imitating to greater or lesser degrees the iconographic programme of the portico attics of the Forum of Augustus; in some cases, the architectural context is well-understood, while in others we only possess relatively contextless fragments of roundels. In the latter category are fragments from Caderousse (Espérandieu I, 272) and Vienne (Espérandieu X, 7627), both of which depict the head of Jupiter Ammon on a *clipeus*, and are equally completely contextless.[44]

Also in Narbonensis, a *clipeus* (Espérandieu IX, 6731) has been found at Arles with very elaborate vegetal decoration and a central head which, while resembling the Ammon-type, in fact appears to be a type of river or water deity; he possesses pointed ears in lieu of horns, and a dolphin and a crocodile are visible in his hair (Fig. 4.5).[45] A fragment of a second *clipeus*, sadly lacking the central portion, was found in the same excavation.[46] The context for these fragments is a little better understood. They seem to have been part of the decorative scheme of a rectangular plaza (there is no evidence of a roof) built against one end of the forum; the plaza was capped at at least one of its ends by a curved exedra furnished with niches, and it is possible that it had a temple along its west side.[47] The *clipei* were found during the excavation of the known exedra, although they were not in position and we cannot know exactly what building they were ornamenting. Despite the *clipei* and the possible temple, the layout of this area, as far as we understand it, does not seem to mirror closely the layout of the Forum of Augustus.

Also somewhat clearer with regard to context – although by no means completely secure – are a series of fragmentary roundels from Avenches (ancient Aventicum), Switzerland, the capital of the Helvetii (Bossert 19a–e;

---

[43] Suetonius, *Aug.* 29.   [44] See Cousins 2016 for figures of these objects.   [45] Constans 1921: 268.
[46] Constans 1921: 268.   [47] Rouquette and Sintès 1989: 46.

Figure 4.5: *Clipeus* from Arles (Espérandieu IX, 6731). (Musée départemental Arles antique, n° inv. X-7928. © Rémi Bénali.)

Figure 4.6: *Clipei* from Avenches. (a) River God(?); (b) Jupiter Ammon.
(© AVENTICUM – Site et Musée romains d'Avenches.)

Fig. 4.6). These were found in association with the temple known as La-Grange-des-Dîmes, located well within the urban environment of Avenches;[48] the temple's decoration has been dated, primarily on stylistic grounds, to the Flavian period.[49] P. D. Horne's reconstruction, now generally accepted,[50] understands the temple as fundamentally Romano-Celtic in plan (i.e. with an ambulatory around a central *cella*), but with a classical-style

---

[48] Bossert 1998: 44.   [49] Bossert 1998: 52–3.   [50] Bossert 1998: 51.

pronaos, including columns and a possible pediment.[51] The placement of these *clipei* in relationship to the temple is not entirely certain. It has generally been assumed that they formed part of the architectural decoration of the temple itself, rather than of surrounding Forum of Augustus-style porticoes.[52] The most recent reconstruction by M. Bossert, which synthesizes earlier work, argues that the roundels were placed in the attic of the temple's ambulatory.[53] If this reconstruction is correct, then their placement in the frontal view of this temple is the closest example known to the placement of the Gorgon at Bath. An alternative suggestion, put forward by Verzàr and accepted by Horne, placed the roundels on the facing of the temple platform;[54] given the fact that all other *clipei* of this type whose contexts are known were placed at elevation, this reconstruction seems less likely.

The roundels themselves seem to show several different deities, including Jupiter Ammon (Bossert 19b) and a probable river god (Bossert 19a). It has been suggested that a third roundel may have been of Medusa, since the edge of the shield (the only extant part) recalls closely the edges of the Medusa-*clipei* from Mérida (discussed later in this section);[55] however, the connection is tenuous and we certainly cannot assume that there were Medusa *clipei* at Avenches. The style of the Avenches *clipei* is overall rougher than the examples from Narbonensis, with the heads carved in a less naturalistic and more geometric manner.

There is no firm evidence for other *clipei* in the style of the Forum of Augustus in this region, but edges of similar roundels have been found at other Swiss sites, particularly Geneva and Versoix;[56] Verzàr suggests that these may have been part of similar decorative schemes at these sites, or perhaps another nearby (with Nyon being an attractive possibility);[57] without the central portions of the roundels, however, this cannot be confirmed.

Moving away from Gaul, further examples of the *clipeus* decorative element are to be found in Spain, particularly in two of the three provincial capitals, Tarragona and Mérida. In Tarragona, fragments of *clipei* depicting Jupiter Ammon have been found associated with the so-called Provincial Forum. Around fifty fragments have been found so far,[58] which would allow at the least four or five *clipei* to be reconstructed. The Forum most likely had as its

---

[51] Horne 1986: 17–18, fig. 2.

[52] Verzàr 1977: 26 and 34; Bossert 1998: 48–51. (Bossert offers his own reconstruction and a review of other attempts, including Verzàr's.)

[53] Bossert 1998: 51.　　[54] Verzàr 1977: 26 and 30 fig. 8; Horne 1986: 16.

[55] Verzàr 1977: 41–4 ; Bossert 1998: 47 and 51.

[56] Deonna 1926, cat. no. 194 (Geneva) and 207 (Versoix). The scale of these pieces is much larger than that of most other extant *clipei*.

[57] Verzàr 1977: 38.　　[58] TED'A 1989: 164.

focus a temple to the imperial cult;[59] the suggestion made by T. Hauschild[60] that the *clipei* formed part of the attics of porticoes leading to the temple, along the lines of the Forum of Augustus, is now widely accepted[61] (although so far no evidence of caryatids have been found[62]). Stratigraphic evidence strongly supports a Flavian date for the complex, rather than the Julio-Claudian date put forward by earlier scholars on the basis of textual evidence for a Julio-Claudian temple to Augustus,[63] although Fishwick, relying heavily on the textual evidence, has argued that a Julio-Claudian dating should perhaps be accepted for the temple, if not the complex as a whole.[64] In either scenario, however, the *clipei* will date to the first century AD.

The two most complete *clipei* both depict Jupiter Ammon; the overall appearance of the head is the same, although there are a few noticeable stylistic differences between the two.[65] Koppel has suggested that another fragment of a face may possibly belong to a *clipeus* depicting Medusa;[66] as at Avenches, however, this identification is far from certain. On the other hand, on comparison with Mérida, the certain presence of at least two types of borders for the *clipei* suggests that there may have been more than one type of face.[67]

The best-attested provincial articulation of the Forum of Augustus, however, is to be found at Mérida, where almost all the elements of the archetype at Rome have been identified. Here, in the principal forum of the colony, porticos with attics of caryatids and *clipei* depicting both Jupiter Ammon and Medusa flank the sides of a plaza leading to a temple of the imperial cult (the so-called temple of Diana);[68] it also seems likely that there was, at the least, a sculpture group of Aeneas and his family leaving Troy.[69] The general date of the temple and porticos seems to be Julio-Claudian, making it slightly earlier than most of the other examples discussed here.[70]

---

[59] TED'A 1989: 141 and 156–7.   [60] Hauschild 1972: 38.

[61] TED'A 1989: 153; Fishwick 2004 (*ICLW* III.3): 14. Koppel 1990: 338–9 marks an exception; she thinks the *clipei* more likely adorned the temple, on comparison with Avenches. As I have discussed, however, the Avenches *clipei*'s position is not secure.

[62] Trillmich *et al.* 1993: 326.

[63] TED'A 1989: 156–7; Dupré i Raventós 1990; Aquilué Abadías 2004: 48.

[64] Fishwick 2004 (*ICLW* III.3): 22–30. Koppel 1990: 337 has also suggested a Julio-Claudian date for at least one of the *clipei*, based on stylistic analysis, but since she uses as her points of comparison a statue in the Louvre and one in the Capitoline, her lack of geographic specificity calls the strength of her analysis into question.

[65] Koppel 1990: 334.   [66] Koppel 1990: 334–5.   [67] Koppel 1990: 336.

[68] Mateos Cruz and Palma Garciá 2004: 43–4. For a complete catalogue of the stonework found in this area, see de la Barrera 2000; the *clipei* fragments are catalogue numbers 229–370.

[69] Álvarez Martínez and Nogales Basarrate 1990: 337; Trillmich *et al.* 1993: 52 and 289–90; Mateos Cruz and Palma Garciá 2004: 44.

[70] Trillmich 1990: 317; Mateos Cruz and Palma Garciá 2004: 41.

As at Tarragona, there are a few different identifiable 'types' for both the Jupiters and the Medusas, not differing greatly in appearance but showing minor stylistic modifications (Fig. 4.7);[71] this is most likely due to the work of different workshops, rather than chronological variation.[72] Amongst other variations, the borders of the Medusa *clipei* are surrounded by vegetal motifs of three types: laurel wreaths, oak wreaths, and floral scrolls.[73] On the Jupiter Ammon *clipei*, however, the egg-and-dart style decoration extends right to the edge of the shield.[74]

What are the implications of these sites and their iconography? The fact that they are part of the same phenomenon or trend has been generally accepted, and the meaning behind that trend widely discussed.[75] As I have discussed above, both the iconographic scheme and the functions of the Forum of Augustus emphasized themes of triumph and victory; in addition, the Forum of Augustus is entwined with the Augustan period's larger interest in linking itself to both the mythological and historical past. We see this of course not only in the famous statue groups of early figures tied to both Roman heritage and the Julian *gens* specifically, but also more broadly in the shields' possible links to Alexander and the imitation of Greek artistic elements such as the caryatids.

How much of the message of the original space can be transferred to its imitations in the western provinces is a different question. It is likely that the connotations changed in a provincial context, with the very fact of imitation of a space from Rome becoming more important than the original space's meaning. As Verzàr puts it when discussing the *clipei* specifically:

En conclusion, alors qu'à Rome, au Forum d'Auguste, les *clipei* étaient en rapport direct avec des événements historiques et présentaient aux yeux du citoyen de glorieuses conquêtes en les symbolisant par une tête d'*Ammon* et par des représentations de princes barbares portant les torques, leur contenu iconographique ne pouvait être la même pour les habitants de Tarragone et d'autre villes provinciales. Il eut manqué tout son effet. En province, ce programme fut consciemment transformé en représentation abstraite du pouvoir du nouvel Empire.[76]

In conclusion, although at Rome, in the Forum of Augustus, the *clipei* were in direct relationship with historical events and presented glorious conquests to the citizen's eyes by symbolising them with a head of Ammon and through representations of barbarian princes wearing torcs, their iconographic content could not have been the same for the inhabitants of Tarragona and other provincial towns. It would have lost all its effect. In the provinces, this

---

[71] de la Barrera 2000: 159.   [72] de la Barrera 2000: 159–60.   [73] See de la Barrera 2000, fig. 30–3.

[74] See de la Barrera 2000, fig. 25–9.

[75] Verzàr 1977: 36–41; Ensoli 1997; Bossert 1998: 54; de la Barrera 2000: 158–62.

[76] Verzàr 1977: 38.

Figure 4.7: *Clipei* from Mérida. (a) and (b): *Clipei* of Jupiter Ammon in two different styles (© Archivo Fotográfico MNAR/Lorenzo Plana and Archivo Fotográfico MNAR/ Miguel Ángel Otero); (c) and (d): *Clipei* of Medusa surrounded by *coronae civicae*; (d) shows the snakes knotted under Medusa's chin. (© Archivo Fotográfico MNAR/Miguel Ángel Otero and Archivo Fotográfico MNAR/Ana Osorio.)

programme was consciously transformed into an abstract representation of the power of the new Empire. (My translation.)

Both Verzàr and others following her have gone further, arguing that we can see in provincial imitations of the Forum of Augustus a frequent and direct link to the imperial cult, with roundels almost universally appearing on or near cult temples.[77] This connection, however, was based on (1) Verzàr's

[77] Verzàr 1977: 39–41.

mistaken interpretation of the temple at Avenches as dedicated to the imperial cult and (2) her tendency to argue for connections at other sites where likely there were none.[78] Despite the fact that Verzàr's theory has been occasionally put forward by others,[79] there is no reason to believe that Forum of Augustus-style decoration was directly linked to the imperial cult.

What the roundels certainly are is part of what might be called a visual language of empire, which seeks to incorporate the public civic spaces which they adorn into the wider web of '*Romanitas*'. The temples to the imperial cult at Tarragona and Mérida, although not the cause of the roundels, are thus nonetheless correlated, with both the homage to the Forum of Augustus and the worship of the emperor serving to bring the centre of imperial power out to the periphery.

Now that I have discussed these provincial echoes of the Forum of Augustus, and the role they played in connecting the provinces to the capital, it is time to turn back to the Gorgon. A strong argument can be made that the contemporary trend of provincial imitation of the Forum of Augustus did play a role in the creation of the Gorgon image. As we move away from the Forum of Augustus *clipei* and into the provinces, the stylistic similarities between the Bath Gorgon and the Jupiter Ammon *clipei* become more striking. With the exception of the fragment from Caderousse, the provincial material demonstrates less interest in three-dimensionality and a greater interest in making the head and its hair reflect the circularity of the shield shape. The clearest parallels to Bath are the *clipei* from Mérida. Although the style of the carving is far more 'classicized', the Mérida Jupiter Ammons can be divided into the same concentric circles of face and hair as the Bath Gorgon, with the moustache and beard of the face blending into the hair in much the same way as well. Meanwhile, the oak wreaths on some of the Medusa *clipei* recall the *coronae civicae* of the Bath pediment; the Medusas themselves, though the classicized female faces are far distant from the Gorgon, do show snakes knotted under the chins in much the same manner (Fig. 4.7). The parallels, indeed, are striking enough that I would suggest that it is not beyond the bounds of possibility that Mérida was the direct inspiration for the designer of the Gorgon.

If we accept that the Gorgon may be linked to *clipei* of this type, the head begins to make more sense within the context of its pediment. As I pointed

---

[78] For example, Arles, where her argument rests only on the fact that we have evidence for the imperial cult from the town generally (Verzàr 1977: 40). With the exceptions of Tarragona and Mérida, there is no firm evidence linking these sorts of *clipei* to temples to the imperial cult. The temple at La Grange-des-Dîmes was almost certainly dedicated to Mercury; see Bossert 1998: 129–30 for a full discussion of the flaws in Verzàr's theory.

[79] e.g. Ensoli 1997: 163.

out above, my discussion of the imperial tropes on the pediment did not take into account the Gorgon; however, the connotations of the *clipei* – their place in the visual language of empire – serve to bring the Gorgon into unity with the other images on the pediment. Instead of being an iconographic anomaly, we can see it working together with the other elements like the winged Victories and the *coronae civicae* to visually define the temple as in a Roman space and symbolic of the Roman empire.

At the same time, the image's blending of a Gorgon with a spring deity is intimately concerned with Aquae Sulis's own sense of place. The unique qualities of the Gorgon serve to ground the pediment's more general imperial imagery in the specifics of this particular site. As Chapter 5 will highlight, Aquae Sulis is special and sacred precisely because of its geographical characteristics: its sacredness could not possibly be transferred elsewhere, because it is rooted in the landscape and the springs which can only be found here. The pediment, including the Gorgon, thus serves to acknowledge these distinctive aspects of the sanctuary, yet at the same time to incorporate it iconographically into the wider network of empire.

This concern with place which brings about the transformation of the head of the roundel into a hybrid Gorgon-spring deity helps to remove a potential stumbling block to seeing the Bath Gorgon as connected to the Forum of Augustus imitations, namely that the head shown is not Jupiter Ammon, the deity depicted most frequently on the roundels, and the one seen on the closest stylistic parallel at Mérida. There are other points which mitigate this objection further. Many sites, including the Forum of Augustus itself, have evidence that Jupiter Ammon was not the only deity figuring on the shields, even if he does dominate our surviving corpus. Medusas are certain at Mérida, possible at Tarragona and Avenches, and have even been suggested at Rome itself;[80] the Forum of Augustus certainly possesses torc-wearing male (barbarian?) heads, and Avenches may also have river-gods. Most tellingly, the *clipeus* from Arles is very clearly part of the series, and very similar in general appearance to the bearded Jupiter Ammon type, but it definitely depicts a river god, rather than Jupiter Ammon, thus demonstrating that the Ammon image itself was potentially mutable.

The triumphal iconography of the pediment and the commitment to Roman imperialism that it implies strengthen, in my view, the probability that the instigator(s) of the sanctuary were connected to the provincial government. While in Henig's interpretation, the imperial iconography of the pediment is to be understood as 'the introduction of a new world order' by a Briton embracing Roman rule, and as 'an elegant compliment to the

---

[80] Ensoli 1997: 163.

Roman achievement by a friend and client of both Claudius and Vespasian,[81] in my eyes this iconography which, as I have discussed, is not just imperial but indeed military, with symbols of victory and conquest, should more appropriately be read as part of the appropriation of the hot springs by the Romans, and a permanent reminder in stone of the means by which this land was incorporated into empire. This aspect comes through particularly strongly when placed alongside the drastic, indeed almost violent disruption of the natural landscape discussed at the start of this chapter. This does not, of course, mean that the sanctuary and its temple remained a symbol of domination throughout its history – indeed, the later votive evidence tells a complex story of ritual integration and cultural negotiation. In its foundation, however, we almost certainly see an imperialist act.

How does this reading of the sanctuary's beginnings reinforce or change our broader understanding of the socio-political dynamics of the early years of Roman rule in Britain? The story of the decades both before and after the Claudian invasion of AD 43 is hardly a straightforward narrative of conquest.[82] Rather, it is a tangled web of competing and often contradictory social processes. We see local elites from the first century BC onwards harnessing Roman power and its material signifiers, to the degree that some of those elites should be conceptualized as 'client kings' of Rome, and Roman military and political support for these elites alternates between aligning with and clashing against drives for imperial expansion motivated by internal Roman dynastic politics. Meanwhile, organized, armed resistance and rebellion against the spread of Roman 'hard power' in the island during the first century AD may culminate in the Boudiccan revolt yet is also contemporaneous with evidence for the active adoption throughout southern England of Roman patterns of urbanism and administration, at both elite and non-elite levels of society. The monumentalization of Aquae Sulis is enmeshed into all of these processes, but perhaps most particularly into this final one. Indeed, the controlling of the spring and the construction of the temple and baths may in some ways be read as a Flavian capstone to the glimpses we have from earlier in the first century about the ways in which religion and ritual could be foci for the tensions surrounding increasing Roman control of the island. Our written sources do indicate, for example, that the druids – whatever their exact nature, and whatever their exact role – lent a religious aspect to resistance to Roman expansion.[83] Meanwhile, an obvious parallel for a

---

[81] Henig 2000: 128; Henig 1999: 422.

[82] For different takes on the social dynamics of conquest and collaboration in this period, see, e.g. Millett 1990: 65ff; Cunliffe 2005: 220ff; Creighton 2006: 46ff; Mattingly 2006: 87ff.

[83] Mattingly 2006: 105–6.

temple as a symbol of Roman imperialism is the temple of Claudius at Colchester, destroyed less than a generation before the temple at Bath was built. At Colchester the temple's role as an instrument of Roman oppression is unquestioned. This is not only due to Tacitus's testimony that it was viewed by the local population as an '*arx aeternae dominationis*', a citadel of eternal domination, and that the resentment of elites conscripted into its priesthood was a key spark for the Boudiccan revolt.[84] The context of the temple within the landscape at Camulodunum also supports this reading. The pre-Boudiccan temple was an extremely large and imposing structure;[85] situated on raised ground, it must have dominated the townscape around it to a very considerable extent, especially during the early years of the *colonia*, when other urban buildings must have been very rudimentary. (The fact that the Norman castle, much later, was placed on the same spot demonstrates the strength of its strategic position.[86]) In addition, the precinct was built outside of the main centre of the *colonia*, in the area previously occupied by the annexe to the earlier legionary fortress.[87] Thus the location, in addition to dominating the landscape through its natural qualities, must also have held strong associations with the military force of Rome that had, just a few years previously, conquered the area, with much resulting trauma and displacement for the indigenous population. Both the temple to Claudius and the temple of Sulis Minerva are, in their own ways, emphatically emblematic of militant imperialism: the one through its dedication to the conqueror of the island, the other through its triumphal iconography. Both are symbolic of charged takeovers of local landscapes: the temple at Colchester is located at a pre-conquest elite power centre appropriated by the Roman military, the temple at Bath at a unique sacred feature transformed by Roman engineering. Local reactions to the temple of Claudius, then, suggest that at the very least the temple at Bath would have been viewed with deep ambiguity, if not actual hostility, by those who had experienced the violence of the 40s, 50s, and 60s AD.

Sulis, Soldiers, and Empire

While the sanctuary's role as a symbol of domination almost certainly faded as the province became more integrated into the Roman empire – a process which I will discuss further in Chapters 5 and 6 – Aquae Sulis nevertheless

---

[84] *Annals* XIV.31–2.   [85] The podium measures 24 × 31.5 meters (*ICLW* III.1: 76).
[86] Hull 1958.   [87] Drury 1984: 22.

remained a place where worshipers, in particular those connected to the military community, used the cult of Sulis as a means of clarifying and reinforcing their position within the hierarchy of empire. It is these dynamics that I turn to now.

In particular, I will be examining the ways in which military activity at Aquae Sulis was structured by, and in dialogue with, religious engagement with the emperor. Central, then, to the second half of this chapter is the role and effect of the imperial cult, broadly defined, in and on provincial religious life. It is therefore useful to begin by laying out my broader theoretical approach to this phenomenon, before turning back to Aquae Sulis specifically. 'The imperial cult' is a modern term and a modern construct, and as such, we can legitimately modify its definition to suit a changing understanding of the role of the emperor and of empire in the religion of the Roman world. Scholars have tended, either explicitly or implicitly, to limit their discussion of the phenomenon only to those aspects which can be defined as direct emperor-worship.[88] However, to limit ourselves to such a narrow definition is to fail to recognize the extent to which the figure of the emperor – and thus the concept of empire – permeated almost all religious activity in the Principate; if we are to truly understand the ways in which the inhabitants of the Roman empire were using religion to define for themselves their relationship to their emperor, then we must broaden our outlook from direct worship of the emperor as a god, and look also at the ways in which the worship of other gods and the use of other rituals are both modified by the appearance of an emperor, and also harnessed to help negotiate the links between subject and ruler. Likewise, as McIntyre has recently argued, a narrow focus on emperor-worship also serves to elide the social importance of veneration of non-ruling members of the imperial family.[89] Underlying this chapter, then, is a definition for the imperial cult that encompasses all aspects of religious engagement with the concept of the emperor and his family, from direct emperor-worship to prayers for the emperor's well-being to honours given to 'Augustan' gods.

Expanding our definition in this way is essential if we are to realize the full potential of religious engagement with the emperor to aid our

---

[88] Those limiting it implicitly often do not offer a strict definition of ruler or imperial cult, but their discussion does not leave the bounds of pure emperor-worship (e.g. *ICLW* and Price 1984). Gradel 2002: 7 does offer a definition, limiting his discussion to categories of *divini/summi/caelestes honores*, although his means of identifying these categories is perhaps open to debate.

[89] McIntyre 2016.

understanding of the communities in which it appears. The imperial cult has often been a specialized area, explored fully neither by those scholars working on themes of cultural change and provincial agency,[90] nor by those studying more traditional forms of religious activity.[91] Meanwhile, studies of the imperial cult often fail to take into account the models and frameworks put forward by those working in these other areas, ignoring issues of social agency, and invariably explaining changes in cult practices and attitudes through the *deus ex machina* of direct imperial, or at the most, senatorial, decisions.[92] This is short-sighted on both sides. For those studying the phenomenon of emperor-worship, it is short-sighted not to take into account the rich complexity of the societies, in particular in the provinces, where emperor-worship appears. For those engaged in wider issues of cultural change and the structuring of provincial society, religion in general, by definition intensely symbol- and meaning-laden,[93] provides a particularly fertile area to explore the changing concerns and social structures within a given community; the imperial cult specifically, with its inherent links to empire-wide social structure, provides a unique opportunity to witness provincial peoples' active weaving of themselves and their communities into the web of empire. In short, religious concerns are linked to larger social concerns, and the imperial cult's connection with political and social hierarchy means that it is likely to be particularly laden with signifiers defining not only the emperor in isolation, but the emperor in relation to his subjects, and vice versa.

Turning back to Aquae Sulis, conscious use of the emperor in religious activity is seen most acutely in the site's epigraphy, which shows soldiers and their dependents uniting veneration of Sulis with religious engagement with the emperor and ritual language connected to the imperial cult. The first such inscription that I wish to examine is *RIB* 152, discovered in Stall Street in 1753. An altar, with square focus and plain sides, measuring .46 × .89 m, it reads:

Locum reli|giosum per in|solentiam e|rutum |virtuti et n(umini) | Aug(usti) repurga|tum reddidit | G(aius) Seuerius | Emeritus c(enturio) | reg(ionarius). (RIB 152.)

---

[90] Woolf 1998 for Gaul, for example, pays mere lip service to the phenomenon; Millett 1990 for Britain mentions it not at all.

[91] Sections on the imperial cult appear in standard works on Roman religion, e.g. Rives 2007 or Rüpke 2007, but such treatments tend to be brief asides rather than fully integrated into the work.

[92] See, e.g. Fears 1981; Clauss 1999, whose analysis is primarily divided by reign of emperor; Gradel 2002: 140ff; *ICLW* III.1: 96.

[93] Geertz 1966: 3–4.

This holy place, wrecked by insolence and cleansed afresh, Gaius Severius Emeritus, *centurio regionarius*, has restored to the Virtus and Divinity of the Emperor. (Translation after *RIB*, with modifications.)

The letters of the inscription are strong but a little irregular in size, particularly in the first few lines (Fig. 4.8). They become more even in the second half of the text (where, perhaps not coincidentally, the stone-cutter's parallel guidelines above and below each line are most clearly visible). The REG for *regionarius* is squeezed in underneath the last line, in smaller letters, as if added in order to clarify the exact position of Severius Emeritus, implying that a precise understanding of his role was perceived to be important.

Several question marks hang over this inscription. The imprecise information concerning its findspot precludes detailed theorizing about the circumstances which led to its erection. Most frustratingly, we are unable to tell what exactly the *locus religiosus* was, or whether its supposed destruction was severe enough to appear in the archaeological record. All that is known is that the altar was found at the 'lower end' of Stall Street, along with two other altars, one to Mars and Nemetona and the other to the Suleviae (both of these are discussed in Chapter 6). Depending on how one construes the phrase 'lower end', the altars could be placed within the precinct of the temple to Sulis Minerva;[94] however, it is perhaps more likely that the phrase refers to the south end of Stall Street, away from the temple,

Figure 4.8: *RIB* 152. (Reproduced from Collingwood and Wright 1965, by permission of the Trustees of the Haverfield Bequest.)

---

[94] Cunliffe 1969: 154.

and that the altars constitute evidence for another delineated religious space within the town walls. The use of '*religiosus*' is compelling here. When used in juristic texts, and in epigraphy from Italy, this word almost exclusively refers to funerary contexts; here, however, both the text itself and the archaeological context seem to exclude a funerary meaning. The implications of this inscription for our understanding of the use of legal language in provincial settings are discussed further in Chapter 6. Another open question is the inscription's date. As I will shortly discuss, other datable stone inscriptions set up by *regionarii* from elsewhere in the Empire mostly come from the third century; however, there is also documentary evidence for *regionarii* in Britain in the first century. The inscription's reference to a *numen Augusti* in the singular[95] indicates that it was set up in the reign of a sole emperor, but does little to narrow the possibilities.

These question marks aside, the inscription is a testament to the complex interplay possible between military officials, local dynamics, and the figure of the emperor. At the heart of this interplay is Emeritus's position as a *regionarius*. This office is still not fully understood, but as far as we are able to determine from the limited evidence, *centuriones regionarii* appear to have been legionary centurions detached from their units and made responsible for the security and probably the administration of a local region.[96] They are primarily known from epigraphic sources, which do not give us a wealth of insight into their specific functions and duties. The attestations, however, span the empire. A *regionarius* is known from his tombstone in Agedincum in Gallia Lugdunensis, and another from a statue-base erected to him by the people of Pisidian Antioch.[97] A third is to be found at Brigetio in Pannonia, setting up an altar on 15 October 210 to Jupiter Optimus Maximus and the *genius loci*, *pro salute ddd(ominorum) nnn(ostrorum)* (i.e. of Septimius Severus, Caracalla, and Geta; the third D and N were scored out at a later date).[98] A fourth *regionarius* is seen as the dedicator on a fragmentary marble inscription to Aurelian from Lauriacum

---

[95] The phrase is abbreviated; however, the patterns for abbreviating *numen Augusti* and its singular and plural variants are well-understood for Romano-British epigraphy (see Fishwick 1969).

[96] Fuhrmann 2012: 222.

[97] *CIL* XIII.2958; *IGRR* III.301. *IGRR* incorrectly records the title as λεγεωνάριον rather than ῥεγεωνάριον; see Calder (1912: 81) for the correct transcription.

[98] *I(ovi) o(ptimo) m(aximo)* | *et genio hu[iu]sce* | *loci. Pro sal|ute ddd(ominorum) nnn(ostrorum)* | *M(arcus) Ael(ius) Honoratus* | *c(enturio) leg(ionis) I adi(utricis) reg(ionarius) sub* | *cura Ful(vii) Maximi co(n)s(ularis)* | *u(otum) s(oluit) l(ibens) m(erito) Id(ibus) octob(ris)* | *Faustino et Rufino co(n)s(ulibus)*. *AE* 1944, 103, expanded on by *AE* 1950, 105. Original publication by Radnóti 1941, who was confused by the REG abbreviation; the expansion to *regionarius* was recognized by Betz 1943. The altar was found re-used in the wall of the fort (Radnóti 1941: 94).

in Noricum, dated likely to AD 271–3;[99] the inscription finishes with the phrase '[*devo*]*tus n(umini) m[(aiestati)que eius]*.' Another *regionarius*, G. Iulius Saturninus, is recorded on two religious dedications from Montana in Moesia Inferior (modern Bulgaria), and several other *regionarii* have been proposed for other inscriptions from the town.[100] One of these parallels the Bath inscription to a certain degree, recording the reconstruction of a temple '*vetustate corruptum*', possibly by order of a *regionarius*, to Jupiter Optimus Maximus, for the *salus* of Marcus Aurelius and Verus.[101] Yet another *regionarius* is proposed, probably quite securely, for Dacia.[102] Meanwhile, centurions performing a role in the administration and peace-keeping of civilian zones are known from Egyptian papyri, although the exact title *regionarius* is not attested.[103]

But a significant portion of known *regionarii* come from Britain. The earliest ones recorded are to be found in the Vindolanda tablets. *Tab. Vindol.* 250 is a letter of recommendation from a man named Karus to Cerialis, the prefect of the late first century fort at Vindolanda, requesting that Cerialis commend a certain Brigionus(?) to the *centurio regionarius* at Luguvalium (Carlisle). The editors of the tablets note, 'It is interesting to find this type of command attested at Carlisle during a period when its military importance will have been great … Perhaps he was in charge of operations in part of the western sector of the Stanegate during the period of the withdrawal from southern Scotland.'[104] Another tablet from the same period, *Tab. Vindol.* 653, is signed by a *regionarius* but the text is too

---

[99] [*Imp(eratori) Ca*]*es(ari) L(ucio) D[omitio* | *Aur]eliano p[io felici* | *Aug(usto)] p(ontifici) m(aximo) trib(unicia)* [*potest(ate)* | *co(n)s(uli)]) p(atri) p(atriae) proc[o(n)s(uli)* … .| …] *Ingenu[us c(enturio) l(egionis) III It(alicae)* | *Aug(ustae)] Vin(delicum) regi[onarius* | *devo]tus n(umini) m[(aiestati)que eius. AE* 1953, 129. It too was found re-used as a building stone, this time in the wall of the *praetorium* (Vetters 1952: 105). As for the function of the object, while the fragmentary portion looks to me not unlike a building dedication, the original publisher considered it to be a votive inscription hung either in the shrine of the standards or in the *praetorium*, presumably on account of its find-spot (Vetters 1952: 106). Since it was found in secondary use, this does not seem to me to be a necessary conclusion.

[100] Saturninus: *CIL* III, 12380, *AE* 1975, 745. For the other proposed *regionarii*, some of which are more convincing than others, see Speidel 1984.

[101] *CIL* III, 12385; See Speidel 1984: 187 for discussion.

[102] *CIL* III, 7625, re-read through autopsy by Piso and Cupcea as *I(ovi) O(ptimo) M(axiom) Dulcen|o P(ublius) Gaius Valerianus (centurio) leg(ionis) × Fre|tensis re|g(ionarius) r(egionis) Neridon|is (–?) v(otum) s(olvit) l(ibens) m(erito)* (Piso and Cupcea 2014: 117).

[103] Alston 1995: 85–96. *CIL* XIII, 2958, cited above, indicates that the *regionarius* title could be transliterated into Greek, so its absence in any of the Egyptian papyri probably indicates that we are dealing there with a separate phenomenon – one which seems to have been a much more standard and habitual role in the governing and administration of Egyptian communities.

[104] Bowman and Thomas 1983: 110.

fragmentary for us to know anything about the contents. Finally, the centurion author of *Tab. Vindol.* 255, Clodius Super, may possibly be a *regionarius*.[105] Clodius Super's letter to Cerialis, requesting cloaks and tunics for (probably) his slaves, ends with a 'somewhat familiar ... closing greeting' – '*domine frater carissime*' – which surprised the editors, who added that 'he could easily have been a legionary centurion appointed *ex equite Romano*, however, and he would then be of the same social status as Cerialis';[106] the same would presumably be true of the editors' later suggested emendation to *centurio regionarius*.

Apart from this possible insight into social status, the Vindolanda material does not aid us much in furthering our understanding of Severius Emeritus. Two inscriptions from Ribchester, however, potentially do. They were set up by two different *centuriones legionis praepositi numeri et regionis*, a regional command which Richmond argued is similar, if not potentially identical, to that of the *regionarius*.[107] The first, *RIB* 583, reads

Deo san(cto) | *[A]pollini Mapono* | *[pr]o salute D(omini) N(ostri)* | *[et] n(umeri) eq(uitum) Sar|[m(atarum)]* *Bremetenn(acensium)* | *[G]ordiani* | *[A]el(ius) Antoni|nus c(enturio) leg(ionis) VI Vic(tricis) domo* | *Melitenis* | *praep(ositus) n(umeri) et r(egionis)* | ... | ... | ... | ... | ...

'To the holy god Apollo Maponus for the welfare of our Lord (the Emperor) and of Gordian's Own Unit of Sarmatian cavalry of Bremetennacum Aelius Antoninus, centurion of the Sixth Legion Victrix, from Meltine, commandant of the contingent and the region ... '

The stone, measuring 0.61 × 1.30 × 0.51 m, is not an altar but rather the base of a free-standing monument such as a column or statue; this is shown, as Richmond noted, by the weathering on all sides, and by the dressing and lewis-hole on its top.[108] The mention of Gordian most likely dates the inscription to AD 238–44.[109] But it is the stone's decoration that is most interesting. The right side shows Apollo with his lyre; the left side has been trimmed and any sculptural decoration lost. The back shows two 'tall and stately female figures', each with a turreted crown.[110] Richmond argued, and the editors of *RIB* agreed, that they should be seen as the personifications of the *regio Bremetennacensis* (centred at Ribchester) in the case of the younger figure, and of *Britannia Inferior*, the province, in the case of the older one.[111]

---

[105] Bowman and Thomas 2003: 157 (Appendix of *corrigenda*).
[106] Bowman and Thomas 1994: 224; 227.   [107] Richmond 1945: 25.   [108] Richmond 1945: 27.
[109] It could potentially post-date Gordian's rule, but given that the *salus* of Gordian's Unit is being coupled with that of the emperor, it seems more logical that the Dominus in question is the same as the patron of the *numerus*.
[110] Richmond 1945: 27.   [111] Richmond 1945: 28; Collingwood and Wright 1965: 195.

Even if one does not accept these precise (yet reasonable) identifications, the iconography is certainly that of personifications of cities or places/regions.

The other inscription from Ribchester (*RIB* 587) is also a religious one. It reads:

... p]ro | [sa]l(ute) im[p(eratoris) Caesaris Al]ex[andri Aug(usti) N(ostri) et | Iul(iae) Mamaeae ma]t[r]is D(omini) N(ostri) et castr(orum) su[b cura] | Val(eri) Crescentis Fuluiani leg(ati) eius pr(o) [pr(aetore)] | T(itus) Florid(ius) Natalis c(enturio) leg(ionis) praep(ositus) n(umeri) et regi[onis] | templum a solo ex response [dei re]||stituit et dedicauit d[e suo]

'To ... for the welfare of our Emperor Caesar Alexander Augustus and of Julia Mamaea the mother of our Lord (the Emperor) and of the army, under the charge of Valerius Crescens Fulvianus, his propraetorian governor, Titus Floridius Natalis, legionary centurion and commandant of the contingent and of the region, restored from ground-level and dedicated this temple from his own resources according to the reply of the god.'

The dedication slab, now measuring 1.47 by 0.66 m, and dated by the emperor and governor to AD 225–35, had been reused as a flag-stone in a building in the south-east quarter of the fort. The editors of *RIB* state that originally it 'must have belonged to a structure outside the fort', but although this is probably the likeliest scenario, the possibility remains that the temple could have been within the fort walls.[112] It is an elaborate inscription; as Richmond put it, 'The size and the grace of the dedication give an impression of lavish expenditure and its lettering is worthy of particular note. It displays not only individuality but an elegance uncommon even in the stately lettering of official military inscriptions.'[113]

Small though the sample size is, all three inscriptions set up by *centuriones regionarii* or *praepositi regionis* within Britain, as well as several others from elsewhere in the empire, have some thought-provoking aspects in common. Many of the inscriptions we possess from *regionarii* honour the emperor in some way, whether they are dedications for his *salus*, in the case of *AE* 1944, 103, *CIL* III, 12385, and *RIB* 583 and 587, or a recognition of his *numen*, as in *AE* 1953, 129, and *RIB* 152. Furthermore, all these inscriptions that engage with the emperor are also to a greater or lesser degree concerned with tying religious loyalty to the emperor to *place*. In Pannonia the *genius loci* is invoked, while in Noricum the format of the stone is best suited to a building dedication. In Britain, Antoninus through the sculptured images on the side of the altar grounds his *pro salute*

---

[112] Collingwood and Wright 1965: 196. For intra-mural temples, see, e.g. the recently discovered *dolichenum* at Vindolanda (Birley and Birley 2010).

[113] Richmond 1945: 26.

dedication to Maponus in the *regio* over which he has jurisdiction. Most interestingly of all, the possible *regionarius* at Montana, Natalis at Ribchester, and Emeritus at Bath are restoring sacred places – in the first two, a *templum*, in the last a *locus religiosus* – and doing so through the use of imperial ritual language.

The nature of these inscriptions, then, supports the idea that the *regionarii* were seconded to their *regiones* at times and places where civilian administration had either broken down or was lacking altogether. But they do more than this: they also give us insight into the ways in which ritual activity, and in particular religious engagement with the emperor, could be used to enmesh provincial spaces into imperial frameworks, and enforce potentially crumbling imperial norms. Whatever else *regionarii* were doing – and presumably they were doing a lot – in their epigraphy they seem to be frequently and actively joining gods, religion, and emperor together in their work to bring their *regio* into the administrative fabric of empire. Notably these inscriptions do not reference the cult of the *divi*, but rather the living, reigning, emperor, who is in each case made manifest by the *regionarius*, through the medium of stone, in a specific place under the *regionarius*'s control.

In this particular inscription, then, we are seeing an official, or at least quasi-official, linkage between the sacred spaces at Aquae Sulis and the emperor by a member of the military. But engagement with the sanctuary in ways which emphasize the broader imperial context extends beyond this inscription into the private epigraphy of the military community as well. Overt links with the imperial cult can be seen, for example, in *RIB* 146, found in 1809 in the cistern of the Cross Bath. Like *RIB* 152, this stone is dedicated to the emperor's numen, and this time Sulis Minerva is directly referenced as well:

Deae Su|li Min(eruae) et Nu|min(ibus) Augg(ustorum) G(aius) | Curiatius | Saturninus | c(enturio) leg(ionis) II Aug(ustae) pro se su|isque | u(otum) s(oluit) l(ibens) m(erito).

To the goddess Sulis Minerva and to the Divinities of the (two) emperors Gaius Curiatius Saturninus, centurion of the Second Legion Augusta, willingly and deservedly fulfilled his vow for himself and his kindred.

The altar measures 0.46 × 1.12 m. Its sides are plain, but on its top are two bolsters running from front to back and a well-defined focus sitting in the centre of a pyramidal ridge running between the bolsters. The lines of lettering are a little uneven but clear, with many abbreviations and ligatures. The double G in AUGG indicates that the *numina* of two emperors are being worshiped; this dates the inscription to the reign of Marcus Aurelius and

Verus (AD 161–9) at the earliest. Interestingly, Gaius Curiatius Saturninus addresses the goddess by her syncretic name; only one other stone inscription from Bath (*RIB* 150, found in the Hot Bath) does so. Most notable here for the religious dynamics of the inscription, however, is the *pro se et suis* formula. This phrase is very rare on inscriptions from Britain which engage with the imperial cult; the only other example is *RIB* 627, a dedication to Victoria Brigantia and the Numina Augustorum by Titus Aurelius Aurelianus, a *magister sacrorum*, in AD 208. Here, it serves to highlight that Saturninus's relationship with the emperor not only extends to his identity as a soldier but is also entwined with his personal connections to his family and dependents.

This use of veneration of the emperor to reinforce or articulate private ties seems to be on display too in three further inscriptions, which also tap into the language of the imperial cult, albeit more indirectly. All three are dedications to Sulis by freedmen, on behalf of the *salus* of their former masters, in each case a legionary soldier. The first two, set up for the *salus* and *incolumitas* of the same man, read:

[D]eae Suli | pro salute et | incolumita|[te] Mar(ci) Aufid[i] | [M]aximi c(enturionis) leg(ionis) | VI Vic(tricis) | [A]ufidius Eu|tuches leb(ertus) | u(otum) s(oluit) l(ibens) m(erito) (RIB 143)

To the goddess Sulis for the welfare and safety of Marcus Aufidius Maximus, centurion of the Sixth Legion Victrix, Aufidius Eutuches, his freedman, willingly and deservedly fulfilled his vow.

Deae Suli | [p]ro salute et| [i]ncolumitate | Aufidi Maximi | c(enturionis) leg(ionis) VI Vic(tricis) M(arcus) | Aufidius Lemnus | libertus (u)otum s(oluit) l(ibens) m(erito) (RIB 144)

To the goddess Sulis for the welfare and safety of Aufidius Maximus, centurion of the Sixth Legion Victrix, Marcus Aufidius Lemnus, his freedman, willingly and deservedly fulfilled his vow.

RIB 143 measures 0.71 × 1.52 m, and has clear but slightly uneven letters and plain sides. *RIB* 144 is slightly smaller at 0.66 × 1.24 m and has thinner and more elegant lettering.

The third inscription is for a different man and uses a slightly different formula:

Dea[e] Suli [o]b s[alutem] sac(rum) | G(ai) Iau[oleni Sa] tur[n|a]is [... | i]m[a]g[in] n(iferi) leg(ionis) II | Aug(ustae) L(ucius) Manius | Dionisias libe(r)t(us) | u(otum) s(oluit) l(ibens) m(erito) (RIB 147)

To the goddess Sulis on behalf of the welfare of Gaius Javolenus Saturnalis ... *imaginifer* of the Second Legion Augusta, Lucius Manius Dionisias, his freedman, willingly and deservedly fulfilled his vow.

Although the formula is different from the altars for Aufidius Maximus's *salus*, the stone measures 0.64 × 1.22 m, almost the same as *RIB* 144, and indeed has strikingly similar lettering, so similar that it does not seem beyond the realm of possibility that both stones were carved by the same hand, or at the least come from the same workshop (Fig. 4.9). The distinctive curved G in line 5 of each stone is particularly to be noted. The shapes and decoration of the altars, too, as well as the size, are almost identical. If the two stones are by the same sculptor or workshop, then that provides additional support for understanding all three of these altars for *salus* together. Even if the suggestion is not accepted, however, they are still thematically tied.

As I have discussed in Chapter 2, there is no need to understand vows for *salus* as a prayer for healing or even only physical health. There is, however, a fair amount of reason to understand the vows here as operating in response to or in relationship with the language and ritual of the imperial cult.

Let us take the *pro salute et incolumitate* formula first. This exact formula appears only one other time in Britain, on *RIB* 2066, a now-lost altar from somewhere on Hadrian's Wall. It was dedicated to the Dea Nympha Brigantia(?), for the *salus* and *incolumitas* of Caracalla and of the *domus*

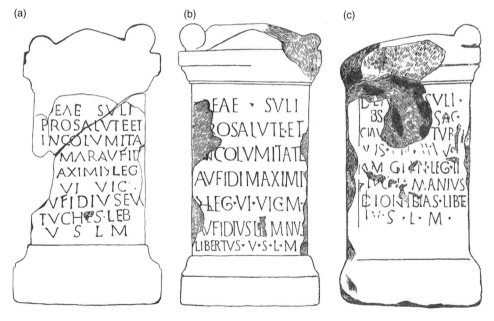

Figure 4.9: From left to right, (a) *RIB* 143; (b) *RIB* 144; (c) *RIB* 147. (Reproduced from Collingwood and Wright 1965, by permission of the Trustees of the Haverfield Bequest.)

divina, by M. Cocceius Nigrinus, a *procurator Augusti*, i.e. the most senior equestrian official in Britain, 'responsible for the collection of taxes and for paying the army'.[114] *Pro salute, tout court*, however, is quite a frequent phrase, especially in dedications on behalf of the emperor.

Of the forty-six other inscriptions from Roman Britain dedicated *pro salute* (not including the Bath pair), twenty-nine are for the *salus* of the emperor or his family. Of the remaining seventeen, six are for the *salus* of a military unit or group of soldiers, two are dedicated by soldiers *pro salute sua suorum*, one is for the *salus* of a woman, Sanctia Gemina, three are altars from Coventina's Well at Carrawburgh Fort, and three are, like the Bath altars, dedicated by freedmen on behalf of their former masters. The final one is for the *salus* of the *vicani* of the fort at Leintwardine, but it too is linked to the emperor since the deities petitioned are Jupiter Optimus Maximus and the *numina* of the Divi Augusti.

There is, then, in almost every single case of the phrase in Britain, a connection either to the emperor or to the army or to both. This strengthens the argument that we must consider the Bath altars in connection with military and imperial culture, rather than healing rite.

Let us turn to the three other British inscriptions set up by freedmen, since they are the closest comparanda for the Bath material.

The first, *RIB* 645, comes from York. A statue base, with the broken remains of Fortuna's feet and skirt above, it reads:

D(e)ae F[ortunae] | pro sa(lute) P(ubli) [Maesi] Auspica[ti et .] | Maesi Au[spicati (?)] | fi(li) d(ono) d(edit) li[b(ertus) eorum] | Metrob(ianus(?)) | m(erito) l(ibens) u(otum) s(oluens)

To the goddess Fortune, for the welfare of Publius [Maesius] Auspicatus and his son [...] Maesius Au[spicatus], their freedman Metrob[ianus (?)] gave this as a gift, deservedly and gladly fulfilling his vow.

In its broken state, the base measures 10 × 20 cm.

The second, *RIB* 1271, found in the fort at High Rochester, reads:

Siluano | [Pa]ntheo | [p]ro sa[lute | Ru]fini trib(uni) et | [L]ucillae eius Eutychus | lib(ertus) c(um) s(uis) | u(otum) s(oluit) l(ibens) m(erito).

'To Silvanus Pantheus for the welfare of Rufines, the tribune, and Lucilla, his (wife), Eutychus, the freedman, with his dependents, willingly and deservedly fulfilled his vow.'

[114] Birley 2005: 298. The expansion of BRIG or BRIC on the stone to Brigantia is not certain; A. R. Birley considered it unlikely that Brigantia would be referred to as a nymph (*op. cit.*).

The last example is from Birrens in Scotland and is also the base for a statue of Fortuna:

Fortunae [pro] salute P(ubli) Campa[ni] | Italici praef(ecti) I[I] Tun(grorum) Celer libertus | [u(otum)] s(oluit) l(aetus) l(ibens) m(erito). (RIB 2094)

'To Fortune for the welfare of Publius Campanius Italicus, prefect of the Second Cohort of Tungrians, his freedman Celer gladly, willingly, and deservedly fulfilled his vow.'

Although the object is now lost, the feet remained when Collingwood drew it in 1928, and the die of the inscription measured 0.38 × 0.28 m.

Conversations about Salus and dedications *pro salute* in scholarship have tended to focus on personifications of the goddess depicted on coins and on the rather obvious fact that the *salus* of the emperor becomes linked to the well-being of the empire and thus of the dedicants themselves.[115] Here, I would like to think a bit more broadly about the implications of this second idea, in particular in connection with *incolumitas*, since the use of *pro salute et incolumitate* at Bath is especially unusual.

Salus and *incolumitas* are two related yet not identical concepts. *Salus* is well-being: It is about ensuring that one's body and health is preserved, but also that one's position in power is preserved (as seen in *pro salute* dedications to emperors after rebellions or assassination attempts), and thus it becomes about those two things being linked: physical well-being becomes tied to status maintenance.[116] A loss of *salus* does not necessarily immediately entail a (total) loss of status. It may however prompt a decay in status or a weakening of it, in the same way that loss of corporeal *salus* does not necessarily result in death but is indicative of a decrease in health, a weakening of physical strength. The point about *salus* is not that it in itself is necessarily the final end goal, but rather that a lack of it leaves one vulnerable to other attacks, whether political, social, or corporeal, and conversely having *salus* does not necessarily prevent such attacks, but does put one in a better position to be able to fend off attacks when they come.

Incolumitas is related but different. It does provide immunity from peril, from attack, and from damage; having *incolumitas* means that the harm or threat does not come near enough in the first place to prompt a need for defence. For someone to be ritually endowed with *incolumitas* is thus necessarily a more loaded action than with *salus*. *Salus* is something that is, ideally, the natural state of everyone. But *incolumitas* is a step beyond, is a state that is not naturally held. Unlike *salus*, which is governed by Fortuna, as we

---

[115] e.g. Winkler 1995; Turcan 1996: 62.   [116] Le Glay 1982.

see in *RIB* 645 and 2094, *incolumitas* is bestowable as a sacred right. This is shown in its various uses in literary texts, where it is often portrayed as a thing either owned or requested by cities, states, and citizens.[117] It is thus even more overtly political than *salus*, whose political connotations and connections to the health of empire were taken on obliquely through the slow association of the person of the emperor with the more abstract aspects of imperial rule.

These points make the language of the Bath altars for Aufidius Maximus more striking. As expressions of social structure and the relationship between master and former slave they are telling. Aufidius Maximus is being treated by his *liberti* as the emperor is treated by his subjects; despite having been given their freedom, Lemnus and Eutuches are still bound in a subservient way to Aufidius Maximus, as subjects to a ruler. Of course, the patronage of former masters and the obligations of former slaves in Roman society can be taken for granted. But the Bath altars remind us that these social relationships could be reinforced through ritual action, and ritual action conducted, moreover, not by the more powerful party in the relationship, but by the less dominant one. Most importantly, through the choice of the phrase *pro salute et incolumitate* in these inscriptions, Sulis is being used *with* the emperor as a constructor and reinforcer of Roman social structure. I reiterate, then, there is no reason from these altars to see Lemnus's and Eutuches's dedications as part of a local tradition of healing cult at Bath. Rather, they need to be understood in an imperial context. The dedications are certainly part of the British ritual landscape because they are in Britain and set up by inhabitants of Britain, and they are part of the Bath ritual landscape and the landscape of the worship of Sulis through their placement (probably) in the precinct surrounding Sulis's temple, but their language and the networks that inform that language are cosmopolitan and imperial, created by the mobility of legionaries and of their dependents and by the permeation of an emperor-defined understanding of power and social position in military culture. This does not in any way lessen the degree to which we should understand these freedmen dedications as part of the local ritual landscape of Bath; what it means is that we should understand that local landscape as one which is partly defined by a much wider web of empire.

We see in the epigraphy, then, soldiers and their dependents repeatedly using the sanctuary at Bath to articulate their role within the empire as personified by the emperor and to define their personal relationships through an imperial ritual lens. There are also a few hints that some soldiers

---

[117] e.g. Cicero *Pro Deiot.* 40; Livy, *Ab Urbe Condita* 25.31.2. See also Tacitus, *Hist.* I.84, where the *salus* of the citizenry is ensured by the *incolumitas* of the Senate, and Alexander 1952 for the relationship between imperial *incolumitas* and personal *salus*.

may have been engaging in similar processes through ritual deposition at the King's Spring reservoir. Ritual practice at the reservoir more generally is the primary focus of Chapter 5. The crucial point for my current discussion is that it seems that much of the votive deposition at the spring should be understood as using the waters to harness and control feelings of loss or decay. One object in particular may reflect engagement by a member of the military with the reservoir's role as a place of ritual relinquishment. This object, a small bronze pan with a handle and a 'rectangular meandering decoration' which would originally have been filled with enamel (Fig. 4.10), is part of a larger category of vessels, found at various sites (including on the continent), which seem to depict the line of Hadrian's Wall;[118] three of this series, the Rudge Cup, the Amiens Patera, and the Ilam Pan, have the names of several of the western wall-forts running in a band below the rim of the vessel.[119] The Bath pan and a similar contextless fragment from Spain (the Hildburgh Fragment) lack this; the Bath vessel, however, does bear a punched inscription on the handle, which dedicates the pan to the Dea Sulis Minerva. The second line, unfortunately fragmentary, begins 'Codon … '; Tomlin supposes this to be the name of the dedicator.[120] Both this personal dedication by an individual and the material, bronze, mark this object out as a private votive separate from the dozen or so pewter and silver vessels

Figure 4.10: Rudge-type cup from the reservoir. (© Bath and North East Somerset Council.)

---

[118] Sunter and Brown 1988: 14–16, cat. no. 23; Breeze 2012: 6–7.
[119] Holder 2012.   [120] Tomlin 1988a: 55.

also found in the reservoir, which, as is argued in Chapter 5, are probably best understood as 'temple plate'.

Rudge-type cups have usually been presented in scholarship as soldiers' mementos, which they took with them into retirement as souvenirs of their time serving on the Wall.[121] So entrenched is this interpretation that a recent volume surveying the known vessels is titled *The First Souvenirs: Enamelled Vessels from Hadrian's Wall*.[122] It is noteworthy, however, that all four vessels for which the context is known potentially come from ritual contexts. The Bath pan, of course, comes from a votive context, and indeed has a dedicatory inscription. The Rudge Cup itself was found in Froxfield (Wilts) in 1725 in a well which contained a mass of other Roman material, including 'several bones of beasts, four or five human skeletons, and some medals of the lower empire'.[123] Although eighteenth and nineteenth century antiquaries suggested that the cup may have been deposited as a votive, Cowen, writing in 1935, dismissed this possibility on the grounds that the animal bones and human skeletons (which could 'only be attributed to a scene of violence'), ruled out a votive interpretation.[124] Now, however, given the work done in recent decades on structured deposits in pits and wells, vast numbers of which include deliberately placed animal bone as well as ceramic and metal vessels and occasionally human remains,[125] the context of the Rudge Cup sounds distinctly ritual. Meanwhile, the Amiens Patera was found buried next to a pipe-clay Dea Nutrix figurine.[126] The context of the Ilam Pan is less clear. It was found by metal detectorists on moorland overlooking the river Manifold in Staffordshire, and subsequent excavation did not reveal any sign of a site at the location.[127] However, other finds were found nearby, including at least twelve first and second century brooches, 'several of which were reported to have been orientated in the same direction, seemingly in some sort of extended linear arrangement', which could possibly suggest a type of structured deposition.[128]

These find contexts have led Ralph Jackson to argue that the pans may have had a ritual component, probably water-related, in addition to being souvenirs.[129] Not only does this seem very likely, but I would suggest taking this interpretation one step further. Rather than being simple souvenirs, some of these pans may possibly have been used in rituals of closure at the

---

[121] Cowen and Richmond 1935: 342; Heurgon 1951; Heurgon 1952: 114–15; Künzl 2012: 18ff.

[122] Breeze, ed. 2012.   [123] Cowen and Richmond 1935: 313.

[124] Cowen and Richmond 1935: 313.

[125] See, e.g. Fulford's examples from Silchester alone, which include one pit with four dog skulls and at least three pits with human remains (Fulford 2001: 201ff).

[126] Heurgon 1952: 95.   [127] Jackson 2012: 42.   [128] Jackson 2012: 42.

[129] Jackson 2012: 58–60.

end of military careers, through the burial or relinquishment of an object embodying the location of the soldier's military service. Similar rituals may have taken place in another part of the north-west provinces: Roymans and Aarts have argued that Batavian soldiers (many of whom would in fact have served on Hadrian's Wall) book-ended their military service with rites at sanctuaries in their homeland, e.g. the temple of Hercules at Empel, although their evidence is not conclusive.[130] Such an interpretation works well for the Bath pan in particular, given the broader interest in ritually facilitated closure which seems to have been on display at the King's Spring reservoir. A few other items from the reservoir which constitute military equipment – a silver-gilt lunate pendant fitting from a cavalry horse harness, and a washer from a catapult, showing signs of wear – could perhaps also fit into this category.[131]

These examples of the engagement of soldiers and their dependents with the cult of Sulis at Bath add texture and depth to existing understandings of the construction of military community and identity in Roman-period Britain. Older models which presented the 'Roman Army' as a monolithic entity to be understood in many ways as a 'total institution'[132] have given way in the last two decades to an understanding of military identity both as part of a distinctive 'imagined community' of soldiers empire-wide,[133] but also constructed by dialogue with more local communities at the provincial, unit, and even fort level, communities in which non-combatants play a critical part.[134] The agency of common soldiers and bottom-up models for the creation of military cohesion and identity have been central to much of this work. Nevertheless, Gardner has recently stressed that within these models it is important not to lose sight of the ways in which inherently hierarchical power dynamics continued to serve as mechanisms for violence and oppression, both within the army itself and between soldiers and those outside the military community.[135] Within this scholarship on military identity, the focus has usually been on understanding these complex community dynamics in fort contexts specifically and their immediate surrounding landscapes. At Bath, we can see many of these social aspects at

---

[130] Roymans and Aarts 2005: 354ff.

[131] Henig 1988: 6 identified the pendant as priestly regalia; however, the parallels with other cavalry fittings are extremely clear (see, for instance, Chapman 2005: 152; Bishop 1988, fig. 47), and indeed the object is currently labelled as such in the Roman Baths Museum.

[132] The term 'total institution' was coined by Goffman, who defined it as 'a place of residence and work where a large number of like-situated individuals, cut off from the wider society for an appreciable period of time, together lead an enclosed, formally administered life' (Goffman 1961: xiii). It was first used in connection with the Roman Army by Shaw 1983, who argued against the model of integration between the army and the local population that had been put forward by Fentress 1979. Haynes 1999 has a brief overview of the debate.

[133] James 1999b.   [134] James 2001; Collins 2007.   [135] Gardner 2013: 10.

play within a different setting: a sanctuary zone set outside ordinary community boundaries – and thus, as discussed in Chapter 3, a peculiarly powerful setting for community self-definition and self-construction. Thus the dedications by the freedmen of Aufidius Maximus and Javolenus Saturnalis, for example, demonstrate the incorporation – indeed, self-incorporation – of dependents into the broader military community. Their use of language echoing dedications to the emperor gains its effect in large part through the ubiquity of such dedications by military units throughout the province and indeed the empire; as such, it also signals the dedicators' place within the imagined community of the military. Severius Emeritus's inscription, meanwhile, is a symbol of military authority at the very least – if not of oppression, then of the re-establishment of ritual order by means of military-defined power. The ritual engagement with the emperor in all the inscriptions discussed in this chapter highlights the ways in which military identity and authority was entwined with broader conceptions of empire and the nature of an imperial society; indeed, through all the monuments discussed here, we see the effect of, as Gardner has put it, 'the double-face of imperial structures as both the medium for and outcome of the actions of people inhabiting them'.[136] In addition, at Bath these expressions and constructions of military/imperial identity are further complicated by their connection either to the cult of Sulis, or to other ritual landscapes at the site. Dedications to the highly localized cult at the sanctuary, *ipso facto* placed outside of *physically* military contexts, thus in fact serve to spread the reach of the *conceptual* military context, and function as locally grounded tent-pegs which help to spread ever-wider the geographic canopy of imperial ontologies ascribed to and constructed by the military community in Britain.

The two halves of this chapter looked at very different material from very different points in the site's history. But what unites them is that in both cases – the monumentalization of the sanctuary in the first century AD, and the subsequent use of the site by members of the military community – in order to understand the dynamics of what is happening it is essential to put Aquae Sulis into a broader imperial context. In other words, without confronting the Roman empire, without taking into account the ways in which being part of an empire shaped provincial societies, it is impossible to make sense of this material.

The opposite is true for the next part of the discussion. In Chapter 5, what people are doing at Aquae Sulis is determined by the intensely local characteristics of the site itself, and by one quality above all else: water from the earth.

[136] Gardner 2013: 13–14.

5 | Water from the Earth

In this chapter, I turn to our evidence for ritual practice at the site, in particular activity centred on the three hot springs. The ritual heart of the site, and the place where the vast majority of evidence for votive activity has been found, is the reservoir of the hot spring now known as the King's Spring. The paucity of evidence from elsewhere in the sanctuary means that this body of material is our principal window into the ritual actions taken by worshipers at Aquae Sulis. If, as I have argued, we need to leave the curative paradigm behind, we now need a new way of understanding Romano-British conceptions of the water's significance at Aquae Sulis. Here, I will propose that much of the votive deposition should be understood as using the waters to harness and control feelings of loss or decay, and that this use of the waters is linked to a chthonic perception of the spring and its deity, a perception seen in other aspects of ritual practice at the site, in particular the report that coal was burned on the altars.

Approaching the Reservoir

The reservoir tank was one of the first things to be constructed at the site in the Roman period, and engagement with it would have been a key aspect of visitor experience throughout the sanctuary's history. Its masonry walls were embedded into the ground surrounding the spring and lined with lead for water-proofing purposes, creating a roughly octagonal tank about fifteen meters by twelve meters in area, with outflow to the large bath complex to its south.[1] The primary approach to it would have been through the precinct of the temple, which lay to the reservoir's north. Visitors would have entered the precinct through an archway on its eastern side. Directly before them would have been the temple of Sulis Minerva, and in front of them and to their left was the spring. As Revell points out, this would have been their first sighting of the sacred spring; the precinct wall would have kept it from view until now.[2] Approach from this point was on a diagonal. Advancing forward and then turning left was impossible, because the large

[1] Cunliffe and Davenport 1985: 39–42. [2] Revell 2007: 218.

'altar' monument, about seven meters in front of the archway and roughly level with the centre of the reservoir, would have been in the way.

In the first, open, period of the reservoir it seems as though access to all sides of the basin was unrestricted, apart from a metal grille. Indeed such a grille or balustrade would have helped to enhance closeness with the water, since visitors could lean on it and thus over the waters, something which would have been trickier and more precarious if there had just been a simple pool.

In the second period, however, the ways in which visitors entering the precinct would have seen and experienced the reservoir changed dramatically, with the construction of a massive roofed structure to enclose it, leaving only a small doorway as the access point from the precinct. The first practical consequence of this is that anyone entering the precinct would no longer be able to see the water from their moment of entry; all that could be seen from most vantage points would perhaps be some steam issuing from the door. This invisibility of the water makes it perhaps likelier that blocks of stone showing a spring emanating from rock were indeed incorporated into the later monumental entrance (the so-called quadrifrons monument) surrounding this doorway, as a visual clue to visitors of what the structure contained.

The only portion of the reservoir which precinct visitors would not have been able to walk around in the first period was its southern side, which was built into the wall of the massive bath complex to the south of the precinct. This wall, however, represents the second access point to the reservoir, this time for visitors within the bath complex. This visual access was granted by three windows set into the wall, one large arched window (2.9 m wide) flanked by two smaller square ones (2.06 m wide).[3]

The changing ways in which visitors within the baths would have approached these windows are complex. In the first phase of the baths, the windows seem to have formed part of a large hall forming a sort of vestibule to the Great Bath immediately to the east. The entrance to the Great Bath, and the other two baths further on which were also fed by water from the spring, was through a door at the far northern end of the hall's east wall; meanwhile, entrance to the hall itself was from the south-west corner. Bathers moving into the Great Bath through this north-east door, then, would necessarily have walked towards these three windows looking over the reservoir, before turning towards the door. In this first phase, therefore, a view of the reservoir was a preliminary to bathing in water from the

---

[3] Cunliffe 1969: 103.

reservoir. There was, however, no direct view of the spring from the baths themselves, even though the Great Bath could surely have been easily built in the hall's position further west, and the windows placed in its walls instead. Furthermore, as Richmond pointed out, the windows 'were no doubt intended to give a vista, but they neither gave access to the pool nor afforded any convenient close view of it'.[4] Either, then, close visual engagement with the spring by the bathers was not thought necessary, or indeed was deliberately avoided.

In the second period, however, this line of movement from view of the waters to immersion in the waters was eliminated. The central portion of the first-period hall was replaced with a circular bath, fed by cold water,[5] while the northern section of the hall – including the north wall windows – was blocked off from view by a new wall.[6] Access to the Great Bath was now through a new door in the southern corner of the eastern wall. From this phase on, there was no point within the baths from which the reservoir could be viewed. The windows remained, however, now forming the north wall of a narrow dead-end passage. The entrance to this passage remains uncertain, as the north-west end of the bath complex has never been excavated. Cunliffe has written, however, that 'One must suppose that would-be suppliants still entered the now-darkened viewing space from the south side of the precinct by a narrow passage leading between the baths and the reservoir enclosure.'[7]

So after the initial open phase of the reservoir, we have two access points: (1) the door leading from the precinct, and (2) the windows, with an uncertain approach path, but almost certainly not from within the bath complex, unlike formerly. Who do we imagine is using each of these access points, and how?

Cunliffe has assumed that use of the doorway from the precinct was restricted to priests, and that private encounters with the spring must have been via the windows.[8] This interpretation, however, must surely be incorrect. Without a detailed plan of the conjunction between the north-western portion of the baths and the temple precinct, we cannot say anything definite, but it is hard to imagine a means of access to this dead-end hall which makes sense within the larger patterns of access and movement within the precinct.

---

[4] Richmond in Cunliffe 1969: 104.   [5] Richmond in Cunliffe 1969: 104.

[6] In 1969, Cunliffe had reservations about Richmond's conclusions that the passage was cut off from the rest of the hall (Cunliffe 1969: 105, n.1), suggesting that initially perhaps the passage was raised, with the wall now visible being in fact a retaining wall. Later he seems to have concluded that the area was indeed walled off from view, as I have described it here (Cunliffe and Davenport 1985: 50; Cunliffe 1988: 359).

[7] Cunliffe 1988: 359.   [8] Cunliffe 1988: 359.

Furthermore, the hall, awkwardly shaped and cramped due to intruding walls from the Baths, seems more of an accidental space created by modifications to the Baths, than the main ritual pathway for worshipers to the sacred waters (Fig. 5.1). Meanwhile, the threshold of the door from the precinct is extremely worn,[9] implying that it saw frequent and heavy use, surely more than would be provided, even over a period of centuries, by an elite group of temple staff (Fig. 5.2). These architectural and spatial considerations, combined with the impressive quadrifrons monument over the precinct door, imply to me that, not only is there no reason to think worshipers could not use the precinct doorway, but also it is in fact likely that this was the main access point for them. Certainly only one or two individuals at a time could view the reservoir via the door, but, as we shall see, such a funnelling fits well with the sort of engagement with the goddess and her waters implied by the votives found in the reservoir.

To sum up reservoir access, then, there are two principal phases:

(1) The reservoir, surrounded by a metal grille, is open on almost all sides to the precinct, with windows in the wall of the baths on the south side providing visual access to the reservoir for bathers heading into the Great Bath. Many people could have seen the reservoir or stood round it at any given moment, and thus also seen any rituals or votive deposition occurring at the reservoir.

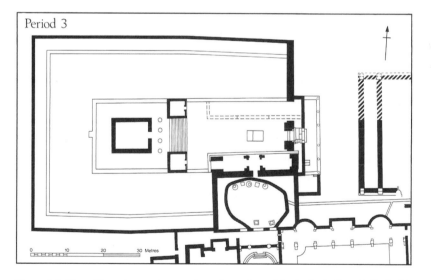

Figure 5.1: Plan of temple, precinct, and north portion of the baths in Temple Period 3.

[9] Cunliffe and Davenport 1985: 52; Elevation 1.

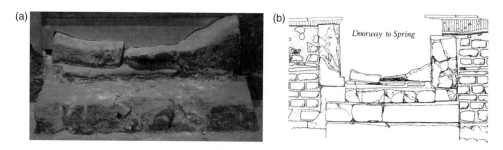

Figure 5.2: (a) Photo of doorway to spring (*in situ*, Roman Baths Museum; photo by author) and elevation. (Cunliffe and Davenport 1985, Figure 132. Reproduced by permission of the School of Archaeology, University of Oxford.)

(2) The reservoir is roofed over and thus made invisible from the precinct except from a narrow doorway, although the building containing it would have loomed larger than the temple. The windows remain, but changes to the baths mean they can no longer be reached by bathers; access to the windows remains unclear, but may have been via a corridor reached from further down the precinct (west). Wear patterns and sightline and spatial considerations imply that the doorway was the main point of access for both priests and visitors. Access, however, would have been restricted to far fewer people at a time than in the first period. Witnessing deposition or rituals by others would consequently be more difficult than in the first period.

The structure and layout of the reservoir can be compared with other sites where a tamed water source was the focus of ritual activity. Coventina's Well at Carrawburgh Fort in Northumberland, although encasing a cold spring rather than a hot one, remains the closest British parallel in terms of both assemblage and context. (The assemblage is discussed at greater length later in this chapter.) Its construction, however, was on a considerably smaller scale than that of the reservoir of the King's Spring. The well itself, made of masonry, measured roughly 2.5 × 2.2 m (8 ft. 4 in. × 7 ft. 2 in.), and was at least 2.1 m (7 ft.) deep; the masonry was lined on the outside with a thick layer of clay, presumably for water-proofing purposes, a considerably simpler technique than the lead lining of the Bath reservoir.[10] There is no evidence that the well at Carrawburgh was ever enclosed, although it does seem to have been placed in a precinct of roughly 12.2 × 11.6 m, delineated by a stone wall about one meter thick.[11] At Bourbonne-les-Bains in France, the well (known as the Puisard) constructed to contain the thermal waters, although still

[10] Clayton 1880: 31; Allason-Jones and McKay 1980: 2.   [11] Allason-Jones and McKay 1980: 3.

much smaller than the Bath reservoir (3.6 m × 2.80 m),[12] provides a better parallel for the engineering efforts required to bring the King's Spring under control. In order to build the Puisard at all, it seems that the main hot spring at Bourbonne had to be diverted, and the whole surrounding area (around 50 × 100 m) was covered with concrete flooring to 'prevent the thermal water from forcing its way to the surface'.[13] Like the Bath reservoir, the Puisard rested on wooden piles; the composition of its walls, although different from at Bath, is equally sophisticated, with four layers, from inside to out, first of limestone ashlar, then concrete, then limestone again, and finally a composite layer of rubble, sandstone, and tiles.[14] However, the Puisard's placement within the site at Bourbonne differs significantly from that of the reservoir at Bath: the Puisard is placed at the heart of the bathing complex, fully integrated into it, while the Bath reservoir, as I have described, becomes in many ways increasingly cut off from the baths.[15]

A similar method of construction to the Puisard and the King's Spring reservoir seems to have been used for a spring reservoir at Sceaux-en-Gâtinais (Aquae Segetae), the site of a sanctuary to Segeta. The reservoir, made of sturdy masonry with a foundation of oak piles, measures 3.3 × 3.3 m and lacks a base; the spring itself rises from the north-west corner.[16] 860 coins were found within it during excavations in 1972; the reservoir was almost certainly part of the veneration of the goddess.[17] The date of construction is unknown; the earliest coins are of Vespasian.[18]

The King's Spring reservoir differs from these parallels in two principal respects: its size and its irregular shape. In both these respects, perhaps the closest parallel is in fact the famous spring basin of the Jardins de la Fontaine at Nîmes.[19] Furthermore, although the methods of construction at Nîmes have been largely obscured by eighteenth century renovations,[20] it does appear that at least part of the basin (the semi-circular staircases on its southern edge) was founded on wooden piles.[21] Bath, however, seems to be unique with respect to the ultimate enclosure of the reservoir. The reason behind its irregular shape is hard to discern. Irvine believed that the tank was 'so singular in shape' that it must have resulted from 'the Roman Architects having preserved the precise shape and general boundary line of the Tank they found used by the Britons before they themselves had arrived', which is an appealing, though unprovable, possibility.

---

[12] Sauer 2005: 6.   [13] Sauer 2005: 6.   [14] Sauer 2005: 6.   [15] Sauer 2005: 12, fig. 10.
[16] Picard 1974: 304.   [17] Bourgeois 1992: 180.   [18] Bourgeois 1992: 180.
[19] Naumann 1937: 29–30; Grenier 1960: 493–7; Bourgeois 1992: 235–8.
[20] Bourgeois 1992: 246–7.   [21] Veyrac and Pène 1994–5: 129.

It is important to note, however, that controlling the water at all is, in fact, a choice. Excavations at the spring sanctuaries at Springhead in Britain, and at the Sources of the Seine and Chamalières in Gaul, all of which were foci for extensive votive activity, have revealed little attempt to control or contain the waters, whether in a reservoir or by other means such as channels or pipes.

Indeed, even the reservoir at the King's Spring is a compromise between controlling the waters and embracing their natural properties. In the pre-Roman period, the spring would of course have been open to the elements, bubbling up through a sandy fissure in the black mud-like surroundings of the river valley.[22] But even in the Roman period, the reservoir had no bottom or filtering mechanism by which the spring water entered it; thus along with the water would come up silt and sand from the spring's fissure. This created a quicksand-like atmosphere at the bottom of the tank, into which objects thrown into the reservoir would sink and move about over the centuries.[23] There is, as a consequence, no real stratigraphic sequence to the votive deposit, and no way of determining, at any rate through stratigraphic means, which objects were deposited earliest. More importantly, in terms of the experience of worshipers in antiquity, the presence of this sand means that objects thrown into the reservoir could not be seen after their deposition. We should therefore not imagine a wishing-well type atmosphere, with coins glinting clearly through clean water. Finally, the heat and steam of spring needs to be emphasized. This would have been an exceptional quality for ancient visitors, especially those native to Britain, where hot springs are extremely rare.

Watery Deposition

Now that we have established how users would have approached the reservoir, and experienced the sight of the waters, it is time to consider what they did there.[24]

The water is central to any model of votive activity at the reservoir. I want to begin, therefore, by discussing the implications of water and watery contexts when it comes to archaeology in Iron Age and Roman Britain. It is, of course, not unusual for archaeological objects to be found in watery contexts, whether they emerge from dredging of modern rivers and ponds, are found in now-dry stream beds, or are uncovered in artificial water spaces

---

[22] Cunliffe 1988: 1.   [23] Cunliffe and Davenport 1985: 43.
[24] Some of what follows has been published as Cousins 2014.

such as wells. Early scholars often focused on, as Bradley has put it, 'practical interpretations' for these finds and their loss in antiquity.[25] A. W. Franks, for example, when presenting the Waterloo Helmet to the London Society of Antiquaries, noted its stylistic resemblance to the Battersea Shield, and suggested that it was 'not impossible that the helmet may have belonged to the same warrior killed in some struggle'.[26] John Clayton, when confronted with the thousands of coins from Coventina's Well in Northumberland, could not believe that they had been deposited as votives, on the grounds that, first, the copper would have spoiled the water, and second, the priests would never have allowed so much money to escape their clutches.[27] He concluded instead that 'some panic' in a time of military crisis must have prompted their concealment.[28] Battle scenarios or accidental loss during river crossings explained the deposition of items of obvious high value; for smaller objects and coins, both the accident scenario[29] and the modern parallel of the wishing well have been invoked.[30] People, it was assumed, dropped these little objects into watery environments as a matter of casual practice, with often no more motive than a little light-hearted superstition or desire for a bit of a good luck.

Prehistoric archaeologists in Britain have recognized for some time that the deposition of artefacts in water in the pre-Roman Iron Age was more deliberate and laden with ritual meaning than earlier scholars were willing to or perhaps even comfortable with acknowledging.[31] While without written sources it is impossible to parse the precise epistemological motivations for these depositions, they seem to form the focus of rituals which both served as a connection between the depositor and the chthonic powers – perhaps even deities – of earth and water, and played a role in the construction of the depositor's social prestige and position.[32] Thus these objects have gone from being understood as casual losses with limited potential for interpretation beyond typological considerations, to being seen as windows into the entanglement of social and ritual in the Iron Age, and into the relationship between human individuals, human communities, and divine or supernatural spheres.[33]

That said, they are opaque windows. Ancient objects found in watery places are usually, by the nature of the medium in which they are found, lacking almost wholly in archaeological context.[34] Paradoxically, that very medium, water, which alerts us to their ritual status, has deprived us of most of our usual tools for reconstructing patterns of meaning and use. The artefact's

[25] Bradley 1998 (1st ed. 1990): 23–8.   [26] Franks 1864–7: 343.   [27] Clayton 1880: 6, 31.
[28] Clayton 1880: 47.   [29] Fitzpatrick and Scott 1999: 117.   [30] Henig 1988: 5; Cunliffe 1988: 361.
[31] Hill 1995; Bradley 1998.   [32] Merrifield 1987: 22–30.[33] Bradley 1998: 181ff.   [34] Bradley 1998: 6.

likely movement through the water from its original place of deposition means that we often cannot begin to reconstruct the ritual's place within the larger natural landscape, and, apart from possible stylistic and typological considerations inherent in the artefact itself, we are usually left with only the vaguest ideas about the dates of various depositions and consequently chronological change in ritual behaviour from one deposition to the next.

These Iron Age concerns with ritual deposition into watery contexts and into the ground certainly find echoes in the Roman period, although the question of direct continuity of practice is perhaps more fraught. Romano-British structured deposition in wells and pits in particular are increasingly well understood, in part because the stratified nature of these contexts allows us to demonstrate that there is an order, a patterning, to assemblages previously seen as simply rubbish in-filling.[35] Late Roman vessel hoards have also been reconsidered in the last few decades, with many scholars no longer seeing them universally as crisis hoards, put away in times of warfare and never recovered. Instead, many might never have been intended to be recovered, and were in fact buried in a form of ritual relinquishment which seems contrary to straightforward economic interest, but which becomes comprehensible when viewed in this broader context of ritual deposition.[36]

Unlike deposits in wells or hoards of plate, the material from the King's Spring was never thought to be secular in nature;[37] not only the spring's location near a temple, but also the inscribed votives found within the spring itself, precluded such an interpretation. But nonetheless the motivations of the worshipers who deposited these votives have not been fully considered in the light of these larger trends of ritual relinquishment I have briefly outlined above. To what extent and in what way should we take these trends into account when considering votive depositions at places like the King's Spring?

The reservoir does clearly differ from rivers and other 'wild' or untamed water contexts in ways apart from its interpretative history. Unlike a river where deposited artefacts might move a great distance over the centuries from their place of deposition, the reservoir is to a large degree a closed context. Some votives probably washed out of the reservoir via the outflow duct or the pipes to the Great Bath, so we likely have lost artefacts, but for those objects which do remain in the reservoir, we know where they were

---

[35] Millett and Graham 1986: 159; Merrifield 1987: 40ff; Clarke 1997; Fulford 2001.

[36] Poulton and Scott 1993; Millett 1994; Gerrard 2009; though see Johns 1994 and more recently Lee 2009: 83–4 for rebuttals.

[37] Haverfield 1906: 251 did believe that some of the objects, 'in particular the jugs and bowls, were doubtless lost by persons who came to draw water for drinking', but on the whole he thought the finds from the reservoir constituted offerings.

deposited – by being dropped or thrown from the edge of the pool, from the access points outlined above. Like a well, and again unlike a natural water feature, the reservoir is man-made, and decisively so; it is, as I have stressed, one of the most impressive feats of engineering in Roman Britain. Herein, however, lies a tension at the heart of the nature of the reservoir. It is a constructed setting, but it was once a natural one, and its power, and the power of its goddess, stems from a continued understanding of it as a place of natural forces. The steaming hot water within it is of the earth – at least as long as it remains in the reservoir. The ways in which perceptions of the role of the spring water may change throughout the site is a topic I will raise again at the end of this chapter.

The Reservoir Votive Assemblage

In all, several hundred artefacts have been recovered from the spring, along with several thousand coins. Many of the objects have no obvious connection to each other, and create no clear pattern. They include items of personal adornment – fibulae, combs, miscellaneous jewellery (including thirty-four intaglios) – as well as objects related to various crafts: spindle whorls, metal ingots, and even a catapult washer. Aside from the three object categories discussed in the next paragraph, the overwhelming impression of the rest of the votive assemblage is one of variety. The breakdown of votive objects (excluding the high volume of tablets and coins, as well as intaglios, the last because their depositional purpose is uncertain) by Nina Crummy's artefact categories[38] can be seen in Figure 5.3.

In addition to these varied votives, there are three more coherent groups of votives recovered from the spring. The first are coins. Coins were by far the most common find from the reservoir; over 12,000 were recovered during the 1979–80 excavations.[39] They span the whole period of Roman occupation, and even include eighteen Celtic coins, though due to the stratigraphic problems of the reservoir, it is impossible to know if those Celtic coins were thrown in before or during the Roman period.[40] The second category is the so-called curse tablets, petitions to Sulis for justice and vengeance, scratched onto thin sheets of pewter, tin, and lead. Around 130 of these have been found, although many are too fragmentary to read. A final category could perhaps be termed 'ritual vessels' – jugs, pans, bowls,

---

[38] See Crummy 1983: 5–6 for the definitions of these categories, and Crummy 1983 and 2012 for their application to the finds at Colchester and Silchester, respectively.
[39] Walker 1988: 281.   [40] Sellwood 1988: 279.

Crummy Types Found in Reservoir	Number of objects
Type 1 – Objects of personal adornment or dress	20
Type 2 – Toilet, surgical, or pharmaceutical instruments	7
Type 3 – Objects used in the manufacture or working of textiles	3
Type 4 – Household utensils and furniture	2
Type 6 – Objects employed in weighing and measuring	1
Type 7 – Objects used for or associated with writing	1
Type 10 – Tools	4
Type 11 – Fasteners and fittings	4
Type 13 – Military equipment	2
Type 14 – Objects associated with religious beliefs and practices	25
Type 15 – Objects and waste associated with metal working	3
Type 18 – Unknown or uncertain function	12

Figure 5.3: Objects from the reservoir by Crummy type.

and plates, mostly made of pewter, but a few of silver or bronze – often dedicated to Sulis Minerva via an inscription, and usually showing signs of wear and tear.

How does the votive assemblage at Bath compare to those at other sites? Is the assemblage typical, or is Aquae Sulis noteworthy in its depositional profile? In what follows, I first present a brief survey of finds at other religious sites in Britain, both watery and not, before moving to the major watery ritual sites of Gaul and finally to the fountain of Anna Perenna in Rome; I then examine the overall patterns displayed at these sites, and discuss where Aquae Sulis conforms to or deviates from the norm. I discuss these assemblages qualitatively, because a quantitative analysis would be misleading in several ways. In particular, the assemblages from some sites, for instance Piercebridge, are not yet fully published, while at others parts of the assemblage went missing before publication (e.g. Coventina's Well, Bourbonne-les-Bains), or it is unclear what was found in a votive context and what was not. A quantitative analysis would obscure the inherent flaws and general 'messiness' of these data sets. This is not a comprehensive look at watery sites in the north-west provinces, but I believe it is a representative one.

The assemblage from Coventina's Well, the only other fully published British enclosed water site with significant votive deposition, is a logical first point of comparison. Coventina's Well is particularly notable for the eleven inscribed and at least eleven uninscribed altars which were found deposited within it.[41] This behaviour is not paralleled at the King's Spring, although altars have been found deposited at both the Cross and Hot Baths. Coventina's Well contained at least 13,490 coins and probably closer to 16,000, a comparable number to Bath (although the Bath deposit has not been entirely excavated). The well also contained a significant amount of pottery, including several entire pots of both imported and local origin.[42] Amongst these were two large vessels, unique in form but possibly incense-burners, inscribed with dedications to Coventina by their maker, Saturninus Gabinius,[43] and a face-jug of a type known elsewhere in Britain.[44] At least ten fragments of glass vessels were also found.[45] With regard to animal bone, five boar's tusks from the well survive in museum collections, and antiquarian accounts inform us that a large quantity of other animal bone, including deer antlers, was found at the well but later discarded.[46] The skull of an adult woman was also found.[47] Ten brooches are recorded, along with sixteen finger-rings and five bracelet fragments.[48] Only one figurine, of a small dog, is recorded, along with three small human masks (possibly mounts) and a two-dimensional horse.[49]

Also in the north of the province, the crossing of the river Tees near the Roman fort at Piercebridge (Durham) seems to have been the site of ritual deposition of objects, with an assemblage found on the river bed far exceeding, in both quantity and quality, what could be expected from accidental loss.[50] The finds from the riverine deposit have yet to be fully published; however, so far 1,319 coins have been recovered,[51] and over 4,000 other objects, including 111 brooches,[52] at least 24 finger-rings,[53] and other items of jewellery. A large number of fittings from military equipment has also been recorded (over 80 so far), although some of these may be present because of accidental loss.[54] Other objects include 3 copper-alloy figurines (2 cupids and a ram), various votive plaques, and over 60 kg of pottery.[55] More than 150 objects made of rolled lead have also been found;[56] although some may be curse tablets the only ones as yet unrolled contained no text.[57]

At the Springhead sanctuary in Kent, 289 coins were recovered from the springs themselves and their immediate surrounding area,[58] and a further

---

[41] Allason-Jones and McKay 1985: 12–19.   [42] Allason-Jones and McKay 1985: 142–50.
[43] Allason-Jones and McKay 1985: 46.   [44] Allason-Jones and McKay 1985: 47.
[45] Allason-Jones and McKay 1985: 39–40.   [46] Allason-Jones and McKay 1985: 37.
[47] Allason-Jones and McKay 1985: 34.   [48] Allason-Jones and McKay 1985: 19–34.
[49] Allason-Jones and McKay 1985: 21–3.   [50] Walton 2008: 287ff; Walton 2016: 191.
[51] Walton 2016: 191.   [52] Walton 2016: 193.   [53] Walton 2008: 290.
[54] Walton 2008: 291; Walton 2016: 192.   [55] Walton 2008: 293, Walton 2016: 193, and pers. comm.
[56] Walton 2016: 193.   [57] P. Walton, pers. comm.   [58] Cooke and Holman 2011: 173, 175.

86 coins from the phase of use of the sanctuary itself, although the excavators did not believe that many of these coins could be attributed to votive activity.[59] Excavations at Springhead also recovered 7 seal boxes.[60] In addition, 49 rings and 309 brooches were found across the site,[61] including 68 brooches in the springs themselves;[62] of the 309, around 60 appear to have been deliberately bent or broken.[63] Other metal objects recovered from the spring deposits include 7 toiletry implements, and 50 fastenings and fittings of various types.[64] Two bronze figurines of Fortuna and one of a horse were found.[65]

Although not a water site, the temple sanctuary at Uley is an obvious point of comparison with Bath, in part because of its relative geographical proximity, but more importantly because it is the only other site in Britain that has produced a comparable number of 'curse' tablets (although the majority of the Uley tablets have not been published). Apart from the tablets, however, the votive assemblage from Uley is notably high in object categories that appear either very rarely or not at all at Bath. These include 94 miniature pots, 52 copper-alloy votive rings (too small to be finger-rings), 14 miniature weapons, and 44 full-size complete or fragmentary weapons.[66] The 40 brooches from Uley also highlight how rare this category is at Bath, as do the 18 bronze figurines:[67] only four brooches were recovered from the King's Spring reservoir[68] and no metal figurines have been found within the precinct, an extraordinary omission for a temple site. Also found at Uley were 29 votive plaques or leaves; no evidence for similar objects have been found at Bath.[69] Finally, 2,996 coins were found in excavations at Uley, although it is unclear how many of these were found in ritual contexts, and how many may be attributed to accidental loss.[70]

The shrine of Apollo at Nettleton (Wilts) is situated on the Fosse Way north of Bath; visitors coming to the sanctuary at Aquae Sulis from Cirencester would have passed by the complex at Nettleton. Although situated by the side of river, the site does not show obvious proof of ritual engagement with water. In total, 112 brooches have been recovered from Nettleton,[71] although some of these may have been lost during the mid fourth century industrial phase of the site. Several objects were recovered *in situ* from the floor of the refurbished late fourth century shrine. These

---

[59] Cooke and Holman 2011: 176.   [60] Schuster 2011: 286.   [61] Schuster 2011: 287, Table 54.
[62] Schuster 2011: 281.   [63] Schuster 2011: 290.   [64] Schuster 2011: 281–2.   [65] Schuster 2011: 272.
[66] Woodward and Leach 1993: 328, Table 19.   [67] Woodward and Leach 1993: 328, Table 19.
[68] Henig 1988: 23.   [69] Woodward and Leach 1993: 103–10; 328, Table 19.
[70] Reece in Woodward and Leach 1993: 86.   [71] Wedlake 1982: 118–35.

include a bronze plaque depicting a bust of Apollo[72], other objects of bronze including a knife, a spoon, and some pieces of jewellery[73], and some iron objects which may have been fittings belonging to a wooden shield.[74] Coins were also found scattered across this floor.[75] Terra sigillata was found throughout the site,[76] as well as 28 spoons or spoon fragments, mostly fourth century.[77] An enamelled seal box was found, although its context not recorded in the site report.[78] Overall, the presentation of material in the Nettleton site report makes it very difficult to separate out objects which may have been found in ritual contexts from those found in other parts of the site, or from periods when the temple was in disuse. However, a large number (55) of bronze bracelets were found,[79] some of which may well be votive, as well as 63 bronze pins;[80] fragments of 11 shale bracelets were also found.[81]

The assemblage from the temple of Mars Nodens at Lydney Park (Glos) is particularly dominated by bronze bracelets (around 270).[82] Since many of the objects from Lydney came from the nineteenth century excavations, it is sometimes difficult to determine with certainty what came from the third and fourth century temple contexts, and which objects belong to the earlier settlement; this is especially true for the several dozen brooches recorded. It is certain, however, that several hundred coins were found within the temple itself, both by the Wheelers and by Bathurst in the nineteenth century. The Wheelers record well over a hundred coins, many of which seem to have been found actually embedded in the floors and walls of the building.[83] Casey and Hoffmann, in their re-evaluation of the site, have postulated that the floor coins may have been ritually re-buried following renovations to the temple; on the other hand, they suggest that in some cases coins 'encrusted with naturally occurring calcareous deposits' may have been misinterpreted as having been embedded in mortar.[84] The nineteenth century excavators found 531 coins, seemingly all in a very small area of the temple.[85] Over a dozen figures of dogs (some have been lost and the exact number is unclear) were found, in both bronze and stone, and it seems clear that the dog was an attribute of Nodens. Contra the Wheelers, I do not think, however, that either the dogs or the 320 pins from the temple are necessarily indicative of healing cult.[86]

---

[72] Wedlake 1982: 143.   [73] Wedlake 1982: 146–8.   [74] Wedlake 1982: 150.   [75] Wedlake 1982: 81.

[76] Wedlake 1982: 154–76.   [77] Wedlake 1982: 203–4.   [78] Wedlake 1982: 207.

[79] Wedlake 1982: 212.   [80] Wedlake 1982: 216.   [81] Wedlake 1982: 223.

[82] Wheeler and Wheeler 1932: 82.   [83] Wheeler and Wheeler 1932: 30–2.

[84] Casey and Hoffmann 1999: 112.   [85] Wheeler and Wheeler 1932: 33.

[86] Wheeler and Wheeler 1932: 41–2. I have discussed in Chapter 2 the flawed association in Romano-British scholarship of dogs with Aesculapius.

Moving to Gaul, while the votive deposit at the Puisard well of Bourbonne-les-Bains, apart from the coins, has not been comprehensively studied,[87] it seems, like Bath, to have produced a comparably small number of brooches (at least three, and possibly five).[88] Only two intaglios were recovered from the Puisard.[89] Other personal items include at least six Roman finger-rings, and at least two belt buckles.[90] A few small fragments of statuettes were also found, and two flat male Bacchic figures climbing vines, clearly designed for attachment to something else.[91] The Puisard also produced a single stone altar, dedicated to Borvo and Damona. Coins dominate the assemblage, with over 4,000 recovered in the nineteenth century;[92] as with Coventina's Well, an unknown number of coins were lost to local visitors during excavation.

The spring sanctuary at Chamalières (Puy-de-Dôme) in central France has produced an estimated 3,500 wooden ex-votos of all sorts of shapes: human figures, heads, parts of the body, including eyes and breasts, models of internal viscera, animals, and almost a thousand rectangular plaques which are likely to have originally borne painted inscriptions.[93] Representations of legs make up by far the greatest portion (68 per cent of the total). The large number of anatomical votives makes it likely that the cult at Chamalières was at least in part focused on healing, although, unlike at the Sources of the Seine (discussed next), almost none of the body parts from Chamalières demonstrate an obvious pathology. In addition to the mass of wooden votives, a fair amount of pottery was found throughout the area around the spring, including several entire pots deposited within the spring itself.[94] Around sixty coins were found, three quarters of them from within the spring.[95] The evidence of both pottery and coins indicate that the site was only in use from the late first century BC to the last quarter of the first century AD – less than a hundred years.[96] Only a few other votive objects were found, including five brooches,[97] a bronze ex-voto plaque of eyes,[98] and, most interestingly, a single lead-alloy tablet in Celtic. Although the precise translation remains obscure, the tablet (*RIG* II.2, L-100) seemingly calls on the god Maponus and chthonic powers, then lists seven names of individuals, possibly enemies in a court of law, to be cursed and possibly blinded.[99] There is no evidence of nearby buildings or of any attempt to tame the spring.

---

[87] Sauer 2005: 168.   [88] Sauer 2005: 171–2.   [89] Sauer 2005: 172.   [90] Sauer 2005: 172–3.
[91] Sauer 2005: 173–4.   [92] Sauer 2005: 3.   [93] Romeuf 2000: 62.   [94] Romeuf 2000: 30.
[95] Romeuf 2000: 30.   [96] Romeuf 2000: 30.   [97] Romeuf 2000: 52.   [98] Romeuf 2000: 52–3.
[99] Lambert 2002: 273–80.

At the Sources of the Seine, north of Dijon, around 300 wooden ex-votos have been found, similar in variety and appearance to those found at Chamalières, and dating to roughly the same period.[100] Over sixty of the ex-votos are plaques depicting viscera, and a few of the statues show obvious pathologies, for instance hernias;[101] as at Chamalières, this does seem to be indicative of healing cult. Significant amounts of animal bone and highly fragmentary ceramic were also found in excavations at the site, in the same layers as the wooden ex-votos.[102] In addition to the wooden statues, several bronze figurines have been found, including a figurine of Minerva and a fragmentary bronze boat with a male passenger.[103] The most notable bronze find, a large model (.615 m high and .40 m long) depicting a woman – possibly the goddess Sequana – standing upright in a boat, was found deliberately buried under a stone, together with a bronze figurine of a faun.[104] An unknown quantity of fibulae and other small objects were apparently found during the excavations at the site in the 1930s, which are poorly recorded.[105] Other evidence of deliberate deposition includes a large ceramic pot, containing 120 bronze eye-plaques and 830 coins (ranging in date from Augustus to Septimius Severus), found during nineteenth century excavations.[106] Some coins have also been found in the deposits around the spring and water channels; although the quantity is again unclear, they do not seem to have been numerous.[107]

The basin at Nîmes also seems to have been the focus of deposition, although the reports are very anecdotal. It appears that around 4,000 coins were found – although never published – in the eighteenth century,[108] and possibly other objects such as rings and intaglios;[109] fragments of pottery (including sherds of amphorae and coarseware as well as sigillata) have also been observed during periodic emptyings of the basin in the twentieth century.[110]

From the fountain of Anna Perenna in Rome come both votive objects to the nymph and an assemblage which can probably be most accurately categorized as 'magical': '549 coins, 74 oil lamps, some of which with *defixiones* inside, some curse tablets scattered in the clay, 9 lead containers with 7 anthromorphic figurines inside, three ceramic jugs, a big copper bowl (*caccabus*) with burn signs, 7 pine cones, egg shells, twigs and tablets

---

[100] Deyts 1983: 154; Romeuf 2000: 143.   [101] Deyts 1983: 104–13; 135–6.   [102] Deyts 1983: 35; 39.
[103] Deyts 1966: cat. 73 and 75.   [104] Corot 1933: 114.   [105] Corot 1934: 197.
[106] Deyts 1966: cat. 101. Numbers of ex-voto and coins reported by Aubin and Meissonier 1994: 149.
[107] Deyts 1983: 48; 59.   [108] Veyrac and Pène 1994–5: 128, n. 19.
[109] Veyrac and Pène 1994–5: 127.   [110] Veyrac and Pène 1994–5: 128.

made of various kinds of wood'.[111] The tablets and containers were in many instances covered with magical formulae and drawings.[112] The rough figurines were made of wax and other organic materials;[113] x-rays of the figurines revealed that each had a single animal bone as a 'skeleton' inside of it.[114] This site is geographically distant from Aquae Sulis; I have chosen to include it here as a point of comparison with tablet deposition at Bath.

Turning back to Bath, we can see that while the votive assemblage from the reservoir seems typical in some ways, there are also some notable presences and absences. To begin, let us examine the ways in which the assemblage is typical. The preponderance of coins is characteristic of many other sites. In particular, coins overwhelmingly dominate the assemblages at the places where a well or reservoir is the focus of offerings: Coventina's Well (at least 13,490), the Puisard (at least 4,000), the fountain at Nîmes (~ 4,000), and the fountain of Anna Perenna (549). Interestingly, while coins are present at the 'untamed' water sites at Springhead (289), Chamalières (~ 45 from the spring), and the Sources of the Seine (number uncertain), they do not form the bulk of the assemblage. Coins are more numerous at the Piercebridge river crossing (1319) than at these sites, but the relative proportion of coins to other finds is still significantly smaller than at enclosed water sites, including the Fons Annae Perennae. I will discuss the ritual significance of coin deposition at much greater length below.

While 'items of personal adornment' are common votives at all sites, including Bath, the proportions vary from site to site. It has been noted that some objects seem particularly common at certain temples:[115] for instance, pins and bracelets at Lydney Park, and brooches at Springhead. There is no obvious comparable favourite in the Bath assemblage, and, indeed, the numbers of all these objects from the Bath reservoir are low compared to the other British sites in particular. With respect to jewellery, for instance, Bath has produced two earrings, three finger-rings, six bracelets, and four brooches; these small numbers seem best paralleled by the Puisard. Brooches are particularly common temple offerings throughout both Britain and other sites in the North-West provinces. However, their numbers do seem lowest at controlled water sites (e.g. ten at Coventina's Well, three to five from the Puisard), so perhaps their low frequency at Bath is a marker of the characteristics of this site category, rather than an anomaly specific to Aquae Sulis. The lack of figurines from Bath, whether pipeclay or metal,

---

[111] Piranomonte 2013: 152.   [112] Piranomonte 2010: 207–11; Piranomonte 2013: 162–3; Figs. 4, 7, 9.
[113] Piranomonte 2010: 205–6.   [114] Piranomonte 2013: 158.
[115] Woodward and Leach 1993: 332; Schuster 2011: 286–7.

may also be characteristic of more general 'rules' governing watery deposition; while such offerings are common finds at temple sites, Coventina's Well produced only one figurine, of a dog, and the Puisard has produced only a few figurine fragments. A potential explanation may lie in the Fons Annae Perennae assemblage. Here, many hand-made figurines were found, but these were obviously the focus of curses and may consequently be thought of as ritually 'drowned'. Was the deposition of figurines depicting a deity into water a symbolically uncomfortable act?

Several object categories, however, are found in significant numbers at Aquae Sulis but hardly at all at other sites. Most notable, of course, are the 'curse' tablets. I discuss the position of the Bath tablets within their wider British and continental context at much greater length in the sections that follow, and again in Chapter 6; however, as mentioned above, the only other site in Britain to produce a comparable corpus of tablets is Uley. Depositional practice at Uley, however, was very different, with water playing no role in the rite. Water deposition of curse tablets is seen at the Fons Annae Perennae in Rome, where it obviously forms part of a process of cursing and witchcraft.[116] As we shall see, the texts of Bath tablets have little in common with the dark magical formulae of continental tablets like those from the Fons Annae Perennae; however, the water, I will argue, does play an equally important, albeit different, role in the 'functioning' of the tablets as enactors of ritualized change.

The metal vessels are also an interesting anomaly. No comparable assemblage has been found at any of the temple sites, in either Britain or Gaul, that I have discussed here. However, structured deposition of metalwork is in fact very common in isolated, individual pits and wells throughout Britain.[117]

The thirty-four intaglios recovered from the reservoir drain at Bath are also noteworthy and deserve a little discussion here; other sites have only produced a few stones, if any. There is debate about whether these intaglios were deliberately deposited, or were lost by visitors to the Baths; however, their chronological profile in particular suggests that they were deposited at the reservoir, which means that they do probably represent an object category peculiar to votive activity at Aquae Sulis. Both their material (e.g. the absence of red jasper) and their style date them to the second half of the first century, most likely to the Flavian period.[118] In both his initial publication of the corpus in Cunliffe 1969 and subsequent reanalysis in Cunliffe 1988, Henig

---

[116] Piranomonte 2010: 204–11; Blänsdorf 2010: 215–16.   [117] Gerrard 2009: 179–81.
[118] Henig 1988: 27.

argued that the gems were all the product of a single craftsman, or at least a single workshop;[119] he has subsequently sought to identify further products of this workshop at other sites.[120] However, the attribution of all the gems to a single workshop, let alone a single hand, is surely not defensible. For instance, the treatment of particular iconographical elements varies significantly from gem to gem; notable examples include the cornucopiae visible on catalogue nos. 4 and 5, or the wings of the cupids on nos. 6–10, none of which (with the possible exception of 9 and 10) are handled in a similar manner.[121] Meanwhile, as Henig himself noted, both the delicacy of the carving and the attention to detail vary considerably.[122] To take one example, the spindly, jointed legs of the horses on cat. no. 19 differ strikingly from the thick single-strokes used to carve each leg of the goat on cat. no. 21 (Fig. 5.4).[123] It cannot be, then, as Henig proposes, that 'a *gemmarius* made a selection from gems he had cut and threw the bag containing them into the spring'.[124] The corpus of gems is almost certainly the result of multiple depositional events. But were those events ritual or accidental?

While none of the gems were found set into finger-rings – and indeed, no finger-rings with a setting for a missing gem have been found from the reservoir – the upper faces of many of the stones show signs of wear consistent with use in rings.[125] As a result, scholars have debated whether we should understand these gems as votive offerings (arriving in the outflow drain via the reservoir), or gems lost by users of the baths (arriving in the outflow drain via the pipes from the baths).[126] The narrow chronological range, however, surely precludes the latter model. If these were gems which had been lost by bathers, we would expect to see gems typical of second and third century assemblages as well. A point of comparison can be made with the eighty-eight gems recovered from the legionary bathhouse at Caerleon, whose presence in the drains there was certainly the result of accidental loss. Based on the dated stratigraphy of the Caerleon drains, the gems can be divided into two groups, the first comprising stones lost between the late 70s and circa 110, the second circa 160 to 230.[127] The materials used for the gems in the first, earlier, category, correspond well with the materials found

---

[119] Henig 1969: 79; Henig 1988: 28.   [120] Henig 1992.

[121] Henig 1988: 30–1; Plate XVIII. I am grateful to G. Watson for calling my attention to these stylistic variations.

[122] Henig 1988: 29.   [123] Henig 1988: 32; Plate XIX.   [124] Henig 1988: 28.

[125] Zienkiewicz 1986: 118, n. 4; Henig 1988: 27.

[126] Zienkiewicz 1986: 118, n. 4; Henig 1988: 27–8. Henig wonders if the signs of use indicate that we should 'see our *gemmarius* as an *annularius* re-setting examples of his own work but dedicating to Sulis a mixed "bag" of new, slightly worn and damaged pieces'.

[127] Zienkiewicz 1986: 119.

in the Bath corpus, in particular the high percentage of cornelian gems, the preponderance of other types of transparent stones, and the complete lack of red jasper, which in contrast comprises almost half of the later group.[128] We can probably conclude, then, that the Bath gems were predominantly, if not all, deposited by visitors to the reservoir. Moreover, based on the dating, the practice of depositing gems took hold very early on in the sanctuary's history, possibly at or immediately after its foundation, but equally rapidly fell into disuse. Was this the result of a change in fashion or of prohibition? If the former, we might expect to see a more gradual decline in gems deposited, rather than the extremely rapid fall-off by the end of the first century. The suggestion that there may have been strict rules or taboos surrounding the deposition of certain types of material into the reservoir is possibly supported by the conspicuous absence of certain other object categories, as I will discuss next.

At the same time that the Bath assemblage conforms in some ways with patterns at other sites, and also has some object categories peculiar to itself, there is a conspicuous lack of certain other categories of artefacts, in particular pottery and (unworked) animal bone.[129] The total absence of any pottery, whether shards or whole pots, is extraordinary, especially considering the frequency of pottery, particularly whole pots, in structured depositions and at other watery votive sites in Britain. Of the watery sites discussed here, Coventina's Well contained large quantities of entire pots,

(a)   (b)

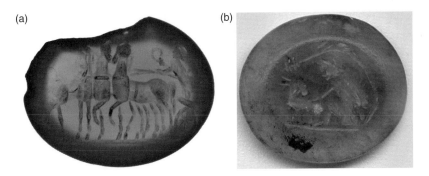

Figure 5.4: Gems from the reservoir demonstrating the different treatment of animal legs. (a) Orange cornelian intaglio with quadriga (Henig 1985, cat. no. 19); (b) Chalcedony intaglio with goat and herdsman (Henig 1985, cat. no. 21). (Images © Bath and North East Somerset Council.)

---

[128] Zienkiewicz 1986: 120, Table 3. Red jasper in general was not widely used before the second century, although it becomes very popular thereafter (Henig 1978: 31).

[129] I am grateful to B. Cunliffe for confirming to me that neither of these categories was found in the 1979–80 excavations at the reservoir.

including pottery seemingly specifically designed for use at that site,[130] and the riverine deposit at Piercebridge has produced around sixty kilograms of pottery.[131] There is evidence for ritual deposition of pottery in pits at Springhead;[132] sherds were also found in the springs themselves, although the excavators doubted whether they were deliberately placed there.[133] In Gaul, entire pots were also found deposited in the spring at Chamalières, and an unknown quantity has been recovered from Nîmes and the Sources de la Seine; it is unclear whether pottery was found at Bourbonne-les-Bains. At smaller watery sites throughout France, pottery is the most common offering, surpassing even coins in its frequency.[134] Meanwhile, at non-watery sites, not only is pottery ubiquitous, but it is very often the focus of ritual deposition and discard.[135]

The lack of pottery at Bath consequently cannot be put down to chance. It seems to me that we must conclude that, for whatever reason, there was a conscious avoidance or even prohibition of the deposition of pottery into the reservoir. Possibly offerings of pottery were placed elsewhere. The discovery of a complete black burnished ware pot placed against the quadrifrons monument at some point during Period 5 (after the sanctuary fell into decay) has led Davenport to suggest that pots were placed as private offerings in the precinct during this final period of gradual abandonment and decay.[136] Perhaps similar practices were already in place at an earlier date. A further possibility is that the role of ritual vessels at Aquae Sulis was largely taken by metal vessels, not pots. Both the anomalous presence of metal vessels in the spring, and the anomalous absence of pottery, might then in fact be linked.

The absence of unworked bone is also surprising, although possibly more understandable than the absence of pottery. (Its absence cannot be put down to environmental conditions, since worked bone and wood survived.) Again, the ritual depositions of animal bone and also entire animal skeletons are extremely common in British structured deposits and

---

[130] Allason Jones and McKay 1985: 41–50.   [131] P. Walton, pers. comm.
[132] Smith, Brown, and Mills 2011: 64–8.   [133] Smith, Brown, and Mills 2011: 69.
[134] Bourgeois 1991: 169–71; 173.
[135] For instance, ritualized burial of both whole and fragmented pots is a recurring theme in a recent volume (Schäfer and Witteyer 2013) on ritual deposition in the ancient world, and the practice spans the Roman empire (e.g. Zuchtriegel 2013: 167–8 for Gabii; Schörner 2013: 175–7 for sanctuaries to Saturn in North Africa; Schäfer 2013: 185–91 for Apulum; Fielder and Höpken 2013: 204ff for Sarmizegetusa in Dacia; Martin-Kilcher 2013: 222 for Thun-Allmendingen in Switzerland; Gassner 2013: 267–8 for Carnuntum). See also Tuffreau-Libre 1994 for an overview of types of treatment and burial of pottery at Gallo-Roman sanctuaries.
[136] Davenport 1991b: 146.

on Romano-British temple sites. Bone was found in quantity at Coventina's Well. The lack of animal bone from the temple precinct raises questions about whether animal sacrifice formed a part of the rituals at the site; the possibility that it did not is increased slightly by the absence of bone from within the reservoir as well, which would surely have been a likely place for the post-sacrificial deposition of bone. Against this argument is the fact that the reservoir fed the baths, and thus the deposition of animal matter into its waters may not have been thought either pleasant or suitable; the remains of sacrifice may have been carefully deposited elsewhere on the site, and these deposits were either destroyed by later activity or remain undiscovered. On the other hand, as I shall argue later, there seems to have been a conceptual disconnect between the water in the reservoir and the water in the baths.

To sum up, the votive deposit from the King's Spring reservoir is in some ways typical of assemblages at other sites, particularly with respect to coin deposition, and the range of personal items (although the number of these is perhaps surprisingly low). It is almost unique in other respects, however, namely in its high numbers of 'curse' tablets, metal vessels, and intaglios, and its complete lack of pottery and animal bone.

The Votive Assemblage: Depositional Meanings

The challenge before us now is how we may best use this votive assemblage to further our understanding of religious activity at Bath. Most discussions of the votive objects have focused on using them as evidence for various aspects of the syncretic nature of Sulis Minerva. Thus the one anatomical ex-voto has been cited as proof of her healing, 'Minerva Medica', side,[137] the spindle-whorls must have been placed there because Minerva was goddess of weaving, the catapult washer because she was the goddess of war, and the various other objects from the '*mundus muliebris*', as Henig put it, because they were appropriate to her as a female deity.[138]

This tactic of matching objects to attributes is a reasonably common approach to syncretic deities, yet in its lack of specificity it is ultimately of limited utility. It is also fundamentally flawed in the assumption that because Sulis (or any other syncretic deity) is Sulis *Minerva* (or any other classical god), she must incorporate into her identity all the various classical incarnations of Minerva – and even Athena – from Mediterranean Greco-Roman culture. The mechanisms which led to the equation of

---

[137] Sauer 1996: 65.   [138] Henig 1988: 5.

particular 'native' deities with Greco-Roman ones are usually unrecoverable, but, as Georg Wissowa himself pointed out in his original discussion of *interpretatio romana*, we should be very reluctant to assume that careful theological inquiries led to these equations, rather than the vagaries of individual experience and understanding.[139] In other words, we cannot assume that the aspect or aspects of Sulis which led to her initial equation with Minerva are easily identifiable in the worship of the later goddess Sulis Minerva. In the specific case of the votives, this means we are probably on more solid ground thinking about what the choice of votives tells us about Sulis Minerva's worshipers, than about what that choice tells us about Sulis Minerva.

At the same time that individual votives from the reservoir have been treated in this way, the larger votive categories which I outlined above have usually been treated separately from each other, with little attempt made to analyse the ways in which they are – or are not – part of a more universal attitude towards ritual at the reservoir. In part this is a side effect of the specialist knowledge needed for full publication of these types of artefacts; intaglios, coins, tablets, pewter vessels, etc., were each studied by different scholars, which rendered synthesis difficult. In the next section, I wish to begin to remedy this lack of synthesis by considering, in particular, the pewter vessels and the 'curse tablets' in conjunction with each other. I start by briefly discussing deposition of the vessels, before moving on to a discussion of the tablets; I then argue that both object categories' presence in the reservoir can be understood as part of a broader practice of 'ritual relinquishment' into the spring's water of meaning-laden possessions.

The Vessels

In total, twenty-four vessels, included bowls, plates, jugs, pans (or *paterae*), and more unique items such as an ink pot and a zoomorphic candleholder, have been recovered from the reservoir or the reservoir drain, both in the nineteenth century and during the 1979–80 excavations.[140] The vast majority are of pewter, apart from two silver pans and one small bronze one. The bronze vessel is the Rudge Cup type discussed in Chapter 4; since it seems likely to have been a private votive (it is the only vessel which was marked with the name of a dedicator), it seems to be in a different category from the other plate.

[139] Wissowa 1916–19: 24ff.   [140] Sunter and Brown 1988: 9–21.

Many of the vessels show signs of wear or even soldered repair, indicating that their deposition in the reservoir was the last act in a longer life history of the object, a life history involving active use. Many also, particularly the jugs and pans, are likely to have been in some way involved in rituals in the cult of Sulis Minerva, and were deposited in the goddess's water at the end of their life history.[141] Six of the seven silver or pewter pans bear inscriptions to Sulis Minerva;[142] their form, the *patera* type often depicted on altars, combined with the dedication, lends support to this 'temple plate' theory.[143] Other vessels show signs of having been deliberately damaged beyond practical use before deposition. One vessel, a bowl with a pedestal, seems to have been deliberately squashed,[144] while the stag-shaped candlestick has been pierced through the body. Another vessel, a plate, was repeatedly perforated with a sharp instrument before deposition (Fig. 5.5). (The damage to this last piece has not, to the best of my knowledge, been discussed or illustrated by anyone besides myself;[145] it is represented only by a profile line drawing in the report of objects from the spring.[146] Its potential for insight into practice at the reservoir has thus gone unnoticed, an unintended but unfortunate consequence, perhaps, of the frequent focus in specialist reports on object typology rather than object context.)

If we are correct to understand these objects as ritual vessels, used in rites at the spring, or perhaps in feasting contexts, then their deposition into the spring at the end of their life-cycle thus represents a way to control the loss of objects of significance. The vessels, having reached the end of their functionality, need to be discarded, but due to their previous ritual significance that discard cannot be casual. They are given over to the goddess, rather than simply thrown away; thus their disposal does not need to entail a potentially painful loss of something of symbolic value – the water enables them to retain their sacred status even after their functionality is gone.

I turn now to the tablets. Both their materiality and texts, along with what we can glean about the rituals surrounding their placement in the reservoir, imply that we can see a similar motivation behind their deposition.

---

[141] Cunliffe 1988: 361.   [142] Tomlin 1988a: 55–7.

[143] The form of the goddess's name on these vessels should be highlighted: all refer to her as Sulis Minerva, whether with the name in abbreviated form (DSM) or written out in full. The ubiquity of the syncretic name on the vessels is noteworthy. When the goddess is named in the curse tablets, she is Sulis more than half the time, and in the stone epigraphy from Bath only *RIB* 146 and *RIB* 150 use the syncretic version. Even the tombstone of the goddess's priest, *RIB* 155, records her only as Sulis; no inscription from the site refers to her solely as Minerva.

[144] Pollard 1985: 60.   [145] Cousins 2014: 58; fig. 1.   [146] Sunter and Brown 1988: 11, cat. no. 11.

Tablet Deposition

The exact steps which led from desire for a tablet to its deposition in the reservoir are still debated. I will therefore briefly go through the various stages of tablet creation and deposition, pointing out each of the various options we have for the exact process and the evidence (or lack thereof) for each.

First, an injury must occur, which prompts the injured to petition the goddess for retribution. British tablets, as I will discuss in Chapter 6, are almost exclusively concerned with avenging acts of petty theft, and the Bath corpus is no exception. The spark for a tablet, then, is usually the theft of a personal item, often clothing, or a few coins, etc. Our first question about this stage is, where did this injury take place? The items are so mundane, that it has been difficult for modern scholars to believe that the thefts took place anywhere but within Aquae Sulis; that is, it is hard to accept that anyone would take an extended journey to complain to the goddess about a relatively inconsequential loss.[147] We should not be too swift in imposing modern ideas about value and practicality on conceptions of appropriate levels of loss in antiquity; nevertheless, a long-distance pilgrimage for the sake of an item such as a cloak does seem far-fetched. The implication of this is that the curse tablets may often (but not always) be secondary ritual at the site; their deposition is perhaps not what brings visitors to Aquae Sulis, but is rather an activity which some visitors engage in, in addition to whatever brought them to the sanctuary in the first place.

So, an event, often a theft, occurs. The petitioner then decides, for whatever reason, to appeal to the goddess rather than to (or as well as) any temporal authority or vigilante justice. He or she[148] decides to do so through the form of a lead alloy tablet. We therefore must assume that the petitioner has some way of knowing or learning that this is the appropriate form for this sort of petition. This implies a communality of knowledge concerning curse tablets within the wider society.

The petitioner then needs to obtain the material. Here we encounter more questions which we cannot answer. Was the lead alloy used in the tablets produced specifically for this purpose? Or is their material the by-product of pewter production? On balance, the second seems more

---

[147] Tomlin 1988b: 80; Jordan 1990: 437.

[148] Both men and women deposited tablets; for examples of female depositors, see, e.g. *Tab. Sulis* 59–61.

Figure. 5.5: Deliberately perforated pewter plate. (Photo by author.)

likely, given the high degree of variability in the levels of lead and tin in individual tablets, which implies that they are not the product of a standardized tablet industry. This issue of composition has further implications. Although tablets of this kind are often casually referred to as lead curse tablets, the corpus from Bath are actually predominantly pewter, i.e. a mixture of tin and lead, with a few containing some copper (never amounting to more than 2 per cent of the composition). Metallurgic analysis has been done on 75 of the 130 tablets from Bath; out of these, only 4 are pure lead, and only 3 more are more than 90 per cent lead.[149] This corresponds almost precisely with the high-tin end of the spectrum; three tablets are pure tin, and a further four more than 90 per cent tin.[150] In between (*contra* Tomlin[151]), there are no definable groups. This lack of uniformity in the composition of the tablets suggests two things. First, from a practical point of view, the production of tablets does not seem to have been a standardized operation; rather, tablets were produced either individually or in small batches, with whatever materials may perhaps have been convenient.[152] This indicates that the 'communality of knowledge' mentioned above is likely to have been the result of informal communication rather than a formalized system. Second, from a ritual point of view, the

---

[149] Tomlin 1988b: 82.   [150] Tomlin 1988b: 82.   [151] Tomlin 1988b: 82.   [152] Tomlin 1988b: 82.

chthonic, indeed sinister, properties of lead, often understood as a key part of the 'magic' of curses,[153] may not have been a key aspect of the ritual at Bath. The very process of making a pewter tablet, particularly the melting required, suggests a different mind-set from that of magical practices known elsewhere, in particular in the eastern half of the empire. According to Jordan, the very process of melting goes against the fundamental rules of how to make a tablet: the lead must instead be pounded.[154] In his review of Tomlin's report, Jordan went so far as to question Tomlin's assessment of some of the tablets as made in moulds, simply on this basis. Yet the fact that the vast majority of the tablets are of pewter, and of necessity must have been melted in order to be made, shows that this apparently fundamental rule cannot possibly apply to Bath. Whether this difference is the result of deliberate choice or stems from continental practices simply being lost in cultural translation is, however, unanswerable.

The fact that the tablets are the result of some sort of metallurgic activity already implies that the process which led to their deposition may be the product of a series of communal acts, however informal, rather than private, secretive ones. This is important, because the secrecy of the creation and activation of curses is another common theme in the discussion of tablets on the continent and in classical literature. It is highly unlikely, however, that all petitioners had the materials and metallurgic knowledge to produce pewter; therefore presumably they were obtaining the pewter sheets from someone.

With the tablet obtained, the text must be written on it. Here as well we have a choice between the petitioner acting alone, or with the aid of another. Given the frequent repetitions of formulae and legalistic language, as well as assumptions about literacy in the general population, it seems likely that most tablet-depositors had help in the composition/content of the text, and also probably the writing of it as well.[155] At this stage, however, we also get our first hints of concealment and secrecy as a key component of the ritual. Some texts are deliberately obscured through jumbled writing, backwards writing, or simply gibberish letters.[156]

This theme continues in the next stage of the ritual – or the next stage as far as we can tell. Whether the tablets were displayed publicly for any length of time before their deposition in the reservoir – and thus could have been seen by the intended victim of Sulis's revenge – is an unfortunately

---

[153] Tomlin 1988b: 81–2; Gager 1992: 4. The argument that lead was understood as a particularly suitable material for curses goes back to Audollent 1904: xlvii–xlix, and is sufficiently entrenched in scholarship to appear as a matter-of-fact statement in modern standard references works (see, e.g. the article 'Defixio' in *Brill's New Pauly* (Versnel 2004)).

[154] Jordan 1990: 438ff.   [155] Tomlin 1988b: 98–101.   [156] e.g. *Tab. Sulis* 44, 60, 62, 98.

unanswerable question.[157] What is certain is that many tablets, after being inscribed, were folded multiple times, concealing the message written on them through the act of folding. Some were also pierced with nails, and one was even cut with a knife.[158] They were then thrown into the reservoir, where they disappeared from view into the swirling sands of the spring. This final deposition also probably lacked witnesses, or at least a great number of witnesses. The material pewter is relatively uncommon in Britain in the early Roman period, and pewter production in the region around Bath is equally a late development.[159] If the tablets are for the most part a secondary ritual at Bath, not the primary reason for a visit, then probably we should think of the procurement of the material as secondary as well, and thus not common until pewter is routinely needed for other things. Therefore, simply because of the chronological peak of supply, the peak of the tablet ritual probably comes after the first, open, phase of reservoir access.

So much for the steps of the ritual. What was it supposed to accomplish? In what way were worshipers asking the goddess to intervene? A typical example can be found in *Tab. Sulis.* 8:

I have given to the goddess Sulis the six silver coins which I have lost. It is for the goddess to exact (them) from the names written below: Senicianus and Saturninus and Anniola. The written page (has) been copied out.

Reverse: An(n)iola / Senicianus / Saturninus

This tablet illustrates some standard features of the way petitioners to Sulis talk about theft. They do not seek to redeem the lost object for themselves – rather they are dedicating it to the goddess.[160] With the stolen item now Sulis's property, it becomes her responsibility to deal with the thieves – not on behalf of the original petitioner, but on behalf of her own self. The practical consequence of this is that the petitioner is able to harness the loss they experienced through the theft, and to reclaim control over the lost

---

[157] The possibility does remain that some, or even all, of the votives found in the reservoir made their way there via a secondary deposition, e.g. as a result of clearing out a storage space for votives elsewhere in the temple precinct. However, given (1) the prominent position of the spring as the ritual focus of the site, (2) the widespread insular practices of deposition in pits, wells, and watery places which I have outlined above, and (3) the almost complete lack of small votives elsewhere at Aquae Sulis, I believe the model I present here is the likelier one.

[158] *Tab. Sulis* 64.   [159] Beagrie 1989: 175–6; Lee 2009: 146.

[160] Of the thirty-six tablets from Bath certainly dealing with theft, fifteen dedicate the object – or occasionally the thief – to the deity, and five demand the lost object be brought to the temple. Four simply demand the thief be punished. Twelve are too fragmentary to tell. None explicitly ask for the lost object to be returned to the victim.

object, without physically regaining the object. Through the use of ritual, the petitioner goes from powerless victim to having agency over the fate of his or her possessions again. The placement in the water presumably plays a part in this, as the final, activating, step in the ritual. Perhaps the medium can be thought of as connected to this transformation from stolen object to dedicated, sacred one, since anthropologically water often appears as an element in flux, and through its own ever-changing state, able to effect transformation in other objects or people.[161]

Deposition of the tablets and vessels, therefore, fulfilled similar functions. The mundane cloaks, gloves, and coins recorded as stolen in the tablets may not have had the same sacred, symbolic value as the vessels during their life history, but once lost they take on an added importance, since their loss brings about feelings of helplessness and violation in their owners. Those feelings are then mitigated by using communication with the goddess and dedication-by-proxy of the object, allowing the victims of theft or of time to regain control of both the situation and the object, and to refashion the loss to be a willing one – a voluntary handing-over of ownership claims to the goddess.

Thus by using the water as a place of ritual deposition, the worshipers are able to relinquish ownership of meaning-laden possessions on their own terms. This motivation differs from votive practices at many Mediterranean temple sites, where a desire for display has often been taken by scholars to be a principal prompt for dedication.[162] At Aquae Sulis, the point is not to gain prestige by having a valuable dedication displayed in a temple – i.e. the point is not the public social after-effects of the ritual. Rather, the aim is to use dedications as a means of closure for tensions concerning ownership, loss, and the material intersection of profane and divine. In its emphasis on deposition into watery ground, practice at Bath may seem superficially more akin to the Iron Age practices I discussed earlier in this chapter. In provincial settings, it is certainly important to ask whether, and how, continuity is maintained between pre-Roman and Roman practices, including not only direct continuity but also processes of hybridity or polysemy, i.e. practices which had the capacity to be read through different lenses of tradition by different groups. These are, indeed, questions that will be of vital importance in the next section, when I turn to the ritual significance of coins. Even so, although the form of the ritual at the King's Spring resembles Iron Age water deposition, I think we are nevertheless dealing with a fundamental difference in purpose, which precludes easy

---

[161] Strang 2004: 61–5, 91ff; Kamash 2008; Oestigaard 2011: 38–42.
[162] Price 1984: 146; Linders 1987; Beard 1991; Rüpke 2007: 154ff.

narratives about religious continuity, or suggestions that ritual at Aquae Sulis was in some way 'native' in nature. Iron Age deposition in Britain seems in fact to have been no less wrapped up with elite conspicuous consumption than were *polis* treasuries at Delphi; indeed, Bradley has argued recently that ritual deposits, from the Bronze Age to the post-Roman periods, are frequently as much about display as concealment.[163] For these sorts of deposits, the ritual's power is constructed from a substantial sacrifice of material wealth; it is a transfer of abundance from the worshiper to the divine. At Aquae Sulis, I have argued, we have almost the reverse: deposition stems from lack, from deficiency, from a place of impoverishment rather than a place of possession.

In addition to the reasons behind their deposition, the tablets and vessels from the King's Spring are also linked by their material, pewter. On the whole, the production of pewter (tin alloys, usually mixed with lead) objects in Roman Britain on a wide scale does not become common until the third century and later.[164] The region around Bath seems to have been a focus for this industry, for instance at Camerton and Lansdown, although there is no proof that the vessels found at Bath were made at these nearby manufacturing sites. Lead, mostly in the form of galena (lead and silver) outcroppings, was also mined in the region, particularly in the Charterhouse valley, only eighteen kilometers from Bath.[165] Pewter vessels of the Roman period have a range of tin contents, with some being more than 50 per cent lead, though broadly speaking the vessels divide into three groups centred on 95 per cent, 75 per cent, and 50–33 per cent tin.[166] Most finds are from the southern half of Britain, and hoards almost exclusively from the Fens and Mendip, but there is evidence for small-scale production (i.e. unlikely to be exported) in many places, particularly in the north, where pewter vessels have not yet been found, so our understanding of the distribution of use may be flawed.[167]

As for Roman attitudes towards pewter, terminology in our sources is usually unclear, but it does seem that there is an (understandable) association between the appearance of pewter and silver. Thus one lead/tin combination is referred to by Pliny as *argentarium*.[168] The association is not necessarily a positive one; Pliny implies that the term *argentarium* can be abused to raise the price of more debased alloys, and Suetonius accuses the emperor Vitellius of replacing gold and silver offerings in temples with ones of brass and tin/pewter (*stagnum*).[169] Our sources, however, perhaps display

---

[163] Bradley 2017: 80ff.   [164] Lee 2009: 50.   [165] Todd 2007.
[166] Beagrie 1989: 172; Lee 2009: 145–6.   [167] Beagrie 1989: 177–8; Lee 2009: 42ff.
[168] *Nat. His.* XXXIV: 160–1.   [169] Suetonius, *Vitellius* 5; Beagrie 1989: 170.

an elite judgment towards the less valuable material; the message to take away may simply be that pewter, in looks at any rate, could be seen as a substitute for silver, and from a materiality standpoint, we can potentially justify thinking about pewter and silver votive objects as a single group sharing aesthetic visual qualities.

This applies particularly to the tablets. In discussions of 'curse tablets', both at Bath and elsewhere, lead has been understood as the standard material, even when, as at Bath, there are as many pure tin tablets as pure lead ones, and most are a mixture. As discussed above, the emphasis on lead stems from a belief that lead had particularly strong chthonic qualities in antiquity, and from the idea that its heaviness and dull colour was, *prima facie*, easily associated with death and suitable to a cursing context.[170] If, however, we think of the tablets as pewter, rather than lead, the connotations change. The tablets, instead of being made with a death-related material, are formed of a wishful version of silver, which, as a material for rich offerings, has much more 'positive' and orthodox religious connotations. The tablets are also then potentially to be grouped with the pewter vessels from the reservoir through their material as well as, as I have argued, through the motivations behind their deposition.

How do the coins, the most common offering at the spring, fit into this model of ritual relinquishment I have put forward here? To answer this, we need to step back once again and examine the place of coins in ritual deposition more broadly.

Coins as Votives in Iron Age and Roman Britain

Until relatively recently approaches to ritual coin deposits on Roman period sites have considered only cursorily the implications of their votive nature. The focus for Roman Britain in particular has been a numismatic one, with dialogue occurring primarily between numismatists, rather than amongst all scholars studying the full range of votive behaviour and votive offerings in Romano-British religion.[171] The faults lie on both sides: while it is true

---

[170] Tomlin 1988b: 81; Gager 1992: 4; Tomlin 1992: 13; see Faraone 1991: 7 for discussion of the weaknesses of this rationale.

[171] See, e.g. Allason-Jones and McKay 1985 for Coventina's Well, and Walker 1988 for Bath. D. R. Walker's initial publication of the Roman coins in Cunliffe 1988 was a seminal work, contributing greatly to our understanding of coin supply to Roman Britain. His main interest, however, was the insight which the Bath coins give into the larger numismatic picture of Roman Britain, rather than the coins' status as votives and the place of coin deposition within the larger realm of ritual activity.

that many numismatists have approached coins from religious sites without consideration for their context, archaeologists with a non-numismatic background have an equally pervasive tendency to ignore coin evidence and to fail to engage with the implications of coinage or to incorporate the coin-as-object into their wider discussions on artefact materiality and meaning.[172]

Yet the use of coins in ritual contexts seems to be an almost universal behaviour not only across the Roman world, but across coin-using societies more generally.[173] Indeed, the ubiquity of coins as religious offerings may be why we have often neglected their votive aspects, assuming, as Myberg Burström has put it, that they are 'too commonplace to deserve much comment in writing'.[174] They become perceived by scholarship as a routine, casual gift, significant only as a means to transfer wealth from the worshiper to the god (or religious institution), rather than as material objects in their own right. A recent volume on ritual uses of coins in European societies from the Iron Age to the present day, however, demonstrates the incompleteness of this picture.[175] The deposition of coins can certainly be a semi-automatic act, without much in the way of explicit ritual awareness.[176] Monetary gifts can indeed play an important role in the economic functioning of sanctuaries.[177] But we can also often see coins being endowed with ritual significance greater than their economic aspect, with the pure monetary value of the coin becoming less important than its entanglement with other social and religious categories of meaning. Wigg-Wolf points out, for example, that late Iron Age worshipers at the Martberg in Gaul almost universally placed chop-marks on the reverse of deposited gold and silver coins, where the image of a horse appeared; he suggests that either this represents a sacrifice-by-proxy of the animal, or perhaps that the horse symbolized the authority of the coin issuer, and its defacement therefore served to negate the coin's monetary value, rendering it appropriate for deposition.[178] In a medieval example, both archaeological and textual sources attest to the importance of folding coins, particularly pennies, as part of a common process of prayers for divine or saintly intervention;[179] the central role of physical manipulation of coins in this practice indicates a ritual concern with their properties as material objects rather than solely as stand-ins for economic value. For the Roman period, Kemmers has explored how the deposition of counterfeit coins in votive contexts, rather

---

[172] Kemmers and Myrberg 2011.   [173] Myrberg Burström 2018: 1.
[174] Myrberg Burström 2018: 2.   [175] Myrberg Burström and Ingvardson 2018.
[176] Houlbrook 2018.   [177] Allen 2018.   [178] Wigg-Wolf 2018: 18–20.
[179] Kelleher 2018.

than being a cynical solution to the economic conundrum of what to do with 'worthless' fakes, may instead be tied up with the construction of local identities through long-standing traditions of coin production and the creation of 'deliberately deviant' coin iconographies.[180]

The ability of coins to take on these complex ritual functions undoubtedly does stem from the particular properties of coinage more broadly. Coins hold within themselves a complex nexus of social relationships pertaining not only to economics but also political authority, social contracts, and technological associations. These social aspects of coins have become particularly important in recent decades to the study of coin use in Iron Age Europe, which in many ways has followed a similar trajectory to the discourse concerning objects found in water which I discussed earlier in this chapter. There has been a move away from seeing Iron Age coinages as simply money in a narrow, economic sense, to arguing that they 'remained largely bound in various kinds of ceremonial and religious usage quite distinct from those with which we are familiar today'.[181] It has been noted, for example, that a significant proportion of finds of Iron Age coins come from religious sites.[182] This holds true across a wide geographical area, as demonstrated by individual studies on the distribution of coins in different regions, e.g. the south Midlands in Britain[183] or western Picardy and upper Normandy in France.[184] These observations on Iron Age coinages' possible ritual significance and need for ritual deposition, at least at the end of their life, are interesting and important to keep in mind for the Roman period as well. Yet even for the Iron Age, observation has for the most part found it difficult to move on to explanation. Looking over the papers in a key volume on the topic, for example, one sees that most contributions are content to list instances of possible ritual deposition – coins in pits, coins in ditches, etc. – without discussing to any great extent the motivations for such deposition.[185] There are a few exceptions. Hingley has tried to link iron 'currency bars' and the uncertainty and danger surrounding iron production and transformation to the deposition of those currency bars in liminal settings in Roman Britain.[186] Roymans and Aarts have argued that deposition of coins at shrines of Hercules in the Lower Rhine region is linked to the military life cycle of Batavian men serving in the Roman Army.[187]

---

[180] Kemmers 2018: 202–4.   [181] Haselgrove and Wigg-Wolf 2005b: 9.
[182] Haselgrove and Wigg-Wolf 2005b: 10.   [183] Curteis 2005: 207–8.   [184] Wellington 2005: 235.
[185] Haselgrove and Wigg-Wolf 2005a.   [186] Hingley 2005: 197ff.
[187] Roymans and Aarts 2005: 354ff.

It is difficult to say to what extent any theories about the ritual function of coinage in the Iron Age should be carried through to our understanding of coin deposition in the Roman period. Giving coins as votives is a practice which is also of course well-known from the Mediterranean world. To take one oft-cited literary example, a letter from Pliny the Younger to Voconius Romanus tells of coins shining at the bottom of the spring at the shrine of Clitumnus.[188] It is probably most useful to conceptualize coin deposition in Bath as informed by both insular and continental understandings of the place of coins in sacred spaces. As with the vessels and tablets, however, the ways in which those influences would have played out would have varied from worshiper to worshiper, endowing the same act with a multiplicity of potential meanings and associations.

Contra this conclusion, Sauer, in his discussion of the deposition of coins at the spring at Bourbonne-les-Bains, has argued strongly against seeing any relation between Iron Age deposition in 'watery contexts', particularly rivers and bogs, and Roman period coin deposition in springs.[189] He makes the valid point that veneration of water is an 'almost universal' human cultural trait, while acknowledging that the form of that veneration may be culturally specific.[190] He also demonstrates that for Gaul and the Germanies, there is no convincing example of unquestionably Iron Age coin deposition at springs.[191] Nonetheless I think he goes too far in his emphasis on the need to prove an 'evolutionary chain' for the 'ritual evolution of the deposition of prehistoric objects in rivers and Roman coins in springs',[192] before we can suggest that practices in the Roman period are in some way connected to earlier non-Roman practice. The concept of the development of human culture as an evolutionary progression which can be tracked in the archaeological record has long been abandoned, and cultural change should be seen as a complex mechanism of give-and-take and dialectical revision, rather than proceeding linearly through well-defined and clearly linked intermediate points.[193]

Apart from this general theoretical point, there are more precise reasons not to discount cultural dialogue between indigenous and imported practices when it comes to coin deposition in water, at least in Roman

---

[188] '*Modicus collis adsurgit, antiqua cupressu nemorosus et opacus. Hunc subter exit fons et exprimitur pluribus venis sed imparibus, eluctatusque quem facit gurgitem lato gremio patescit, purus et vitreus, ut numerare iactas stipes et relucentes calculos possis.' Letters* VIII.8.2.

[189] Sauer 2005: 95–100.   [190] Sauer 2005: 97.   [191] Sauer 2005: 100–4.

[192] Sauer 2005: 100.

[193] For Romanization specifically, see, e.g. Barrett 1997; Woolf 1998: 7–23; for a historical overview of theoretical trends see Trigger 2006: 436ff.

Britain. As discussed above, there is ample evidence that coins in the late Iron Age had an inherent ritual meaning, and their use had an inherent ritual component, at least at the end of their life cycle. This ritual aspect to Iron Age coinage seems to have been stronger and more pervasive than the ritual aspect to Roman coinage – i.e. Iron Age coinage was never part of a pragmatic monetary economy even to the extent that Roman coinage was.[194] Thus, even if the particular practice of putting coins into spring contexts was brought in by newcomers at the commencement of Roman rule, there seems every reason to think such a practice would also be understood – and even adopted – by the indigenous population in the light of their earlier experiences with coins.

Moreover, Sauer's objection that there is no certain Iron Age coin deposition at springs does not hold true for Britain. At least one such site, at Stoke (Kent), is known, where at least fifty-eight Iron Age quarter staters and one Augustan *denarius* have been found in a spring on a low hill overlooking the Medway estuary;[195] the lack of later Roman coins would seem to indicate that the activity definitely took place in the pre-Conquest period. Iron Age deposition of coins is also very likely at the temple site at Springhead (Kent), where a large number of pre-Roman coins has been found, including twenty-nine in the (now-dry) spring deposits.[196] It may even be present at the King's Spring, where, as I have noted, eighteen Celtic coins have been found; though the lack of other Iron Age material in the reservoir may suggest these were deposited in the Roman period.

Taken together, these general and specific points justify, I think, taking Iron Age precedents for both water deposition and ritualized coinage into account when discussing the implications for the votive coins at Bath.

For the Roman period itself, it is clear that the practice of depositing a coin or coins into sacred water was widespread in Britain, as of course was offering coins at non-watery temple sites. As I have discussed earlier in this chapter, several Romano-British sites besides Aquae Sulis have evidence of votive coin deposition on an expansive scale, including Coventina's Well at Carrawburgh Fort (Northumberland),[197] and the riverine deposit at Piercebridge (Durham).[198] Based on both the British and Gallic evidence, I

---

[194] We should be wary of applying modern ideas about money and coins even onto the Roman world (Reece 2002: 115–17; Walton 2012: 8–9).

[195] Holman 2005: 275–7. The coins in question have been found by metal detectorists, and not all have been reported, so the exact numbers are uncertain, but it is certain that they were found within the spring itself.

[196] Cooke and Holman 2011: 171.   [197] Allason-Jones and McKay 1985: 50ff.

[198] King 2008: 30–1; Walton 2012: 152ff.

have also tentatively suggested that coin deposition may have been more popular at enclosed water sites than at 'natural' ones. Coin deposition into these wet contexts potentially differs from other offerings of coins at temples. As King points out, 'although coin deposition at temples may usually have been deliberate, it is not always the case that there was no intent of recovery': for instance coins given as offerings may then have been used to purchase sacrifices.[199] A stone 'offertory box' at Bourbonne-les-Bains bears witness to this type of practice at a site which also had watery coin deposition.[200] However, there is some evidence that gifts of coins at watery and dry religious sites may have shared similar ritual practices. Although coins are frequent finds at dry temples in Britain, as I have discussed above, the distribution of the coins across the site is often hard to reconstruct.[201] However, the distribution maps of coins at several temple sites on the continent, in particular in modern Switzerland, seem to indicate that many if not most of the coins were deposited by worshipers tossing the coins into the temple *cella* or its surrounding area. This pattern can be seen, for instance, at the sanctuary at Thun-Allmendingen (CH; around 400 coins)[202] and Fanum I at Martigny (CH), where 2,742 coins were found,[203] as well as at the Mithraeum at Martigny, where the vast majority of the scattered coins were of low value, leading Wiblé to suggest that higher-value coins were given directly to the priests or placed elsewhere, while the lower denominations were tossed primarily as symbolic act.[204] Tossing coins into *cellae* and then letting them be left on the floor of the temple replicates the dropping or throwing of coins into a reservoir, with the *cella* taking the place of the enclosure of the water. The coins at these sites may well have been psychologically out of circulation, even though they remained technically recoverable.

Nevertheless, re-introducing coins into circulation – whether for sacred or for profane reasons – would have been a complete impossibility at a site like Aquae Sulis; once in the spring, the coins were completely unrecoverable.[205] This point provides a link between the coins and the tablets and vessels I have discussed above. These offerings, and indeed every offering thrown into the reservoir, would have been permanently lost as soon as they entered the water. Once again, we see that display of offerings was apparently not a factor in the ritual recognition of Sulis's spring. Ritual

---

[199] King 2008: 25.   [200] Sauer 1995: 13–14.

[201] Wythe 2008: 48–9 attempts to analyse coin find-spots at British temples, but since he uses averages compiled from seventy-five different sites, his charts showing distribution can give little insight into practice at individual sanctuaries.

[202] Martin-Kilcher 2013: 220–1.   [203] Wiblé 2013: 242–3.   [204] Wiblé 2013: 246.

[205] Sauer 2005: 111; King 2008: 38.

at the reservoir appears to be entirely about the moment of the action, and not concerned with recording that moment for future visitors.

What may have been the motivations for the deliberate discard of coins at Aquae Sulis? As discussed above, the modern example of almost thoughtlessly tossing coins into a wishing well is often used when imagining the motivations of coin deposition in water in antiquity. Given the clear signs of strong intent and motivation behind the deposition of curse tablets and pewter vessels, however, this anachronistic analogy almost certainly trivializes what was probably a much more conscious act. Although the dedication of stolen property and of used pewter vessels seems to have been used to harness the distress of loss, loss of value is nonetheless still occurring for the worshiper in these rituals. Perhaps the coins should be seen in a framework in which interactions with the goddess or prayers to her are always to be accompanied by sacrifice or gift; sometimes an object directly related to the situation is sacrificed or given, at others a coin or coins takes its symbolic place. Gerrard has pointed out that some of the late coins could possibly represent, not individual dedications, but an actual hoard, of the type often found buried in the ground.[206] If true, this would reinforce the idea that the coins are not being casually thrown in as the feeling takes a passer-by, but do instead represent a deliberate dedication. In any case, the sheer number of coins recovered from the reservoir, outnumbering by far any other offering category, indicates their perceived worth – whether monetary or ritual – as a gift or sacrifice to the goddess. For at least part of the sanctuary's history, coins are likely to have been the default physical marker of devotion to Sulis.

Coin deposition as a form of 'ritual relinquishment' is also supported by the presence at Aquae Sulis of a small number of coins which have been deliberately slashed, cut, or otherwise mutilated.[207] A full study has not been done, but of those examined by Kiernan, which included the coins up through Vespasian and a few later ones, several had undergone some form of mutilation, for example deliberate bending or slashing of the coin's surface.[208] While by no means common – the percentage of deliberately damaged coins is less than one per cent – the practice, as Kiernan has pointed out, does reinforce the point that worshipers at the reservoir were deliberately putting coins out of common use.[209] Such mutilation of coins can also be paralleled. While not at all common, there is evidence for the occasional deliberate

---

[206] Gerrard 2005.

[207] Kiernan 2001. Kiernan only examined coins through the reign of Vespasian, however; the prevalence of mutilation in later periods is still unknown (Kiernan 2001: 19, n. 19).

[208] Kiernan 2001.   [209] Kiernan 2001: 33.

defacement of coins in Iron Age Britain, notably in two hoards of Durotrigan coins from Hampshire.[210] A small number of coins from Bourbonne-les-Bains also seem to have been deliberately damaged,[211] and the practice appears at other sanctuary sites in Gaul, including Juvigné (Mayenne) and La Villeneuve-au-Châtelot (Aube).[212] Most interestingly, out of the 2,742 coins found at the aforementioned Fanum I at Martigny, 1,330 had been hacked into pieces, and some were further disfigured by cutting or hammering;[213] this supports the conclusion that these coins were being deliberately put out of use when thrown into the *cella*.

Chthonic Meanings at Aquae Sulis

A core component of the model of ritual relinquishment put forward in this chapter is that the reservoir is a place of chthonic significance, a place where objects can disappear through the swirling steam, hot water, and quicksand into the depths of the earth. This chthonic conception of Sulis's *numen* may also be supported by our one ancient literary reference to Bath. Solinus, the late third or early fourth century[214] author of the *Collectanea rerum memorabilium*, reports that in Britain

'*fontes calidi opiparo exculti apparatu ad usus mortalium: quibus fontibus praesul*[215] *est Minervae numen, in cuius aede perpetui ignes numquam canescunt in favillas, sed ubi ignis tabuit vertit in globos saxeos.*

Hot springs are sumptuously equipped for human use: the divine spirit of Minerva presides over these springs, and in her temple the perpetual fires never decay into ashes, but rather when the fire has died out it turns into rocky balls.'[216]

The consensus has long been that Solinus is referring to Aquae Sulis in this passage; not only does Aquae Sulis match his description extremely well, it is the only site in Britain which does so.[217] It has also long been pointed out that the 'rocky balls' are likely to be chunks of coal from outcroppings near to the

---

[210] de Jersey 2005: 104.   [211] Sauer 2005: 79–86.   [212] Aubin and Meissonier 1994: 144–8.

[213] Wiblé 2013: 242.

[214] Hofeneder 2008: 138–9. Solinus was dated by Mommsen to the mid third century (Mommsen 1864: v-viii) but more recent scholarship has argued for a later date.

[215] It has occasionally been suggested that this line should be emended to read '*praeest Sulis Minervae numen*' (see Hofeneder 2008: 151–2 for an overview). While there is no need from a manuscript perspective for an emendation, the suggestion, according to S. Oakley (pers. comm.), is 'neither absurd nor implausible'. There is, then, a possibility, albeit faint, that Solinus had not only heard of Bath, but also knew the full syncretic name of the goddess.

[216] Solinus, *Collectanea rerum memorabilium* 22.10. My translation.

[217] Haverfield 1906: 221; Cunliffe 1969: 7, who points out that the equation goes back to Geoffrey of Monmouth in the twelfth century.

site.[218] Solinus certainly had access to information about Britain; the rest of his discussion of Britain contains some surprisingly accurate details – for instance, that Britain is a source for jet.[219] If his reliability as a source is accepted, there are two points to make: first, that coal was burned in honour of Sulis and second, this was considered to be a notable, and characteristic, feature of the goddess's temple – noteworthy and distinguishing enough that word of it reached Solinus. Indeed, the coal's behaviour would likely have been striking to anyone used to the combustion of wood; a correspondent of J. G. Frazer described his first-hand experiences with Somerset coal in this way: 'I lived some 30 years ago at Frome in Somerset, and it took me some time to get used to the peculiar behaviour of the local house-coal, which after giving off its gases in the form of flame, leaves the grate full of dead coke, which soon goes out completely unless there is a good draft.'[220]

There is a small amount of archaeological evidence supporting Solinus's statement. Although no burnt coal was found during the twentieth century excavations,[221] Irvine noted a find of 'a quantity of coal ashes ... and thrown on it a large Roman cup' in the north-west corner of the temple precinct.[222] No coal from Bath has been tested so far, but tests of coal from other sites in the region around the Severn imply that local sources of coal were being used by the inhabitants of the area.[223] Evidence for the use of coal in ritual contexts in Britain, however, is exceedingly rare. Coal has been found in fourth century layers at the temple at High Nash (Glos.);[224] on the other hand, coal from the shrine at Nettleton (Wilts.), although occasionally cited as evidence of coal in a ritual context,[225] seems rather to be associated with the site's transformation into an industrial settlement.[226] While it is possible that the use of coal at other ritual sites has either gone unrecognized, or has left no archaeological trace (either because the coal was entirely consumed or it was completely cleared from the site after use), the archaeological evidence as it now stands supports the impression from Solinus that the burning of coal was a singular part of ritual practice at Aquae Sulis – not merely rare in comparison with Solinus's continental experiences, but rare

---

[218] Lysons 1813: 3; Scarth 1864: 3; Haverfield 1906: 221.   [219] Solinus, *Coll.* 22.11.

[220] Letter, Thomas C. Cantrill to J. G. Frazer, 24 May 1921. Recorded in an MS note by Frazer on the last page of his personal copy of Mommsen's edition of Solinus (held in the Classical Faculty Library, University of Cambridge).

[221] Unburnt coal was found in the Period 5 layers (i.e. after the temple had fallen into disuse) (Cunliffe and Davenport 1985: 35).

[222] Cunliffe and Davenport 1985: 35.   [223] Smith 1996: 379.

[224] Dearne and Branigan 1995: 92.   [225] Travis 2008: 159.

[226] Wedlake 1982: 68, 220; Dearne and Branigan 1995: 94.

within Britain itself. Perhaps, then, coal, a material emerging from the ground, was seen as a particularly appropriate fuel for Sulis's cult: taken together, both the coal and the spring place heat from the earth at the heart of worshipers' experience of Sulis.

As the water left the spring and entered the baths, however, perceptions of its purpose may have changed from the ritual functions I have discussed here, to a more mundane appreciation of the physical pleasure it could afford to bathers: the 'sumptuously equipped' waters of Solinus's description. As discussed above, in the baths' initial phase, bathers would have had a view onto the reservoir of the sacred spring as they passed through the central hall to the Great Bath; the experience of bathing and the experience of viewing the sacred heart of the site would have thus initially been intertwined. In the second phase, however, these two experiences were disconnected by the changes made to the layout of the central hall, which blocked the windows to the spring from view. This suggests that, although the baths were technically fed by the hot water from the reservoir, as time went on the activities taking place in the baths were consciously separated from the ritual activities taking place at the reservoir edge, and may have formed a draw to Aquae Sulis which was distinct from its religious significance. Although of course Roman bathers would have been accustomed to artificially heated bathing complexes, the sheer volume of steaming hot water provided by the three hot springs would have been on an entirely different scale to anything visitors could have experienced elsewhere in Britain. This fact alone is enough to explain the early construction of the main bath complex at the King's Spring. As I have discussed in Chapter 4, the initial development of the area around the King's Spring was planned by people thoroughly immersed in Roman cultural standards. Given the importance of bathing in Roman society, is it any surprise that they chose to exploit the hot springs in this way?

6 | The Local Writ Large

Introduction

In Chapter 4, I focused on the way in which Aquae Sulis was used in the construction of Roman imperialism and the self-positioning of individuals within Roman power networks. Chapter 5's themes were at a much more localized scale, concerned as it was with the role of water, central to the site's sacrality, and the ways in which worshipers used the water to negotiate highly personal concerns and needs. In this chapter, I want to explore the ways in which we can bridge our understanding of these different scales: the local, the regional, and the empire-wide. There has been a shift in recent years in the study of the ancient world generally, and perhaps especially within classical archaeology, towards a focus on the local, and in particular on emphasizing variety and diversity from site to site, rather than on big-picture generalizations. This book is indeed part of this trend, focusing as it does in depth on a single site, rather than on ritual practices throughout the province of Britain, or watery cults in the north-west provinces as a whole. And yet, the methodological challenge remains: are we doomed to understanding sites as isolated and unique points in the landscape, unable to be connected to larger trends, unless by so many caveats that the generalization is rendered meaningless? Or are there ways in which to embrace site-specific uniqueness, while at the same time understanding how that uniqueness both stems from, and feeds back into, a broader-brush yet still intellectually legitimate picture? This chapter attempts to create such an understanding for Aquae Sulis, examining in particular how iconography and certain ritual practices may be read through, as I put it, concentric circles of ever-increasing locality – like zooming in on the earth from above.

Imagining the Gods: Local and Supralocal Iconographic Networks

The buildings and monuments of Aquae Sulis are emblematic of the way in which the sanctuary was shaped by the broader networks of both Britain and the other north-west provinces. In the first part of this chapter, I want to explore how these networks are manifested in the site's religious iconography, beginning once again with the temple to Sulis Minerva. The temple is a prime example of how the environment of Aquae Sulis reflected the hybrid, dynamic networks of the western empire. As has been discussed, Blagg showed in 1979 that the pediment was carved by craftspeople from north-east Gaul.[1] The distribution of Forum of Augustus imitations discussed in Chapter 4 does not overlap with the territory which may have produced the sculptor(s); Avenches is the northern-most instance. This lack of overlap, however, highlights an important point which has been overlooked in discussions of the pediment focused on artist and artist's origin. The iconography of the pediment cannot be linked to iconographical trends specific to north-east Gaul and the Rhineland; the flavour, as it were, of the pediment comes more from the empire's centre. The winged Victories, *coronae civicae*, etc. are not provincial reworkings of Roman models: they are the Roman models themselves. The same can be said for the very fact that the temple possesses a sculptured pediment at all, which, as I have discussed, makes it unique amongst the temples of the north-west provinces. The temple of Sulis Minerva and its iconography may have been carved by someone rooted in the north-east of Gaul, but it was designed by someone whose visual and architectural lexicon came from the more deeply established portions of the empire, and who not only had a familiarity with the urban spaces of the western empire nearer the Mediterranean (perhaps even with Rome itself), but was indeed thoroughly immersed in them and drew on them as a matter of course.

Whether the carver and the designer were the same individual (which perhaps seems unlikely) is not necessarily material. Whether one hand or multiple were responsible, the merging of style and iconography from different continental sources demonstrates the complexity of the interprovincial links which came together in the creation of Bath as a sacred space in the Roman period. The Bath Gorgon is, as we have always known, a syncretic image. But it is not merely a syncretism between two simple concepts, 'Roman' and 'Celtic'; rather it brings together a multiplicity of threads from a multiplicity of places, from the conceptual to the technical, and from the local to the empire-wide.

In addition to the temple, other images from Bath besides the temple demonstrate clear links to continental iconographic traditions and provide strong indicators that Aquae Sulis was embedded in supraregional networks of architectural and iconographic production. One of these is the so-called

---

[1] Blagg 1979.

head of Sulis Minerva. This life-size head of gilded bronze, presumably part of a larger statue (it is broken at the neck), was found in 1727 during building works somewhere in Stall Street, in central Bath. The exact location is unknown, since the work in question ran some length down Stall Street, including through the area of the temple precinct and part of the bath complex.[2]

The work is of high quality, with calm, composed classical features (Fig. 6.1). The head is deliberately truncated, finishing at the line of the hair; it is assumed that a separately cast helmet would have been placed on top.[3] It has sometimes been suggested that this head belonged to the cult statue of

(a)   (b)

(c)

Figure 6.1: (a) Front, (b) profile, and (c) back of the head of Sulis Minerva. ((a) © Bath and North East Somerset Council; (b) and (c) photos by author.)

[2] Haverfield 1906: 259; Cunliffe 1969: 34.   [3] Toynbee 1964: 79–80.

the temple.[4] Given the uncertainty over the find spot, and the weight such an interpretation would carry, we cannot accept this without question. On the other hand, the scarcity of life-size bronze sculptures in Britain, particularly gilded ones, suggests that this was an important statue, and that if it was not the cult statue, the cult statue itself likely was even more elaborate.[5]

Here, however, I want to focus not on the statue's precise location within the sanctuary, but instead on where it came from before. Toynbee considered that the head, 'if not of Mediterranean provenance, must have been cast in one of the leading and most romanized bronze-working centres in Gaul'.[6] Henig, on the other hand, has argued that it shows 'local features' (although he does not specify what these are) and clearly favours seeing the head as a British manufacture.[7] Neither Toynbee nor Henig, however, lay out the steps which led to their conclusions, and one may suspect that, despite their respective unquestionable expertise on Romano-British art, Toynbee's favouring of a Gallic workshop and Henig's of a British one are more the result of their separate scholarly biases than of rigorous stylistic analyses. Toynbee routinely assigned geographic origin by perceived degree of classicism,[8] and Henig has openly acknowledged his agenda to restore the reputation for excellence of Romano-British artists.[9] It is, in fact, remarkable that no one, as far as I have found, has ever offered comparanda for the Bath head (beyond the rather facile comparison with the head of Minerva from the Walbrook in London, only made because they are the two remaining life-size heads of the goddess from the province).

The best parallel I have been able to find is the so-called Apollo of Vaupoisson, now in the Musée de Troyes (Espérandieu IV, 3216; Fig. 6.2). This smaller than lifesize statue (1.08 m) was found in 1813 in a field outside the village of Vaupoisson (Aube) in north-eastern France.[10] The findspot has never been properly excavated, but other Roman finds were found in the immediate vicinity throughout the nineteenth century, including building foundations and fragments of bronze laurel leaves.[11] The nature of the buildings found is unknown, but the possibility remains that the statue comes from a small temple.

---

[4] Cunliffe 1969: 34; Cunliffe and Fulford 1982: 9; Cunliffe and Davenport 1985: 114; McGowen 2007: 82.
[5] B. Croxford, pers. comm.   [6] Toynbee 1964: 80.   [7] Henig 1995: 84; 97.
[8] Toynbee 1964: 4–5.   [9] Henig 1985: 2; Henig 1995: 10–11.   [10] Le Clert 1898: 2.
[11] Le Clert 1898: 3.

(a)   (b)

(c)

Figure 6.2: (a) Front, (b) profile, and (c) back of the Apollo of Vaupoisson. (Troyes, Musée des Beaux-Arts et d'Archéologie. Photo Carole Bell, Ville de Troyes.)

Stylistically there are quite strong similarities between the head from Bath and the head of the Vaupoisson statue. While the lines of the Bath head are slightly softer, there is a similar cast to the calm, composed features. The lines of the bridge of the nose continue into the lines of the eyebrows in much the same way, and the 'coronet' of hair parted in the middle on the Apollo also strongly brings to mind the hair of the Minerva. The most striking similarity, however, is that the Apollo displays precisely the same sort of truncated upper head as the Bath head.[12]

These stylistic similarities between the Vaupoisson statue and the Bath head are strong enough to make it plausible that they are the product of, if not the same workshop, at least the same region. The workshop which produced the Vaupoisson statue has been linked by Boucher to a network of workshops active in this part of north-east Gaul.[13] We may have here, then, further corroboration of the artistic links between Aquae Sulis and north-east Gaul. At the least, the Vaupoisson statue offers a more concrete reason for associating the Bath head with a Gallic workshop than has previously been offered.

The links the Bath head demonstrates differ from the links seen in the pediment or those in the corner blocks of the so-called altar, discussed next. While both the pediment and the corner blocks are made of local stone and were probably carved by itinerant craftspeople, the bronze sculpture would probably have been imported already finished from its workshop across the continent. Its creators might never have visited Aquae Sulis. It is thus as much an example of the economic networks and trade routes which linked Britain to the continent as it is of artistic links. It is unfortunate that we cannot date the head, especially since it may be the cult statue. There is thus no way of knowing whether it is contemporaneous with the temple, or whether it is a later import.

A separate set of connections are seen in a monument which stood in the temple precinct, the base of the so-called altar, and the carved corner blocks associated with it. Although I shall challenge the assumption that this monument was necessarily the temple altar shortly, for the sake of convenience and consistency with previous scholarship I shall continue to use the term for the moment.

---

[12] This in fact raises a question about the identity of the Vaupoisson statue. The Minerva's truncated head is explained by a separately cast helmet, which would have been placed on top. What may have necessitated such truncation on Apollo is harder to imagine. He may have had a laurel crown, but while the laurel leaves would have needed to be cast separately, it is doubtful the whole top of the head would have needed to be. One possible solution is that this statue is not in fact of Apollo. The French antiquaries were torn upon its discovery over whether the statue was Apollo or Bacchus (Le Clert 1898: 4). Apollo was eventually settled upon, and so he is known today, but this identification is based more on tradition than hard iconographic evidence. If, however, he is Bacchus, then the top of the head might have been in the style of the bronze Palazzo Massimo Bacchus (whom, indeed, the Vaupoisson statue closely resembles in pose and style); the part of the head from the headband up may well then have been separately cast. For another provincial bronze of Bacchus with similar headgear, this time from Avenches, see Leibundgut 1976: Plate 7.

[13] Boucher 1976: 130.

The 'altar' stood on a base of lias limestone roughly 2.86 m², which was raised about 15 cm above the level of the precinct; wear on this base indicates the 'altar' itself was about 2.2 m².[14] Three of its four corners have been found, each decorated with two figures of deities in relief. It would seem by the cramp-holes that these corners were incorporated into a larger monument, with a moulded stone capping (Fig. 6.3). Of the corner blocks, one was discovered in 1790, another near the location of the altar base in 1965, and the third was built into Compton Dando church, 11 km from Bath, at some point in the medieval period.[15] It has generally been assumed that the limestone base – and by extension the blocks – dates to Period 1 of the Temple Precinct, i.e. the late first century.[16] Certainly the base predates the pennant paving of later phases.[17] However, no direct relationship between the Period 1 lias paving and the blocks which made up the base could be observed, since the Period 1 paving did not survive in this area.[18] The assumption that the blocks in question belong in this spot rests largely on the discovery of one near – though not on – the limestone base, in the

Figure 6.3: Reconstruction by Cunliffe and Davenport of the 'altar'. (Cunliffe and Davenport 1985, Figure 66. Reproduced by permission of the School of Archaeology, University of Oxford.)

[14] Cunliffe and Davenport 1985: 118.   [15] Cunliffe and Davenport 1985: 118.
[16] Cunliffe and Davenport 1985: 37.   [17] Cunliffe and Davenport 1985: 63.
[18] B. Cunliffe, pers. comm.

rubble layers post-dating the destruction of the temple;[19] since none were *in situ*, the possibility does remain that they belonged to a monument placed elsewhere. However, they were clearly part of a rectangular monument and fit well into the dimensions of the base, and I am willing to accept that this was their most likely location.

The first block, found in 1965, shows Bacchus on one side, pouring liquid into the mouth of a panther sitting by his feet, and a goddess on the other, who is also pouring liquid from a jug onto the ground in front of her, and seems to be holding a cornucopia on her right arm (*CSIR* I.2, 29; Fig. 6.4). The second, found in 1790, shows Hercules Bibax, holding a cup and leaning on a club, and Jupiter, standing with a sceptre and a staff, and with an eagle at his feet (*CSIR* I.2, 30; Fig. 6.5). The third block is extremely weathered after having been exposed to the elements at

Figure 6.4: Block showing (a) Bacchus and (b) a female deity. (Photos by author.)

[19] Cunliffe 1966: 201.

Figure 6.5: Block showing (a) Jupiter and (b) Hercules Bibax. (Photos by author.)

Compton Dando for centuries (*CSIR* I.2, 31; Fig. 6.6). Nonetheless, the figure of Apollo, with a lyre resting on his bent left knee, is clearly visible on one side; the other side shows a naked male figure holding unclear attributes. It has occasionally been suggested that this figure is another Hercules.[20] A second Hercules, however, on a monument seemingly so interested in portraying a range of figures would seem unlikely. From personal autopsy, I agree with McGowen that a more likely identification is Neptune, which would make the worn attribute cradled in his right arm a dolphin.[21]

Taken as a whole, these blocks are unusual for Roman Britain. The choices of Jupiter and Apollo in particular are noteworthy; depictions of either god from the province are extremely rare.[22] Depictions of Bacchus in

[20] Toynbee 1964: 153; Cunliffe 1966: 201.   [21] McGowen 2010: 26.
[22] Toynbee 1964: 152–3.

Figure 6.6: Block showing (a) Apollo and (b) an unknown male deity (Neptune?). (Photos by author.)

stone are also very infrequent.[23] Not only are the choices of deities atypical, but the very format in which they are depicted is as well, i.e. stones displaying on multiple sides individual deities with their attributes. However, when we turn to the continent, parallels are abundant. The style of the altar blocks, with classical deities in niches, bears a striking resemblance to the so-called *Viergöttersteine*, the lowest blocks on the base for Jupiter columns.[24] Found in great numbers in the Rhineland and surrounding areas, the *Viergöttersteine* demonstrate all the features which are to be found on the Bath blocks.

Each side of a *Viergötterstein* depicts a standing deity, almost invariably classical, holding attributes; the deity either stands against a plain backdrop

[23] See Chapter 2, note 43 for a summary of iconographic evidence for Bacchus in sculpture from Britain. *CSIR* 1.7, 1 is the only other undoubted representation in stone from the province.

[24] The resemblance has been noted before by McGowen (2010: 86–7), although she did not pursue the implications very far.

Figure 6.7: Two sides of a *Viergötterstein* from Mainz, depicting (a) Juno and (b) Minerva. (© GDKE, Landesmuseum Mainz, Ursula Rudischer.)

or in a niche (Fig. 6.7). Given the extreme rarity of this form of representation in Britain, and its ubiquity in the Rhineland, it seems very likely that the Bath stones were carved by mason(s) who were well-acquainted with this form, and thus either from the Rhineland themselves or trained by men who were: in this monument we are once again seeing iconographic links and thus artistic or commercial networks tying Bath to the continent. This conclusion is strengthened when we examine the few pieces from Britain which can be seen as parallels to the Bath blocks. Most of them in fact constitute our evidence for the few Jupiter columns known from Britain;[25]

[25] e.g. *RIB* 89 from Chichester (Sussex), *CSIR* I.7, 5 from Great Chesterford (Essex), and *CSIR* I.7, 46 from Irchester (Northamptonshire). A block from Housesteads fort (*CSIR* I.6, 23) is carved on four sides with images of Mars, a Genius, Victory, and Vulcan, and is stylistically very similar to *Viergöttersteine*, but, at .515 m × .235 m × .255 m, is probably too small to be the base of a Jupiter column (Coulston and Phillips 1988: 10).

Jupiter columns outside the Rhineland can usually be shown to be monuments set up by visitors or immigrants from that area, rather than indigenous.[26] A further British parallel similar in iconography, if not in form, is the monumental London Arch; this too has demonstrable links with the iconography of Jupiter columns, which as Blagg put it, 'show a common source for the repertoire, and a connection in subject matter and thus possibly in purpose'.[27]

The clear parallels between the Bath blocks and the Rhineland *Viergöttersteine* raise a serious question about the established date of the Bath blocks. While the Great Jupiter column at Mainz, widely regarded as the prototype for later Jupiter columns, dates to the reign of Nero, the vast majority of the other columns date to the late second and third centuries; this is their period as a 'type', rather than isolated phenomena.[28] As I have discussed above, it has always been argued that these blocks form part of the precinct layout for Period 1, i.e. the late first century. We are therefore left with two possibilities: (1) the Mainz column itself was the prototype which inspired the design of the Bath monument, or (2) we must reconsider our dating of these blocks, and consequently their place with the visual space of the precinct.

The first possibility can be safely ruled out. Although the Mainz column must have been the model for the later type of Jupiter column in the Rhineland,[29] its style, particularly with respect to the ornamentation around the deities' niches, rules it out as the direct inspiration for the Bath monument (Fig. 6.8). If the masons who carved these blocks had the Mainz column in particular, rather than the general category, in mind, we would surely see, e.g. echoes of the decorative bands which edge the niches; we know from the architectural ornament on the pediment that such elaborate decoration would have been well within the capabilities of masons working in Bath in the first century. We would also most likely be dealing with a direct copy of the column, rather than a monument which both adopted and adapted its visual language. As with the London Arch, it is the general type which the Bath monument resembles, rather than any particular column; this strongly suggests that the blocks date to the period when that type was so well-established that its signature elements would be both used and modified by those familiar with it from their design of monuments elsewhere. We must therefore conclude that these blocks could not have been part of the initial

---

[26] Woolf 2001: 118.   [27] Blagg in Hill, Millett, and Blagg 1980: 178–9.
[28] Bauchhenß 1981: 26ff; Noelke 1981: 309ff.   [29] Woolf 2001: 119.

Figure 6.8: One side of the *Viergötterstein* of the Great Jupiter column at Mainz.
(© GDKE, Landesmuseum Mainz, Ursula Rudischer.)

iconographic scheme of the sanctuary, but rather date to the late second century at the earliest. This means that if the blocks do indeed belong with the 'altar' base, either the base cannot be dated to Period 1, or we must assume that the blocks were a replacement for an earlier, original structure.

We must also question the assumption that the blocks formed part of the temple's sacrificial altar. This is an assumption which may need to be reconsidered whether or not one accepts they were placed on this base. The assumption that the base in question formed the base for an altar has never been questioned in print.[30] Although the base's position directly in front of the temple supports the altar theory, other aspects of its positioning call it into question, especially in light of the necessities of sacrificial performance. The base is considerably closer to the precinct entrance than it is to the temple. Many, if not all, of the sacrifices performed at the temple would presumably have been large events, attended by a crowd of worshipers and pilgrims. If the base is for the altar, then the majority of this crowd would have needed to be standing between the officiating priest and the temple. In order to watch the sacrifice – a highly performative act – they would have needed to have their backs to the temple (and thus to the goddess); moreover, they would form a large barrier between the priest and the goddess. This is perhaps not an impossibility, but given our understandings about the theatrical nature of sacrifice, and also the hierarchical aspects of its performance, spatially an arrangement of temple → altar/priest → audience makes more sense. Second, in a later precinct phase we know that at least one statue was erected immediately behind the base.[31] This would have served to cut off even more efficiently the sightlines between the monument on the base and the temple, rendering even more questionable the idea that rituals were performed there which intimately connected monument and temple. On the other hand, if the base were for a different type of monument, there is ample room in the rest of the precinct in which we might place the main altar, including both immediately in front of the temple steps and on the podium itself, both positions which would better fit the ritual requirements of sacrifice.

If the blocks do not belong to an altar, what else might they be? They certainly do not belong to a Jupiter column of traditional form; although their design echoes the *Viergöttersteine*, they are not in fact *Viergöttersteine*. Nonetheless, clamp holes on the tops of the blocks do make clear that something was attached to the top of them. This is usually assumed to be a simple stone capping forming the altar's surface; a piece of stone found nearby has been interpreted as part of this capping.[32] If, however, we want to entertain the possibility that these blocks were part of a larger monument, possibly one which either resembled or borrowed further from the lexicon of the Jupiter columns, is there material from the site which could be part of such a monument? In fact, there are indeed pieces of sculptured stone

---

[30] Blagg considered the possibility that the base may have been instead for the niched quadrangular monument, but ultimately abandoned this theory before publishing it. (Blagg 1990: 430, n. 48; B. Cunliffe, pers. comm.)

[31] Cunliffe and Davenport 1985: 37.   [32] Cunliffe and Davenport 1985: 36.

which could have been part of a larger monument incorporating the blocks, although either proof or more precise reconstruction is impossible.

One example is the as yet unplaced monument known as the niched quadrangular monument (*CSIR* 1.2, 84–85). Two pieces from this monument were found in 1895 in the temple precinct; wear on them, however, indicates that they were probably reused as paving stones, so we cannot know for sure that the monument was originally in the precinct. The two pieces belong to the top part of 'a quandrangular monument with semicircular niches in each side'; little of the niches remains on either piece, but on one a spear head and part of the helmet of a standing figure can be seen.[33] It therefore seems probable that each niche contained the figure of a deity. The overall width of the monument when complete (1.83 m) would have been slightly too large to fit on top of the four corner blocks if they had simply been joined together, but might easily have fitted on them if there were any further blocks between them. Another piece of stonework, *CSIR* I.2, 27, shows a hand holding either a trident or a thunderbolt (Fig. 6.9); this piece was found underneath the altar corner found in 1965.[34] Finally, a

Figure 6.9: Hand holding thunderbolt. (Photo by author.)

[33] Cunliffe and Fulford 1982: 20.   [34] Cunliffe and Fulford 1982: 9.

fragment of a relief found in contexts of re-use during the 1981–3 excavations shows a hound and part of a bow, and is most likely from a relief of Diana (Fig. 6.10). Diana is frequently seen with a hound on material from the Rhineland. Whether any or all of these pieces were indeed part of a larger monument which incorporated the corner blocks, or what form that monument may have taken, it is now impossible to say. Nevertheless, these stones and their iconography are yet another reminder that even our most fixed theories about Aquae Sulis and the sanctuary's layout are open to reconsideration.

Like the temple pediment and the head of Sulis Minerva, the corner blocks reveal links between Aquae Sulis and the artistic traditions of the continent. They do not, however, reveal the same links. Although the precise meaning of Jupiter columns is still debated,[35] despite their use of traditional classical iconography they do seem to be rooted in mythological and cosmological traditions peculiar to the Rhineland.[36] Thus, to put it crudely, the pediment of the temple draws from the empire's 'centre', while the corner blocks come from another part of the 'periphery'. If I am correct to re-date the blocks from the first century to the second/third, they may reflect Aquae Sulis's – and indeed Britain's – greater and more natural

Figure 6.10: Fragmentary relief showing Diana's hound and bow. (Photo by author.)

[35] Woolf 2001.   [36] Nöelke 1981: 391ff.

integration into empire at this later date. To employ another dichotomy, the pediment is more 'political', using a religious space to communicate a message of imperial power in the early days of the province, while the blocks, dating to a time when Roman appropriation of the hot springs may have been less charged, should rather be seen as 'religious', part of the rich fabric of provincial religious acculturation in the middle and late empire.

As for any theological or mythological meaning behind the choice of deities, without the fourth corner – or indeed without knowing what the superstructure may have been – there is little that can be said. Given the proximity of the spring, however, it is worth noting that several of the figures are interacting with liquid in some way: we have not the generic Hercules, but specifically Hercules Bibax; we have Bacchus pouring liquid directly into the mouth of a rather thirsty panther; and we have the female figure pouring a libation from a pot onto the ground. Finally, as I have said, the unidentified male figure may be Neptune.[37] This water/liquid motif might be one of the ways in which the *Viergötterstein* model was being adapted for the setting at Aquae Sulis.[38]

A final object demonstrates considerably more local iconographic connections (Fig. 6.11). This relief deserves some attention, in part because of the place images like it have taken in several recent reinterpretations of Romano-British iconographic material. The central focus of the relief is two standing figures, one male and one female;[39] although worn, various characteristics and attributes are distinguishable. The female, on the left, seems to be wearing some sort of headgear, and holds a sceptre of some sort in her left arm. The details of her clothing on the upper half of her body are not apparent, but her full skirts are shown, with strong patterned lines depicting the folds. At her right side is what appears to be a barrel. She holds in her right hand an object which is rather ambiguous; possibly it is a small dish. The male figure on the right has either wings or horns sprouting from his head; a cap might possibly be visible, so perhaps wings are the most

---

[37] McGowen 2010: 26.

[38] Hercules, for example, is very common on *Viergöttersteine* from the Rhineland, but as far as I have been able to find there are no instances of him as Hercules Bibax: apart from his club and lion skin his most common attributes on the German material are the Apples of the Hesperides.

[39] Contra Toynbee 1964: 158, Ross 1967: 207, and Cunliffe and Fulford 1982: 11, it seems clear to me that the goddess is standing, not seated; no trace of a seat can be discerned on the relief, and she is of the same height and limb proportions as the standing male figure. (This interpretation seems to have arisen from a misunderstanding of the barrel at her side as a seat. Both internal (the placement of her hand; the height of her body) and external (comparison with similar barrel reliefs) factors show it is not a seat; the slight offset of the goddess's lower half is there for compositional reasons, to make room for the barrel by her side.)

Figure 6.11: Relief of Mercury and unknown goddess. (Photo by author.)

likely possibility. On his left arm he holds a *caduceus*, which mirrors the line of his companion's sceptre. I am unconvinced by claims that he holds a purse in his right hand;[40] as Ross points out, this is an illusion created by the combination of his upper leg and the corner of his cloak.[41] He would appear to be nude apart from a cloak flung back from his shoulders and seemingly pinned underneath his neck. Underneath this pair is another register containing further figures, carved at a smaller scale. On the left is a quadruped, moving left; on the right are three small hooded figures of the type usually referred to as *genii cucullati*. Very little beyond the general outline of their cloaks and hoods is discernible; they appear to be standing rather than moving, leaning slightly to the right.

[40] Toynbee 1964: 158; Cunliffe and Fulford 1982: 11.   [41] Ross 1967: 207.

What deities does this relief depict? I agree with scholars who have accepted that the male figure is Mercury with a caduceus and wings, rather than a 'Celtic' horned god.[42] The question of the female figure's identity is entangled with the place this relief and others like it have taken in recent scholarship; it is thus necessary to examine this scholarship before discussing her identity.

The first thing to note is that reliefs depicting Mercury and a female goddess with similar iconography to the Bath relief have been found elsewhere in the region, with a notable cluster at Gloucester (*CSIR* I.7, 78–80). In one of the Gloucester reliefs a tub or bucket similar to the one on the Bath relief is visible (*CSIR* I.7, 78; Fig. 6.12); images of a goddess with

Figure 6.12: Relief of Mercury and a goddess from Gloucester. (© Gloucester Museums Service.)

---

[42] Toynbee 1964: 158; Goldberg 2005: 89. Ross 1967: 207, 271 suggested that the couple should be seen as Mars Leucetius and Nemetona, but this is based only on Peregrinus's dedication at Bath to these deities (*RIB* 140), and since Peregrinus was from Trier, and this relief is demonstrably part of a British iconographic phenomenon, there is no reason to associate the relief with the inscription. Certainly they were not found in the same location.

similar vessel, but with no male figure, have been found elsewhere in Britain, e.g. at Corbridge (*CSIR* I.1, 115).[43] It seems, then, that this relief should be understood as part of a regional 'cult' or worship (whether organized or not) of a goddess (or potentially a god and goddess pairing), whose name – if she possessed a single name – is as yet unknown. The regional character of the iconography marks out this small relief from much of the large-scale sculpture which defined the precinct's visual environment; there, as we have seen, the networks indicated by the iconography have a much broader geographic remit.

While both Toynbee and the *CSIR* for Bath refrained from identifying her,[44] the female goddess accompanying Mercury on these reliefs has often been referred to by others as Rosmerta (with or without scare quotes). Rosmerta is found paired with Mercury with relative frequency on votive inscriptions from north-east Gaul and the Rhineland;[45] she is, however, unknown on inscriptions in Britain. Nonetheless, this lack of British epigraphic evidence has not prevented many scholars from casually referring to Mercury's consort on British material with the Gallic goddess's name. This tendency seems to have begun with Green, who groups the Gloucestershire reliefs with the continental material in her discussion of the 'divine marriage' between Mercury and Rosmerta, but without offering any justification for doing so (or indeed mentioning that Rosmerta is only epigraphically attested in Gaul);[46] Webster followed Green's example in her own discussions of the 'divine marriage', writing that '[i]n Britain the couple are not documented epigraphically but do occur iconographically'.[47] Henig, in the *CSIR* volume for the Gloucestershire reliefs, chose to put the name in scare quotes, saying simply that 'In Classical mythology Mercury is associated with his mother Maia, but it is more likely that his consort here is a deity of the same type as the Gallic Rosmerta attested in Eastern Gaul, where she is representative of plenty.'[48] This language seems to imply

---

[43] See Goldberg 2005: 88 for further examples.

[44] Toynbee 1964: 158; Cunliffe and Fulford 1982: 11. On the other hand, the Roman Baths Museum currently suggests she is Rosmerta.

[45] Bémont 1960: 29; Bémont 1969: 23; see Keune 1914 for a catalogue of inscriptions known at the time.

[46] Green 1989: 54–61. Haverfield did write in 1906 that '[P]recise identification is impossible. The pair of deities often found together in Germany, Mercury and Rosmerta, has occurred to me, but the attributes are not decisive'; since, however, Toynbee does not pick up on Haverfield's suggestion and Green does not cite him, we can probably consider his remark unrelated to the later trend (Haverfield 1906: 259).

[47] Webster 1997a: 172ff; Webster 1997b: 326–7. As we shall see shortly, identifying Rosmerta based on her attributes is fraught with difficulties.

[48] Henig 1993: 27.

that Henig does not mean the British goddess to be the same as the Gallic one; his use of the name in his description of all the subsequent stones, however, carries with it a certain force.

On the surface, the Rosmerta identification, both at Bath and elsewhere, is not ipso facto problematic. We do have evidence for other mainly continental gods being worshiped at Bath, for example Mars Leucetius and Nemetona, known principally from the region of the Treveri, and indeed worshiped at Bath by a Treveran citizen, Peregrinus (*RIB* 140). However, when we turn to the continental material, we find that Rosmerta herself lacks any attributes which can distinguish her, in the absence of corroborative epigraphy, from any of the other goddesses with whom Mercury was paired, in particular Maia and Fortuna.[49] On reliefs which unquestionably depict her, Rosmerta sometimes carries Mercury's own attributes of the purse and *caduceus*, and somewhat more frequently holds a *patera* and a *cornucopia*;[50] both attributes are seen with a wide range of other goddesses, including non-classical ones, for instance a goddess frequently seen with the 'hammer-god' Sucellus.[51] The conclusion we must reach was put best by Bémont:

La banalité de ces attributs, celle des modes de figuration nous prouvent simplement que nous devons manifester la plus extrême prudence en ce qui concerne l'attribution de reliefs à Maia-Rosmerta. Toutes les déesses associées en Gaule à Mercure tendant, vraisemblablement, à reproduire sous une forme féminine les puissances de prospérité dont dispose le dieu, pourront très aisément porter les symboles soit de cette association, soit, plus encore, de cette abondance. **Cela explique que nous nous interdisions, provisoirement au moins, de comprendre dans notre catalogue les monuments dont les lieux de découverte sont situés hors de l'aire actuellement déterminé par les inscriptions de Maia et Rosmerta.**[52] (Emphasis mine.)

Translation: The banality of these attributes and of the modes of depiction simply prove to us that we need to exhibit extreme caution in attributing these reliefs to Maia-Rosmerta. With all the goddesses associated with Mercury likely tending to reproduce in female form the powers of prosperity that the god holds, they could all very easily bear the symbols either of this association, or, even more likely, of this abundance. **This therefore explains why we have forbidden ourselves, at least provisionally, from including in this catalogue those**

---

[49] Bémont 1960: 36.   [50] Bémont 1969: 31.   [51] Green 1989: 49–51, figs. 19–20.
[52] Bémont 1960: 38.

monuments whose findspots are outside the area currently defined by inscriptions naming Maia and Rosmerta. (Emphasis mine.)

In other words, *contra* Webster, without further epigraphic discoveries there can be no iconographic justification for identifying a goddess as Rosmerta on any British material. Furthermore, the British reliefs do not even show the goddess with some of the more common attributes of Rosmerta; for instance, while the *patera* appears, the *cornucopia* does not.

Removing the name of Rosmerta from these British reliefs is important, because it deconstructs another instance of a methodology which should now be accepted as irredeemably flawed: the unconsidered and acontextual use of material from throughout the 'Celtic' west to create a 'pan-Celtic' narrative which in fact bears little to no relation to ancient reality. In the case of the Bath relief, by erroneously connecting this relief to the continent, this methodology muddies the continental links which we do see in other material from Bath, and obscures the potentially more important local and regional links of this particular image of god and goddess. In fact, a contrast, rather than a parallel, should be drawn with Peregrinus's inscription to Mars Leucetius and Nemetona. These deities are mainly found epigraphically in the territory of the Treveri, and Peregrinus's self-identification as a *civis Trever* further reinforces their foreign nature and emphasizes Peregrinus's choice to venerate the cult of his homeland in a Romano-British space. Peregrinus's dedication, then, demonstrates exactly the sort of epigraphic proof that is needed in order to place continental deities and religious traditions in Britain, proof which is lacking in this relief.

Another recent theory about the relief deserves some consideration. Goldberg has argued that the tubs/barrels on this relief and others like it in fact represent butter churns, and that the iconography of this goddess or goddess-type is linked in with the importance of pastoralism and sheep husbandry in Roman Britain.[53] He also suggests that *genii cucullati* like those on the Bath relief, in particular their heavy cloaks, may well be linked to wool production.[54] Goldberg's theory is appealing because it nuances familiar yet facile arguments about the fertility roles of native goddesses in particular, and also the *genii cucullati*; as he points out, a generalized fertility role has been the dominant interpretation for these figures until now.[55] Indeed, fertility interpretations for goddesses are so clichéd, and so lacking

[53] Goldberg 2006: 88.　[54] Goldberg 2006: 91.　[55] Goldberg 2006: 84–6.

in rigorous contextual proof, that up until now I have not seen fit to engage with them at all. The divine powers or spheres of influence which could fall under the heading of 'fertility' are so myriad that the term is rendered practically meaningless.[56]

Accepting Goldberg's theory, however, hinges on his interpretation of the tub as a butter churn. The object in question certainly bears a strong resemblance to traditional upright churns.[57] Whether that resemblance is merely coincidental is another question. While sheep herding and pastoralism generally were certainly a major part of the agricultural production of Roman Britain, the evidence for butter production is much less certain. H. Cool points out that our recipe evidence from the Mediterranean suggests that cheese was used when we would now expect to use butter, but there is no evidence to say whether this was the same in the northern provinces.[58] Since churns are usually of organic material, if butter was being produced it would often leave no archaeological trace, so our lack of material evidence cannot necessarily be seen as significant.[59] Even if sheep and goat milk was being turned into butter, however, it is unlikely that cow's milk was regularly so used; bone assemblages from the Roman period indicate that cattle were more likely being exploited predominantly for meat than for milk.[60] On the other hand, deposits of 'bog butter' have been found in Ireland which have been carbon-dated to the early centuries AD;[61] this at least supports the possibility that there was knowledge of butter-production methods in Roman Britain as well. The possible ritual explanations for Irish and Scottish bog butter deposits perhaps gives a small amount of support to the idea that butter production may have had a ritual component in Britain;[62] I am, however, extremely reluctant to use evidence from the unconquered areas of Ireland and Scotland to interpret ritual finds from Roman Britain, even if that evidence is contemporaneous.

On the whole, Goldberg's interpretation remains an intriguing possibility, but cannot be unconditionally accepted. Some aspects of his methodology, however, are worthy of emulation, in particular his emphasis on the regional

---

[56] Weather, flocks, and childbirth are just a few of the very disparate arenas which could have a 'fertility' connotation.

[57] See Davidson 1999: 93 for images of such churns. Whether these churns – in use until the nineteenth century – were already to be found in the Roman period is an unanswerable question. On the other hand, the continuity of many other forms of basic domestic tools – from agricultural implements to spindle whorls – suggests that this is not beyond the bounds of possibility.

[58] Cool 2006: 94.   [59] Cool 2006: 94.   [60] Cool 2006: 93–4.

[61] Cronina *et al.* 2007: 1015.   [62] Downey *et al.* 2006: 33–4.

character of this iconography, and his willingness to push beyond the generalized categories of both 'fertility' and 'Celtic' imagery (he too rejects the Rosmerta identification).[63]

The presence of craftspeople at Bath who were exposed to visual traditions from elsewhere in Britain and the north-west provinces can not only be deduced through these iconographic connections, and through technical stylistic considerations, but also directly through the site's epigraphy. *RIB* 151, a statue base, 0.46 × 0.58 × 0.30 m with a rectangular socket on the capital, reads:

Suleuis | Sulinus | scultor | Bruceti f(ilius) | sacrum f(ecit) l(ibens) m(erito).
   To the Suleviae Sulinus, a sculptor, son of Brucetus, gladly and deservedly made this offering.

The letters are for the most part strong, well-formed and even, with the exception of the L M of the last line, which had to be unevenly squeezed in. The letters of SVLEVIS and SVLINVS which comprise the first and second lines are almost twice as large as those of the other three, and the initial 'SVL' and final 'S' of each word are placed directly above/under each other, creating a strong visual connection, indeed almost a patterning, between the two words. Sulinus, being a sculptor, or as Haverfield put it 'rather a superior mason than what we would call a sculptor'[64], may well have carved the altar himself, or at least given very specific instructions for it; in any case, whoever did the carving seems to have been seeking through the use of this mirroring to create not only a linguistic but also a visual link between Sulinus and the deities to whom the statue was dedicated.

The connections between his name, the Suleviae, and Sulis Minerva are uncertain. Certainly there does not seem to be a direct etymological link between the Suleviae and Sulis; the Suleviae appear in number in Upper and Lower Germany, often as a version of the Matres, and consequently seem to be an imported cult to Britain, where only four inscriptions to them are found, two of which are from our Sulinus.[65] The structure in particular of the Bath altar seems to suggest that Sulinus perceived a link between himself and the Suleviae; it may well be that he perceived a similar link, even though there technically was none, between the Suleviae and Sulis at Bath. What effect that may have had on his understanding of these goddesses, or on his decision to place a statue near Sulis's sanctuary, cannot be known.

[63] Goldberg 2006: 87.   [64] Haverfield 1920: 182.   [65] Birley 1986: 53.

But the crucial point is that Bath is not the only place where we encounter Sulinus the son of Brucetus setting up a dedication to the Suleviae. A second altar dedicated by him, *RIB* 105, was found at Cirencester in 1899, together with two reliefs of the Matres and various other pieces of worked stone, including some other fragmentary sculptures and architectural stonework.[66] The Cirencester altar shares the mirroring of the initial 'SVL's, although the overall effect is not as strong as in *RIB* 151. The original excavator, W. J. Cripps, believed the finds to be unsold products of Sulinus's workshop, on the grounds that the objects were all too unweathered to have ever been in use;[67] Haverfield rather more convincingly argued that they formed the contents of a shrine to the Suleviae (whose walls would presumably have been destroyed by later disturbances mentioned by Cripps).[68]

The progression of events in Sulinus's life which led him to both Bath and Cirencester are of course unreconstructable. Cripps painted a pretty picture of 'an honest mason of Cirencester, who resorting to Bath for its healing waters, and receiving the wished-for relief, dedicated an altar there to the tutelary deities he was in the habit of worshipping at home';[69] however, given what we know about the high levels of mobility of masons in Roman Britain, Sulinus might well have been originally from neither place.[70] Another inscription found in the Great Bath, *RIB* 149, records a similar itinerant craftsman:

Priscus | Touti f(ilius) | lapidariu[s] | ciues Car[nu]|tenus Su[li] | deae u(otum) [s(oluit) l(ibens) m(erito)]

Priscus, son of Toutius, stonemason, a tribesman of the Carnutes, to the goddess Sulis willingly and deservedly fulfilled his vow.

Priscus's dedication, like virtually all the inscriptions from Bath, is un-dateable. The territory of the Carnutes, however, was centred on Chartres in northern Gaul. The original masons who worked on the temple of Sulis Minerva came from northern Gaul, as noted, though rather more to the east than Chartres;[71] it is slightly tempting to place Priscus, if not in this first wave of Gaulish masons, then at least in a tradition of continental stone-workers coming to Bath at some point in their careers.

Who was funding the monuments built by these craftspeople remains for the most part an open question. I have argued in Chapter 4 that the initial

[66] Cripps 1900: 183–4; the names Sulinus and Brucetus are sufficiently rare that it is acceptable to assume we are dealing with the same person (Haverfield 1920: 182).
[67] Cripps 1900: 183.   [68] Haverfield 1920: 182.   [69] Cripps 1900: 179.   [70] Blagg 2002: 186.
[71] Blagg 1979.

support for the sanctuary's construction most likely came from the highest levels of provincial government. Later on, however, especially as the region around Aquae Sulis became a locus for rural wealth, we can presumably assume the involvement of more local figures. The only clear evidence for later euergetism, however, comes from the dedicatory inscription associated with the Façade of the Four Seasons.

The inscription, as fragmentary as the façade's decoration, consists of two portions. The first (*RIB* 141 (d) and (e)) was placed in at least two of the gaps between the pilasters of the monument (the relevant portions of the other gaps have not survived). The only legible portion reads:

G(aius) Protaciu[s ... | deae Sulis M[ineruae

The second portion (*RIB* 141 (a), (b), and (c)) is assumed to be part of the same monument in large part because it is stylistically almost identical with the Protacius portion;[72] in reconstructions it has been placed in a frieze above the main pilastered section (Fig. 3.7). In three separate fragments, of which two conjoin, it reads

(a) ... C]laud[i]us Ligur [... | ...]ae nimia uetust[ate ...

Claudius Ligur ... excessive age ...

(b) (c) ... c]olegio longa seria [annorum ... | ... sua pec]unia refici et repingi cur[auit ...

... the guild in long sequence of years ... at his own cost had it repaired and repainted ...

The inscription as a whole clearly refers to the refurbishment of a building. A guild and at least two individuals are in some way involved. Beyond this, the specifics of the situation are a little harder to reconstruct. Commentators have often assumed that the building in question was the temple of Sulis Minerva.[73] There seems no reason for this, however. It is much more likely that the inscription refers instead to the refurbishment of the building attached to the Façade, whatever that may have been, especially since a new façade would be a natural choice for such a project.

Thomas and Witschel have shown that the sort of language seen in this inscription is very often rhetorical.[74] *Vetustas* is often used even when the periods involved were actually quite short,[75] while 'in certain cases, the term

---

[72] Haverfield 1906: 267; Cunliffe 1969: 31.

[73] Haverfield 1906: 239; Cunliffe 1969: 31; Cunliffe and Davenport 1985: 126.

[74] Thomas and Witschel 1992, although see Fagan 1996 for a rebuttal.

[75] Thomas and Witschel 1992: 146.

reficere projects a general idea of reconstruction onto what would have been more accurately described as modification'.[76] In other words, we cannot take for granted that Claudius Ligur and Protacius financed an entire new building, although it seems reasonable to accept that the Façade at least is a result of their euergetism. What the inscription does show is that 'local' people with money – whether actually from Aquae Sulis, or from further afield – did invest in the development of the sanctuary.

Networks of Ritual Knowledge

I discussed in Chapter 5 the links – and distinctions – between ritual practice at Aquae Sulis and other watery sites. Here I want to elaborate on the ways in which the evidence from Aquae Sulis reflects other ritual practices which may be found in a general way empire-wide, but which are nonetheless locally constructed at the site in ways which are bound up with regional understandings, manipulations, and variations that are informed by their provincial setting. The first of these (*RIB* 3049) is the well-known epigraphic attestation of a *haruspex* at Bath. It reads, in well-cut letters with frequent ligatures:

> *Deae Suli | L(ucius) Marcius Memor | Harusp(ex) | d(ono) d(edit)*
>
> To the goddess Sulis, Lucius Marcius Memor, haruspex, gave (this) as a gift.

This inscription has often been cited casually as evidence that Roman officiants such as *haruspices* existed in Britain, and thus that ritual in the province was 'Romanized'.[77] In fact, it would appear to support precisely the opposite conclusion, i.e. that *haruspices* were virtually unknown in Britain. The word *haruspex* in the third line was originally abbreviated as HAR; the VSP was added later, as shown by its asymmetrical positioning.[78] Furthermore, the addition was possibly carved by a different hand, since the ligature between the V and the S is different from that used in line 2.[79] This would seem to imply that the original abbreviation was not intelligible enough to the intended audience, which would indicate that the position was not one with which the usual visitors to the precinct would have been familiar.[80] It may well be possible, then, that L. Marcius Memor was a visitor

---

[76] Thomas and Witschel 1992: 152.

[77] e.g. Henig 1984: 34, 135 (where the single *haruspex* recorded epigraphically is morphed into an entire group attached to the temple), 153; Hassall 1980: 82, where Marcius Memor is pictured using a bronze liver like the one found at Piacenza, an object in reality half a continent and at least four centuries distant from Bath.

[78] Cunliffe 1969: 189.   [79] Tomlin, Wright, and Hassall 2009: 64.

[80] Haack 2006: 82; Tomlin, Wright, and Hassall 2009: 64.

to Britain from an area more accustomed to rituals involving *haruspices*, rather than being a permanent member of Bath's religious community.[81] Thus we may have here evidence that the rituals performed in honour of Sulis Minerva differed from 'standard' Roman practice, rather than adhering to it.[82]

Memor's dedication is not only noteworthy from the perspective of practice at Bath; it is also at odds with much of our evidence for *haruspices* generally. We have epigraphic evidence for over one hundred *haruspices* from around the empire. The majority of these inscriptions are tombstones, but votives comprise a significant proportion of the total.[83] While several *haruspices* set up votives to members of the traditional Roman pantheon,[84] and engagement by *haruspices* with the cults of Mithras and other eastern deities such as Jupiter Dolichenus or the Magna Mater is not unknown,[85] Marcius Memor's dedication is the only one we possess which is dedicated to a deity who is both non-eastern and not native to the Italian peninsula. It is also the only dedication we possess to a deity with a localized cult. Memor's dedication is not even to the syncretic version of the Bath goddess, but to Sulis alone. Regardless of whether Memor was attached to the temple or not, this fact is noteworthy. If Memor was a priest of Sulis, this local cult is possibly unique in the north-west provinces in having the permanent service of a *haruspex*. If he was not, then the cult of Sulis must be considered of remarkable importance or uniqueness, since Memor deemed it significant enough both to visit the site and to dedicate a statue to the goddess while he was there, even though similar behaviour by *haruspices* is seen nowhere else in the empire. The importance of the presence of a *haruspex* at Aquae Sulis, whether permanent or temporary, is underscored by their apparent rarity in the north-west provinces generally. Four *haruspices* are known

---

[81] A. R. Birley has suggested he may have been on the governor's staff (Birley 2011: 683). However, Haack has argued that gubernatorial *haruspices* were usually drawn from the ranks of the elite sixty-member *haruspex* college at Rome, and identified as such in their epigraphy; given the lack of any such designation on Memor's inscription, or indeed any further information about his social position, Birley's theory may be less likely (Haack 2003: 103–7).

[82] Cunliffe 1995: 37–8.

[83] See Haack 2006 for the complete catalogue and prosopography of known *haruspices*, including those known through literary sources.

[84] e.g. a dedication to Hercules from Ostia (Haack cat. no. 31), a dedication to Jupiter Optimus Maximus from Raetia (Haack cat. no. 47), or three votives by the same *haruspex* in Dacia, to Sol Invictus, Venus Victrix. and Nemesis Regina, respectively (Haack cat. no. 48).

[85] e.g. a tombstone from Rome for a *haruspex* identified also as a priest of Sol Invictus, Jupiter Dolichenus, and Liber (Haack cat. no. 47), a record of a *taurobolium* performed in the presence of a *haruspex* (Haack cat. no. 28), and dedications by *haruspices* to Mithras in Upper Germany (Haack cat. no. 69; Haack cat. no. 73).

epigraphically in Upper Germany, and one from each of the Three Gauls, with a further one in Gallia Narbonensis.[86]

Memor's dedication, therefore, while on the surface emblematic of the spread throughout the empire of ritual practices and priesthoods native to the Italian peninsula, takes on new meanings when it is in read in context, with the rarity of *haruspices* in Britain lending an air not so much of conformity but perhaps instead of exoticism to practice at the sanctuary.

Another example of a monument which needs to be read in a provincial context is the inscription of Gaius Severius Emeritus, the *centurio regionarius*. I have mentioned in Chapter 4 that Emeritus's use of the term *locus religiosus* in this inscription is at odds with perceived normal usage; here I wish to explore this issue a little further.[87]

The definition of the term as it appears in the Roman jurists is clear: it refers to privately owned land which has been consecrated for burial, and is distinct from public land which has been consecrated to the gods, which is in turn designated as *sacrum*.[88] This definition is also that reflected in other epigraphic attestations of the term, all of which (that I have found) come from Italy and record the dedication of a private cemetery, or the burial of an individual on private ground.[89] It seems clear both from the archaeological context of *RIB* 152 – within the monumentalized, walled zone of Aquae Sulis – and its text – the dedication of the space to the emperor's *numen* – that Emeritus is *not* using the phrase in accordance with its juristic, funerary meaning, but rather in a sense more closely synonymous with *sacrum*. A parallel for the usage which Emeritus seems to be employing can, however, be found in Pliny's correspondence with Trajan. In letters 70 and 71 of Book X, Pliny asks permission to build over the ruins of a house which had been bequeathed to the Emperor Claudius (and therefore to the city) by a private individual, who also ordered the dedication of a shrine (*aedes*) to the emperor in the peristyle. Trajan in response asks Pliny to clarify whether the shrine had in fact been dedicated, adding '*Nam si facta est, licet collapsa sit, religio eius occupat solum*' ('For if that was done, his *religio* inhabits the ground, even if (the shrine) is

---

[86] Upper Germany: Haack cat. no. 1 (Mainz); Haack cat. no. 39 (Bad Wimpfen in Tal); Haack cat. no. 69 (Stockstadt); Haack cat. no. 73 (Speyer). Gallia Belgica: Haack cat. no. 23 (Trier). Gallia Lugdunensis: Haack cat. no. 66 (Lugdunum). Aquitania: Haack cat. no. 29 (Poitiers). Gallia Narbonensis: Haack cat. no. 68 (Narbonne).

[87] I am grateful to Jill Harries and Kim Czajkowski for discussing the legal aspects of this inscription with me.

[88] Gaius, Institutes 2.2.5-7a; Digest 1.8.9 (Ulpian); 1.9.6, 8–9 (Marcian).

[89] e.g. *CIL* XIV, 2147; *CIL* X, 2015; *AE* 1914, 219.

collapsed').[90] This seems to align quite closely with Emeritus's case: we have a dedication to the deified emperor in one case, and to the *virtus* and *numen* of the living emperor in another, which both had the effect of bestowing *religio* on the ground in question. The provincial context in both instances is almost certainly key. In his discussion of *loci religiosi* in the *Institutes*, Gaius suggests that procedures are different in provincial settings: since ground in the provinces belongs either to the Roman people or to the Emperor, it can never properly become '*religiosus*' (since it is not private to begin with), but may simply be regarded as such.[91] This does not in fact align particularly well with what we see in *RIB* 152 or in Pliny, but does indicate that Gaius, from his perspective in the centre, had some awareness that matters were generally different in the provinces. Even so, if we adhere to Gaius's interpretation of the legal meaning of *religiosus*, *RIB* 152 is in fact 'incorrect' usage. Such a judgment, however, does insufficient credit to the validity of provincial culture in the empire. The crucial point is rather that *RIB* 152 and Trajan's letter both reflect the ways in which other legal discourses besides those of the jurists were enacted, and *RIB* 152 in particular demonstrates how provincial inhabitants were capable of ascribing their own meanings to technical language in ways which were independent of and unconcerned with academic debates at the centre. The regional nature of understandings of *religiosus* is reinforced by the fact that the Italian epigraphy *does* align with the juristic definitions.

A third example of an empire-wide practice modified by regional context, which I want to examine at some length, is the phenomenon of the 'curse' tablets. I have discussed in Chapter 5 the ways in which these objects are used at Aquae Sulis in the context of rituals harnessing loss or decay at the spring. This is their site-specific, highly localized function, but it is a function informed by the broader practices surrounding tablet language and deposition in Britain and the north-west provinces. By looking at the

---

[90] Pliny, *Letters* X.71.

[91] '*Sed in prouinciali solo placet plerisque solum religiosum non fieri, quia in eo solo dominium populi Romani est uel Caesaris, nos autem possessionem tantum et usumfructum habere uidemur; utique tamen, etiamsi non sit religiosum, pro religioso habetur: item quod in prouinciis non ex auctoritate populi Romani consecratum est, proprie sacrum non est, tamen pro sacro habetur.*' (But it has been held by most people that on provincial land the ground does not become *religiosus*, because in that land the ownership belongs to the Roman people or to the emperor, and we seem only to have ownership and usufruct of it; however, even if it is not *religiosus*, it is held as if it were *religiosus*; just as that land which is in the provinces is not consecrated by the authority of the Roman people, it is not held as properly *sacrum*, but it is held as if it were *sacrum*.) *Institutes* 2.2.7.

function of tablets in the ancient world more broadly, and then narrowing in on the north-west provinces, and then on Britain itself, we can see the way in which the tablets at Bath represent the final stage in a series of increasingly localized concentric circles of meaning and use.

The Bath tablets are the largest fully published corpus of 'curse' tablets from Britain. A similar number of texts have been found at the sanctuary at Uley,[92] but only a fraction of these texts have been published so far. In addition to these two large sets of sanctuary finds, around thirty other British tablets with legible texts have been published (Fig. 6.13). So far, all tablets have come from the southern half of the province, with Ratcliffe-on-Soar (Notts) currently the northernmost findspot. Individual finds are evenly distributed throughout the southern zone, although it should be noted that the two major corpora both come from temple sites in the west of the province. Only three tablets have been recovered from military sites (Caerleon, Leintwardine, and Chesterton). (Over a hundred pieces of rolled lead (or lead alloy) are known from the votive riverine deposit at Piercebridge (Durham). It is possible that some of these may be inscribed tablets, but to date only a few have been unrolled and only one had any markings, which were unintelligible as letters, although they may have been numerals.)[93]

The British tablets have often been represented in scholarship as substantially different from those of the continent (even while their interpretation has rested on continental paradigms).[94] The principal differences which have been noted are three-fold: material, linguistic, and thematic. Certainly the Bath tablets, as will be discussed shortly in this section, have markedly different aims and ways of addressing the deity to achieve those aims than do Greek *katadesmoi*. When we turn to corpora closer to Britain, however, i.e. to the Latin tablets found in Gaul and Germany, the differences diminish, weakening the claim that Britain is a (literal) island of anomalous practice.

The practice of inscribing a lead (or lead alloy) tablet with a request for divine manipulation of an interpersonal problem seems to have begun in the Greek-speaking world, with the earliest examples appearing in Attica and Sicily in the fifth and fourth centuries BC – seven hundred years or so before the Bath tablets.[95] Early formulae were simple, often listing only the name of the target, although any verbal part of the ceremony is of course unrecoverable.[96] By the Roman period, however, Greek texts on tablets had become extremely complex. As Gager puts it, '*voces mysticae* and other

---

[92] Tomlin 1993: 113.   [93] P. Walton, pers. comm.
[94] Tomlin 1988b: 60; Mattingly 2004: 19–20; Mattingly 2011: 228–30.
[95] Gager 1992: 5.   [96] Gager 1992: 5.

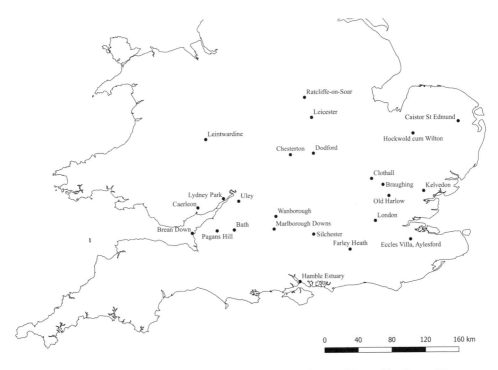

Figure 6.13: Map showing distribution of curse-tablet finds in the UK. (Created by George Watson from data collected by the author from reports of finds in site reports and in the annual reviews of archaeology in Roman Britain in *JRS* and *Britannia* through 2014. Coastline shapefile from Ancient World Mapping Center.)

forms of "unintelligible" writing can take up as much as 80 to 90 percent of the tablet ... the names and invocations of the gods and spirits are notably longer, more complex, and aggressively international ... drawings of human and animal figures, along with the probably astrological *charaktêres*, become omnipresent.' This passage describes texts roughly contemporaneous with, yet strikingly foreign to, the British corpus; these are the sorts of tablets which appear in the Fons Annae Perennae in Rome. The Bath tablets, however, have none of these characteristics. They address no list of arcane gods, only single deities (usually Sulis, once or twice Mars or Mercury). They contain no imagery or visual symbolism, astrological or otherwise. Finally, their texts, while sometimes inverted or tangled in their spelling, are nonetheless identifiable as understandable Latin, or, in a few cases Celtic;[97] the long passages of made-up words and incantations which dominate the Greek texts are utterly absent.

[97] Mullen 2007a and 2007b.

The Greek east is far removed from the Avon valley, however, and when we turn to comparanda in Gaul and Germany, as noted above, the differences are not so acute. There are still differences. Tablets in Gaul and Germany are more likely to be addressed to gods of the underworld, and found in graves, for instance.[98] By contrast, only one tablet so far in Britain has been found in a grave,[99] and none address the gods of the underworld.

However, the motivations, when known, for writing a tablet in Gaul and Germany are often similar to those in Britain. Kropp's corpus of Latin *defixiones* lists forty-eight tablets in total from Gaul, twelve of which make explicit the conflict which led to the curse.[100] Of those twelve, six are categorized by Kropp as 'prayers for justice', i.e. the category of judicial prayer first laid out by H. S. Versnel, and into which Tomlin placed the Bath tablets.[101] (These 'judicial prayers' are marked out from more general '*defixiones*' in several ways: They often contain supplication, or a vow, rather than coercion or ordering of the deities or daemons;[102] the intended victim is perceived as guilty of a crime, rather than simply a rival of the curser[103]; and the curser him- or herself, rather than being anonymous, is often named, again implying a sense of right- rather than wrong-doing.[104]) Four more Gallic tablets are concerned with success in law courts; of the remaining two, one is concerned with love and the other with a competition. Of Germany's fifty-three tablets (all found in Germania Superior), fifteen have clear motives; eleven are concerned with law cases (nine of these, however, were found together in one or possibly two funerary urns at Kreuznach[105]), three are judicial prayers, and the last concerns a competition. So while many of the Gallic or German tablets are either silent about the impetus behind the curse, or too fragmentary for us to reconstruct the text adequately, in the roughly one quarter for which we do have the motive, judicial prayer is quite common, and, while there is more variety of motive than in the British tablets, where judicial prayers are almost universal when motive is clear, there is still less variety than in tablets from the Greek east. In short, the Gallic and German examples

---

[98] e.g. Kropp 4.3.1/1 from Chagnon, to Pluto and Proserpina; Kropp 5.1.2/1, from Frankfurt to the Manes and Dii Inferi; Kropp 5.1.4/7–11, from Kreuznach and addressed variously to the Dii Inferi and the Manes.

[99] The rather unsettling *RIB* 221 from Clothall, Herts., pierced with five nails and reading *vetus | quomodo sanies | significatur | Tacita deficta* – 'Tacita, hereby accursed, is labelled old like putrid gore.'

[100] Kropp 2008.

[101] Versnel 1991; Tomlin 1988b: 59, n. 3, using an advance draft of Versnel's 1991 piece; Tomlin 2002: 67.

[102] Versnel 1991: 62.   [103] Versnel 1991: 62.   [104] Versnel 1991: 62.   [105] Audollent 1904: 148.

represent a midway point between the extremes of British and Eastern practices, rendering the still undeniable uniqueness of the British texts a little less jarring and exceptional.

So much for the wider continental context: how do the Bath tablets fit in the landscape of British tablets in particular?

Almost all British tablets meet Versnel's requirements for 'judicial prayers' rather than curses, and the vast majority of those whose subjects we can discern are specifically concerned with the theft of personal items and either the recovery of those items or the punishment of the thief. There are very few exceptions to this rule. *RIB* 221 (see footnote 99 above) is almost a textbook curse. A text from Old Harlow, found in a pit or well, is addressed to Mercury but seems to be concerned with success in an illicit love affair – a topic common for curses on the continent, but otherwise unknown in Britain.[106] Meanwhile, two texts from London also seem to be straightforward curses, with no petitions to deities or justification for the curse.[107] Apart from these texts, however, and a curse against perjury from Bath (*Tab. Sulis* 94), all British tablets whose subject matter can be discerned (apart from those which simply list names), are concerned with the theft of personal possessions. This concern manifests itself in two different ways (although both ways may appear in the same text):

(1) The desire for the return of the stolen property, usually to the temple of the god being petitioned;
(2) The punishment of the thief.

The punishment of the thief sometimes is to end if the stolen property is returned. This is not always the case, however, as for instance in a text found on the shore of Hamble Estuary:

Lord Neptune, I give you the man who has stolen the *solidus* and six *argentioli* of Muconius. So I give the names who took them away, whether male or female, whether boy or girl. So I give you, Niskus, and to Neptune the life, health, blood of him who has been privy to that taking-away. The mind which stole this and which has been privy to it, may you take it away. The thief who stole this, may you consume his blood and take it away, Lord Neptune.[108]

This text is part of a small group of tablets addressed to Neptune. Two more come from river contexts in Norfolk; the first, from Hockwold-cum-

---

[106] Wright and Hassall 1973: 325, no. 3.   [107] *RIB* 6 and 7.
[108] Tomlin 1997: 455, no. 1. N.B. I have deliberately chosen not to include the Latin of the tablets, relying instead solely upon translations. This is due to a) the specialist knowledge both to read the original and decipher the often obscure language and b) the frequently extremely fragmentary nature of the texts.

Wilton, gives the thief to the god,[109] while the second, from Caistor St. Edmund, lists several stolen items, then declares 'If you want the pair of leggings, they shall become yours at the price of his blood.'[110] Whether the other items also go to the god is unclear from the text. A fourth tablet, found on the north shore of the Thames near London Bridge, and asking for revenge on a list of names, may be included in this group; it is address to 'Metunus', which Tomlin argues is a corruption of Neptunus.[111] This small group are the only British tablets apart from the Bath corpus which are associated with watery contexts (with the potential exception of the possible corpus at Piercebridge). Unfortunately, because they are so few and so scattered geographically, little can be said about them. Given their deposition near or in water contexts, however, we may wonder whether tablets to Neptune were in fact more common than the number of finds would suggest, with the majority having been lost to the sea or river bed.

Giving the god an incentive to pursue the thief by offering part of the lost property, as seen in the Caistor St. Edmund tablet, is relatively common practice. Although the syntax of the Caistor St. Edmund text leaves it unclear whether all the stolen property or only the leggings is to be given to Neptune, several other tablets are explicit about the proportion to be given to the god – the finder's fee, as it were. In a tablet from Lydney Park (Glos.), for instance, Senicianus offers Nodens half the price of his gold ring.[112] A text from Pagans Hill, also in Gloucestershire, offers half of 3,000 lost *denarii* to an unnamed deity 'on condition that you exact it from Vassicillus … and from his wife'.[113] Other examples come from London[114] and Ratcliffe-on-Soar.[115] Finally, a text from Uley, notable for the legalistic nature of its language, gives a third of some stolen cloth to Mercury 'on condition that he exact this property which has been written above'.[116] These cases thus clearly demonstrate that the goal of some tablets, at least, was the physical recovery of the stolen property.

I have argued in Chapter 5, however, that the motive behind tablet deposition at Bath is not necessarily physical recovery, but rather a more hypothetical recovery of ownership of lost items via a formula of dedication. The presence of these 'finder's fee' tablets at other sites does not necessarily negate such a reading. 'Finder's fee' language still is centrally about the writer using the tablet and the agreement with the god to reclaim their ability to control their lost property and its disposition. Furthermore, although it is

---

[109] Hassall and Tomlin 1994: 293, no. 1.   [110] Hassall and Tomlin 1982: 408, no. 9.
[111] Hassall and Tomlin 1999: 360, no. 1.   [112] *RIB* 306.
[113] Hassall and Tomlin 1984: 336, no. 7.   [114] Hassall and Tomlin 2003: 362, no. 2.
[115] Hassall and Tomlin 2004: 336, no. 3.   [116] Uley 2 (Tomlin 1993: 131).

clear that British tablets overall follow roughly similar guidelines of language and intent, we nonetheless should not think that all tablets in all places obeyed the same rules: this is where the Bath tablets' regional context can be placed in dialogue with their site-specific context. The lack of 'finder's fee' language at Bath, despite many tablets which could have easily used such formulae, when combined with water deposition, seems in fact to indicate a different mode of thinking behind the ritual than that present at sites where the tablet was not deliberately relinquished into water.

Both the connections and the distinctions between tablet-deposition at Bath and at other sites in Britain are neatly symbolized by *Tab. Sulis* 10. This text, written in elegant rustic capitals, reads:

Docilianus (son) of Brucerus to the most holy goddess Sulis. I curse him who has stolen my hooded cloak, whether man or woman, whether slave or free, that ... the goddess Sulis inflect death upon ... and not allow him sleep or children now and in the future, until he has brought my hooded cloak to the temple of her divinity.

The contents of the tablet fit well with the more general corpus from Aquae Sulis. Yet the tablet also aligns in a surprising way with Uley, where a text (Uley 43) written by a 'Docilinus', in the same handwriting, has been found.[117] This tablet reads, 'To the god Mercury (from) Docilinus ... Varianus and Peregrina and Sabinianus who have brought evil harm on my beast and are ... I ask you that you drive them to the greatest death, and do not allow them health or sleep unless they redeem from you what they have administered to me.'

The almost perfect match in handwriting, as well as a similarity in phrasing (both use the unique phrase '*letum adigat*') makes it almost certain that we are dealing with the same person at both Bath and Uley.[118] We thus have a fortuitous glimpse of an individual engaging in the same ritual practice, but in relationship to two different deities at two different sanctuary sites. This would imply that Docili(a)nus had a 'tablet-writing habit' in the same way that others in the Roman world had an 'epigraphic habit'. If tablet-writing was regularly incorporated into the religious practice of Docili(a)nus and people like him, this reinforces the point that, despite their seemingly mundane concerns, we should not view British tablet writing and deposition as essentially opportunistic and occasional, a kneejerk reaction to petty theft at the bathhouses, but rather as a regular aspect of some Romano-Britons' engagement with the divine. Yet Docili(a)nus's experience of tablet-writing at each site would simultaneously have

[117] Hassall and Tomlin 1989: 329, no. 3.   [118] Hassall and Tomlin 1988: 433; Tomlin 1993: 114.

been a familiar, perhaps even comforting ritual act, but also shaped and distinguished by the different religious settings, most notably, of course, by the presence or absence of watery deposition.

Conclusion

This chapter has explored some of the ways in which Aquae Sulis can be understood as 'the same yet different' – a place where practice and environment are hardly in a vacuum, are naturally linked to trends elsewhere in its world, but where in order to understand the site-specific function of broader cultural symbols and behaviour, we need to examine the ways in which they would have been transformed or reshaped by increasingly localized contextual forces. These processes have implications for how we can understand the site as a whole, and use it to shed light on other rituals and religious places in the western empire. It is these implications – the way in which we can feed a highly localized understanding of Aquae Sulis back into our models of provincial religion – which I will examine in Chapter 7.

Conclusion: From Aquae Sulis to Bath

This book has examined the full range of epigraphic, iconographic, and archaeological evidence from Bath to produce a more holistic understanding of the site in the Roman period. In so doing, it has demonstrated the complexity of ritual activity and of the ritual environment at Aquae Sulis, which enabled the varying ways in which Sulis Minerva and her sanctuary were used to structure differing aspects of her worshipers' lives, from their position within broader Roman society to their more private concerns about loss and personal violation. I want to begin this concluding chapter by revisiting some of these complexities.

As we have seen, from the late first century onwards Aquae Sulis was a place of ever-increasing architectural grandeur and sophistication. At its height, the sanctuary was probably one of the most elaborate built environments in the province – certainly in terms of the density of its classically sophisticated buildings. But the principal interest lies in the processes through which that built environment was created. The architectural and iconographic worlds of the site need to be understood in relationship with their continental connections. The Roman-period sanctuary's genesis seems to lie in a cultural takeover of a sacred landscape by someone either sympathetic to, or actively involved in, the conquest of Britain by the Roman empire. To suggest that the sanctuary began through an act of domination, however, is not to argue that it continued that way. The architectural developments which can be dated to the second and third centuries show a much more organic integration of the site and its patrons into the wider networks of the empire, and especially the other north-west provinces. As the evidence for lower-level euergetism shows, in particular the Façade of the Four Seasons, the sanctuary at this point was certainly no mere 'pet project' of the politically or militarily powerful. Meanwhile, later structures such as the *tholos* continue to ground Aquae Sulis in the architectural traditions of the classical sanctuary, others, such as the construction of an ambulatory and flanking rooms at the temple, or of a monument possibly modelled on the Jupiter columns, may have served to bring it closer to more regional conceptions of the organization of sacred space.

Even so, self-conscious engagement at Bath with Roman imperialism did not begin and end with the Gorgon pediment. As we have seen in Chapter 4, members of the military community in particular used dedications to Sulis to articulate their ritual relationship with the emperor and their position within the structures of imperial power – both in their private personae, in the case of the freedmen M. Aufidius Lemnus and M. Aufidius Eutuches, and in their official one, in the case of the *centurio regionarius* G. Severius Emeritus.

Indeed, the way in which the imperial cult, or religious engagement with the emperor, becomes entangled with other forms of religious activity is, as I have discussed, an understudied phenomenon; as the Bath inscriptions show, such entanglement can give great insight into the role played by cults in the construction of social identity, particularly through the harnessing of the inherently public and performative nature of stone epigraphy. Stone altars are physical embodiments of spoken words or actions, and through their physicality they render the transient durable. They are set up in visible locations, and stay in those places long after their dedicators have moved on. In a sanctuary setting, where worshipers came and went and few were likely to stay for long, stone dedications are thus especially important in the construction of the sanctuary's sense of history and continuity. They are mementoes of what has come before, but as well they are active agents, especially if they are sacrificial altars which might remain in use, serving both as a reminder of the original ritual, but also as a locus for the recreation of that ritual in perpetuity. This 'conversion of an *occasional* sacrifice into a *permanent* relationship', as Mary Beard has put, has often been seen as the principal driving force behind religious inscriptions.[1] Severius Emeritus's altar, for example, stands as a record of his acts of purification, and in so doing, serves to perpetuate the sacralization of the *locus religiosus* in which it stood.

These concerns about permanence and perpetuation so present in the stone epigraphy seem absent, however, at the reservoir. The distinction can be elucidated by comparing the function of writing in the stone epigraphy versus in the 'curse tablets': on stone inscriptions, the written words are intended to be read and consequently work commemoratively. In the tablets, which were almost certainly rolled up and deposited shortly after being inscribed, the act itself of writing, rather than reading, is the focus – text is being used not to commemorate, but to accomplish, to enact. This is

---

[1] Beard 1991: 48.

in keeping with the general nature of the reservoir, which this book has argued is principally a place of ritualized transformation and relinquishment brought about by the natural qualities of the hot spring environment. The enclosure of the reservoir – a rare feature at spring sites in both Britain and Gaul – may be another indicator that performers of ritual at the water's edge were uninterested in public performance or inserting any particular ritual act into public memory.

The study of ancient religion generally is increasingly focusing on the importance of lived experience of the divine and of ritual practices.[2] Key to the narrative I have presented here is a people-centric approach, which seeks to foreground the ways in which worshipers experienced religious spaces, and how sanctuaries provided a space for social contestation and self-construction. In Chapter 3, I discussed the value of thinking of Aquae Sulis as a set-apart destination which consequently enabled the crystallization and confrontation of societal concerns. We have seen worshipers harnessing this aspect of the site at a variety of different levels, from intimate expressions of loss and transgression in the tablets to fundamental questions about one's place within the structure of empire. But an emphasis on people, and their concerns both as groups and individuals, has not been confined to my analysis of Aquae Sulis; it was also core to the opening chapters of this book, where understanding the concerns and motivations of men like Pownall, Warner, Irvine, and Mann is fundamental to understanding both why and how they wrote about Roman Bath.

Connected Localism: Religion in the Roman Provinces

Before concluding with the last days of Roman Aquae Sulis, I want to address briefly some wider issues concerning religious change in the north-west provinces, and in particular the problems of '*interpretatio romana*' and 'syncretism.' Understanding the changes in pantheons, mythologies, and ritual practices that occurred in Britain, Gaul, and Germany as a consequence of Roman rule in these areas, and the reasons for those changes, remains a significant challenge for scholars of religion in the north-west provinces. It is a topic that is naturally bound up in and influenced by broader debates about processes of 'Romanization' and the construction of provincial society in the Roman period. The study of religion in the provinces has

---

[2] e.g. Rüpke 2016; Kindt 2012.

responded to wider theoretical developments with varying degrees of sophistication. The term 'Celtic', for instance, particularly when used to refer to the people of the British Isles, has been shown in recent decades to be primarily a modern construction, and it is not demonstrable archaeologically that the Iron Age peoples of western 'Celtic' Europe shared a coherent material culture, let alone a consistent ethnic identity.[3] As James has put it, 'even as a general cultural description rather than an ethnic term, "Celtic" is to be rejected because it brings an expectation of a single, universal, normative cultural model which does not fit the diverse evidence'.[4] The effects of rejecting a monolithic trans-Western Celtic paradigm have been seen in this book: by focusing on the careful tracing of not only the parallels, but also the differences, between the iconographies and the deities of the north-west provinces, the incontestable continental influences on monuments such as the temple of Sulis Minerva or the precinct 'altar' cease to be examples of the same simple story of Celtic artistic expression, but rather represent multifaceted and chronologically differentiated cross-Channel flows of artisans, artistic styles and techniques, and modes of religious expression. Yet 'Celtic' is still frequently used as a descriptor by some scholars, particularly for religious and artistic traditions, and the cultures of Britain and Gaul are still treated too often (although certainly not universally) as an undifferentiated whole.[5] In a related problem, some work on provincial religion has perhaps remained more prone to being concerned with origins, and with teasing out 'indigenous' religion from Roman, even as the wider scholarship has rightly moved away from using Romanization as a heuristic model for understanding provincial society.[6]

This is particularly clear with respect to the study of the so-called *interpretatio romana* and deities with syncretic double names (one name from the Roman pantheon and one 'indigenous'), a topic of particular relevance to the worship of Sulis Minerva at Bath. The phrase *interpretatio romana* is found in Tacitus's *Germania*, where it is used to equate two

---

[3] James 1999a; Koch 2007; Cunliffe 2011.   [4] James 1999a: 90.

[5] This approach finds its purest distillation in the writings of Aldhouse-Green (e.g. Green 1989; Green 1995; Green 1996; Aldhouse-Green 2004). For other recent instances in scholarship, see, e.g. Groh and Sedlmayer 2007, Watson 2007, and Adams 2009, in addition to much of the work in the various publications of the F.E.R.C.AN. (*Fontes Epigraphici Religionis Celticae Antiquae*) workshops (collected in the following volumes: Gorrochategui and de Bernardo Stempel 2004; Spickermann and Wiegels 2005; Hainzmann 2007; Haeussler and King 2008b; d'Encarnação 2008; Sartori 2008; Arenas-Esteban 2010).

[6] Haeussler and King 2008a: 7–11; Haeussler 2008.

Germanic gods with the Roman Castor and Pollux.[7] It was taken up by Georg Wissowa in the early twentieth century,[8] and in the century since then *interpretatio romana* has come to be an academic shorthand for the Roman habit of identifying the gods of other cultures with their own, and of bringing the worship of these foreign deities into Roman culture, transforming the gods and rituals into more familiar forms in the process. However, as Ando and Woolf have shown, the use of the Tacitean phrase in this way is problematic in 'the unreflective way in which Tacitus is made to serve its proponents',[9] particularly by ignoring the ways in which the phrase operates both within the wider discourse by Latin authors on the power of transformation through translation,[10] and within Tacitus's own complex engagement with 'foreign' religion and ethnography in the *Germania* itself.[11] Moreover, although the precise phrase is found only once in all of Latin literature, this classical origin nonetheless gives a possibly unintended legitimacy to modern models of religious change which invoke the term. Webster, to name one example, in several articles has stated that Tacitus defines the term in the *Germania*, as the 'interpretation of alien deities and of the rites associated with them' – giving the impression that the Tacitean passage contains a discussion of the theory behind *interpretatio*, which, as can be seen in note 7, it most certainly does not.[12] The attribution of this definition to Tacitus, however, serves, intentionally or not, to strengthen her arguments concerning *interpretatio* as a means of subjection by incoming Romans, by representing the practice as a more conscious one. Furthermore, as Derks has rightly pointed out, by using the phrase *interpretatio romana*, we prioritize Roman understandings and experiences over native ones, leading us 'whether or not intentionally, [to] hold the Roman authorities responsible for the associations'.[13] The solution is not, as some have done, to begin speaking of *interpretatio celtica*, or *gallica, punica, christiana, thracica*, or many others which have appeared in scholarship. Far from giving voice to the subaltern, these neologisms create a reductionist model of the

---

[7] *Apud Nahanarvalos antiquae religionis lucus ostenditur. Praesidet sacerdos muliebri ornatu, sed deos interpretatione romana Castorem Pollucemque memorant. ea vis numini, nomen Alcis. Nulla simulacra, nullum peregrinae superstitionis vestigium; ut fratres tamen, ut iuvenes venerantur.* 'In the land of the Nahanarvali is shown a grove, the seat of a prehistoric ritual. A priest presides in female dress, but the gods commemorated there are, according to *interpretatio romana*, Castor and Pollux. That, at least, is the power manifested by the godhead, whose name is Alci. There are no images, no trace of any foreign superstition, but nevertheless they worship these gods as brothers and young men.' (*Germ.* 43; translation after Ando 2005.)

[8] Wissowa 1916–19.   [9] Ando 2008: 45.   [10] Ando 2005; 2008.   [11] Woolf 2013: 135, 146.

[12] Webster 1995a: 153; 1995a: 175; 1997b: 331.   [13] Derks 1998: 100, n.103.

transformation and appropriation of deities in the ancient world, eliding the complex processes which must have been occurring in each time and place of cultural contact, and reducing them all to variants on a theme. For these reasons, *interpretatio romana* and its variants are terms I have consciously avoided in this book.

Discussions of *interpretatio romana* have often been bound up in the study of double-named deities, another area fraught with methodological difficulties. Divinity names in general have frequently been forced by scholars to carry more interpretative weight than they can easily bear. This is in part due to the fact that a large proportion of our evidence for Roman religion is epigraphic, and often little more information beyond the name of the deity can be gleaned from the text of an inscription. There are many gods in Roman Britain whom we know only from a few, or even a single, inscription. There has, therefore, been an understandable tendency to attempt to understand the nature and purview of these deities through linguistic analyses of their names.[14] Sulis Minerva at Bath has not escaped this. The name is presumed to be related to the Celtic root for 'eye', although other suggested links with Celtic words meaning 'sun' are considerably less likely.[15] Mars Leucetius and Nemetona, venerated at Bath by Peregrinus in *RIB* 140 and also worshiped on the continent, are another useful example: the etymology of Nemetona's name suggests an original affiliation with a sacred grove, while the epithet Leucetius does seem to be related both to the Celtic root meaning 'white' or 'shining', and to other deities found throughout the Celtic-speaking parts of western Europe whose names have Luc- or Lug-roots.[16] It is unclear, however, that these etymologies, even if correct, add greatly to our understandings of these deities. To use a modern example, if all a given individual knew about Christ is that the name means the 'Anointed One', he or she would be able to reconstruct very little of the story and significance of Jesus within Christianity. Meanwhile, it is far from clear that if worshipers in antiquity did understand a god's name as meaning something, they would have chosen the meaning which linguists have identified as etymologically correct. The frequent appearance of false etymologies in classical literary texts can serve as general proof of this. A further example

---

[14] e.g. Tolkien 1932 for Mars Nodens, Siegs in Bosanquet *et al.* 1922 for Mars Thincsus and the Alaisiagae, E. Birley 1986: 55–9 for Maponus, A. R. Birley 2008: 27–30 for Veteris/Hvitir, de Bernardo Stempel 2008 for British deities generally.

[15] Croon 1953: 81; Rivet and Smith 1979: 256; Cunliffe and Davenport 1985: 177; T. Meissner, pers. comm.

[16] Hutton 2011: 74. Hutton rightly points out, however, that this does not mean we can assume, as many have, that a coherent pan-Celtic deity lies behind the frequent appearance of this root.

can be cited from the Bath of our own days, in which contemporary pagans who revere Sulis translate her name as 'gap, opening, or orifice', a meaning which seems have come about through a confused understanding of 'eye' as a metaphor for the opening of the spring.[17] Overall, as Revell has discussed, a focus on deity names has too often led to simplistic dichotomies of Roman vs. native.[18] For example, Van Andringa's discussion of gods in Gaul, although learned, is hampered by a framework which relies on investigating the apparent transformation into the Roman Mercury, Apollo, Minerva, and Mars of the principal Gallic deities recorded by Julius Caesar.[19]

Furthermore, the use of double or syncretic names specifically is not straightforward. To begin with, within the epigraphic corpus dedications to gods with syncretic names are in fact quite rare: in Britain, for example, the number is around 8 per cent,[20] and in Lower Germany, less than 4 per cent.[21] Meanwhile, the processes which lead to the same end result – a deity with both a Roman and 'native' name – may vary significantly depending on context and geographical location. Derks and Zoll examining the same phenomenon of double-named deities in two different places, Hadrian's Wall and the regions around the northern Rhine, came to vastly different conclusions about the social mechanisms underlying double-naming in their respective study areas.[22] In Lower Germany, Derks argued that the preponderance of male gods equated with Mars and Hercules, and the lack of female double-named deities, was a consequence of martiality in local culture, and that local elites were for the most part responsible for the double-naming.[23] Similarly, for a second study area in Gallia Belgica he concluded that syncretic forms of Mars and Hercules in particular are the product of cults connected with various local *civitates* and *pagi*, and that the choice of Mars over Hercules by some groups, or vice versa, depended on aspects of those gods, specifically Mars's association with agriculture, and Hercules's with cattle, which would have appealed to the different types of farming and cattle-herding communities in the region.[24] Meanwhile, Zoll determined that epigraphic patterns not only on Hadrian's Wall but indeed in Britain more generally indicate that double-naming in the province was most often performed by members of the military, and does not usually represent an indigenous appropriation of incoming gods, at least when it comes to epigraphic practice.[25] Even the timing for such equations may vary. From Wissowa onwards, most studies have assumed

[17] Bowman 1998: 25.   [18] Revell 2011: 112–14.   [19] Van Andringa 2002: 133–53.
[20] Zoll 1994: 35.   [21] Extrapolated from Derks 1991: 243, Table 2.   [22] Derks 1991; Zoll 1994: 38.
[23] Derks 1991: 257.   [24] Derks 1998: 97, 102ff.   [25] Zoll 1994: 38–9; Zoll 1995: 136.

that the double-naming occurs at or soon after the initial encounter of a new god. However, at the sanctuary of Jupiter Poeninus on the Grand Saint Bernard pass, the god seems to have been equated with Jupiter only at the end of the first century AD, well after the Roman conquest of the area, and does not appear as Poeninus Jupiter Optimus Maximus until the second half of the second century.[26]

Examining the nature of Sulis Minerva at Bath reinforces the point that double-naming has little interpretative utility when examined in isolation, though somewhat more when placed into a wider ritual context. The equation of Sulis with Minerva at Bath seems to have been established at a very early period, judging by the presence of imagery related to the Roman goddess on the pediment of the temple. Solinus's description of the hot springs, presided over by Minerva, demonstrates that this equation was maintained at least through the third century. But who was doing the equating? The epigraphic record at Bath for use or non-use of the syncretic name shows no consistency with regard to social position or occupation. Of the three stone inscriptions recorded to Sulis Minerva, one (*RIB* 146) was dedicated by a soldier, the second (*RIB* 150) by Sulinus son of Maturus, possibly not a Roman citizen, and the third (*RIB* 141d) forms part of the inscription of the Façade of the Four Seasons, whose two known dedicants, Claudius Ligur[…] and Gaius Protacius […], are probably Roman citizens and members of an unidentified guild. Soldiers and their dependents show little inclination to use the syncretic name, even when, as we have seen, their dedications incorporate other very culturally Roman acts such as engagement with the imperial cult; this represents a counterpoint to the trend encountered by Zoll in the military zones of the north.[27]

Just as it is does not seem straightforward to divide preference for Sulis versus Sulis Minerva along socio-cultural lines, so a division according to place or ritual practice within the sanctuary is not apparent. At first glance, the temple may seem to emphasize aspects of Minerva, more so than any other area; this is especially true if the inscribed vessels from the reservoir, all of which record the syncretic name, were indeed used as temple plate, and if the bronze head of Minerva was the cult statue. Against this, however, is the fact that both of our inscriptions from priestly officials, L. Marcius Memor the *haruspex* and the *sacerdos* G. Calpurnius Receptus, whose tombstone (*RIB* 155) survives, list the goddess as Sulis. Meanwhile, the presence of both Sulis and Sulis Minerva in the tablets indicates that the incarnation of the goddess presiding over the hot spring was neither

[26] Wiblé 2013: 237.   [27] Zoll 1994.

necessarily syncretic nor non-syncretic. As discussed above, there are limitations to the conclusions we can draw from deity names, and this is obviously true in Sulis Minerva's case as well. A few tentative points may be suggested. The presence of Minerva imagery on the pediment may be linked to the apparent attempts to define the hot springs as a Roman space in its earliest period. The fact that, despite this, the priests honouring the goddess later on did not use the Roman name may be part of the same shift we see in the monumental iconography and architecture. Sulis, by that point long-worshiped in a Roman(o-British) setting, was a part of, rather than a threat to, Roman(o-British) society. Second (with the exception of the passage from Solinus), the goddess is never addressed simply as Minerva. The ubiquity of the presumably local (if not necessarily indigenous) name Sulis is perhaps a reflection of the way the local landscape is essential to the cult's existence, a point I have repeatedly stressed in this book.

A scholarly focus on syncretism, then, whether emphasizing deity names, iconography, or ritual strikes me in many ways as ultimately a provincializing red herring, which continuously leads us back to an over-emphasis both on 'Romanization' and on strict dichotomies between conceptually problematic 'pure' and 'original' forms. I would argue that we should instead embrace an understanding of provincial deities and their cults which focuses not on their role as markers of degrees of acculturation, but rather as part of the ubiquitous practice across the ancient world of understanding universal gods through local contexts – in other words, through the lens of connected localism which has been explored in Chapter 6. Such a shift in outlook does not entail a synchronic approach, which denies consideration of change. Indeed, if it is to be considered at all at Aquae Sulis, syncretism must be understood above all as a process, an on-going renegotiation and remixing of iconography, of the organization and use of ritual spaces, of votive choices, and even of the identities of worshipers, which begins rather than ends with that initial equation of Sulis with Minerva. *Who* (or what) is being syncretized with *whom* changes as Britain's own position in the empire changes and develops over time. Ritual paradigms which may have originated as a – perhaps uneasy – blending of Iron Age and Roman practices become normalized by the passage of time, and new concerns emerge: we pass from the aggressive appropriation of wild hot springs to the re-consecration of a profaned *locus religiosus*. In amongst all these, the next major religious renegotiation appears on the horizon: the choice will no longer be between Sulis or Minerva, but, as one tablet puts it, *gentilis* or *christianus*.[28]

---

[28] *Tab. Sulis* 98.

Moving Further: the Next Steps

If we are to build up a more nuanced understanding of the social function of religion in the Roman provinces, one which successfully depicts the ways in which diversity of religious experience and expression was connected to broader aspects of provincial life, then other sites can and must benefit from the sort of story-telling I have done for Bath. Uley, as another large Romano-British sanctuary site in the Cotswolds region, located some twenty miles north of Bath, is an obvious point of comparison with Aquae Sulis. Unlike at Bath, there is extensive evidence of pre-Roman Iron Age and even possibly Neolithic ritual use of the site.[29] Although the temples were of roughly the same size,[30] the built environment of the sanctuary at Uley was markedly different to that at Bath. It is not simply that the temples themselves are very different in plan, with Uley belonging to the 'Romano-Celtic' tradition of *cella* surrounded by ambulatory; the buildings which surround the principal temples also differ. While at Bath we have a range of monumental structures, some of which were likely to have been sacred precincts in their own right, at Uley there is little evidence either for monumentality or for other religious structures apart from the main temple. Indeed, the evidence from both excavation and geophysical survey seems to indicate that the temple was surrounded by a fairly ordinary settlement comprised of buildings used for domestic and industrial purposes, with the possible exception of a large structure which the excavators postulated served as a hostel for temple visitors.[31] Uley and Bath also occupy different positions in the natural landscape, with worship at Bath defined by a watery, confined valley setting, and Uley by the site's position on a hill with extensive views over the surrounding area.[32]

These differences make the similarities between Uley and Bath all the more interesting. Both are sites dedicated to a syncretic deity, although the Celtic name associated with Mercury at Uley remains elusive.[33] Uley and Bath are also the only sanctuary sites yet known from Britain where the deposition of tablets formed an important part of religious engagement with the god; the only two large assemblages of tablets from Britain come from these two sites. Given their proximity, did this practice spread from one sanctuary to the other, or did it reach them coincidentally through independent paths?

---

[29] Woodward and Leach 1993: 303–10.

[30] Including ambulatory, the temple at Uley measured 14 × 12 m, compared to 9 × 12 for the temple at Bath; the inner cella at Uley measured 7 × 8 m internally (Woodward and Leach 1993: 33).

[31] Woodward and Leach 1993: 314–15.   [32] Woodward and Leach 1993: 314, fig. 216.

[33] Tomlin 1993: 115.

Coventina's Well, outside the fort of Carrawburgh in Northumberland, is another locus of ritual activity which may benefit from fresh investigation. While a full analysis of the site is hampered by the fact that our records of the nineteenth century excavation of the well are incomplete[34] (in particular, we have very inadequate knowledge of the animal bone, which was discarded after excavation), certain questions, some of them raised by my analysis of Bath, are probably answerable. As discussed in Chapter 5, Coventina's Well represents the enclosure of a natural spring, with evidence for the ritual deposition of a wide variety of objects, and in particular a very large number of coins. At least 13,490 coins, and possibly as many as 16,000, were discovered when the well was emptied.[35] As at Aquae Sulis, coin deposition may well have been the most common way in which worshipers engaged with Coventina, yet so far the primary approach to the coin evidence has been numismatic.[36] Deeper analysis of the ritual aspect of coins at Carrawburgh is required. It also seems probable that closer analysis of the other votive material from the well might reveal patterns of depositional intention, in the same way my analysis of the ex-votos from the reservoir at Bath has. Furthermore, Coventina's Well's place within the wider ritual landscape at Carrawburgh, and even Hadrian's Wall itself, should be considered. The *mithraeum* at Carrawburgh is one of the best-excavated temples on Hadrian's Wall, and we have evidence for at least one other extra-mural shrine at the fort.[37] How would these various ritual *foci* have interacted, and what can their joint study teach us about the place of religion at the fort and its *vicus*?

Meanwhile, a large-scale, in-depth, study of religious practice at watery places in Roman Britain is long overdue. Activity at sites such as the river crossing at Piercebridge,[38] the temples at Springhead,[39] Coventina's Well, and others should be placed within the wider context of watery deposition in the province. At the same time, the goal should not be to create an overarching model of watery deposition, cobbled together from practices at different sites. On the contrary, as this book has shown, the principal interest lies in the rich variety of practice, and in the ways in which ritual engagement with water is affected by difference in cult and landscape. As Collingwood once put it, religion in Roman Britain was 'kaleidoscopic, fissiparous … a land fertile in [gods]'[40]: our scholarship should reflect that.

---

[34] Allason-Jones and McKay 1985: 1–2.   [35] Allason-Jones and McKay 1985: 50.

[36] Allason-Jones and McKay 1985: 50ff. Some of the flaws in McKay's approach were discussed by Casey 1989. Note, however, that Walton 2012: 157–61 has attempted a brief analysis of the coin profile of Coventina's Well in comparison with Bath and the riverine votive assemblage at Piercebridge.

[37] Richmond and Gillam 1951; Smith 1962.   [38] Walton 2008 and 2016;

[39] Andrews *et al.* 2011; Biddulph *et al.* 2011.   [40] Collingwood and Myres 1937: 269.

Finally, a word should be said about Buxton. Based on its Roman name, Aquae Arnemetiae, and the presence of warm springs at the town (28°C, a little more than half the temperature of the King's Spring), it has occasionally been suggested that Buxton, like Bath, may have been the site of a water sanctuary, possibly dedicated to a goddess Arnemetia, whose name would be related to the Celtic word *nemeton*, meaning grove;[41] an altar (*RIB* 281) to 'Arnomecta' has been found at the fort at Brough-on-Noe, a dozen or so miles from Buxton. However, the evidence for Roman occupation is very limited. The remains of a Roman bathhouse were sighted in the eighteenth century, and what may have been a temple podium was found in 1787.[42] Neither of these is now visible. Little has come to light since, although a possible votive deposit of 232 coins, 3 bracelets, and a wire clasp was found in 1975.[43] There was, therefore, clearly Roman activity at Buxton, but given the paucity of finds it is difficult to say anything about either its extent or its nature; I am loath to identify it as a water sanctuary based on the name alone. On the other hand, if Buxton were shown to be a hot spring site lacking in a sanctuary, that in itself would be significant and noteworthy.

What about Gaul? While there are certainly connections between ritual practice in parts of Britain and parts of Gaul, particularly northern Gaul, we should naturally err on the side of caution when it comes to religious homogeneity between the two provinces. When using Gallic sites as comparanda for British ones, or vice versa, we must be careful to prove connections, and be very alert to significant differences. In particular, we must never assume that a Gallic practice (or deity) must have been present in Britain, or again, vice versa, if there is no evidence for it, simply on the basis that the two provinces were culturally linked. On the other hand, given the ubiquity of water veneration on both sides of the Channel, a detailed comparison of practices at water sanctuaries in Gaul and Britain would be particularly worthwhile, especially given the amount of work which has been done by French scholars on these types of sites.[44] The similarities in votive deposition between Bath and Bourbonne-les-Bains, for example, as discussed in Chapter 5, render the differences in the layouts and general use of the two sites particularly compelling, and potentially fruitful for further study.

---

[41] Rivet and Smith 1979: 254–5; Burnham and Wacher 1990: 176.

[42] Rooke 1789; Haverfield 1905: 220–7; Burnham and Wacher 1990: 178.

[43] PastScape Monument Number 306059. L. Allason-Jones (pers. comm.), who is preparing the *CSIR* for Derbyshire, has confirmed that, while she has found a surprising amount of stonework and altars from other sites in the region (compared to what was previously known), there is no material whatsoever from Buxton itself.

[44] e.g. Formigé 1944; Grenier 1960: 477–955; Bayard and Cadoux 1982; Deyts 1983; Gros 1983; Roth-Congès and Gros 1983; Aupert 1991; Bourgeois 1991; Scheid 1991; Bourgeois 1992.

The End of Aquae Sulis

Rarely in this book have I been able to give changes at the sanctuary anything more than a very approximate date. The temple, reservoir, and almost certainly the baths were there from the first century onwards. Over the next several centuries, the story, in general terms, is one of increasing architectural elaboration and expansion, but the individual details will always remain elusive.

So it is, in some respects, with the end. We know that by the middle-to-late fourth century the inner precinct was beginning to be neglected. Mud and silt, probably from episodes of flooding, were building up, despite attempts to keep the area clear through repeated, though rough, re-cobbling.[45] At some point in this stage the temple must have been in disrepair, since pieces of its pediment were used in the repairs of the precinct floor.[46] Apparent hack-marks on the neck of the head of Sulis Minerva may suggest a deliberate dismantling. Carbon-dating done in the mid-2000s of animal bone from this phase (Periods 5d and 5e) has indicated that the final collapse of the reservoir enclosure, the last stage in the dilapidation of the central area of the sanctuary (Period 6), took place sometime between AD 450 and 500.[47] Why and how the enclosure collapsed we do not know. Guesses have ranged from earthquakes to deliberate destruction by the late antique Christian population.[48] What we do know is that by AD 500, the temple of Sulis Minerva and its precinct were no longer a usable place.

Gerrard has discussed the ways in which the end of Aquae Sulis might shed light on broader questions to do with the nature of social change in the fifth century, and narratives concerning the end of Roman Britain.[49] The evidence from Bath, limited though it is, supports broader readings of the religious culture of Britain at the time, which emphasize the lack of a clean demarcation between Christian and 'pagan' practices, or clear unequivocal rejections of the theologies and rituals of previous centuries:[50] even as the sanctuary's monumental structures began to decay, deposition at the King's Spring seems to have continued into the fifth century, as demonstrated by a small group of late fourth century clipped *siliquae*, which may represented a single hoard, and a penannular brooch datable to between 450 and 550.[51] Gerrard has wondered whether the final dismantling may have been deliberate, and 'the temple and baths, as a potent symbol of *Romanitas*, might have been a target in a world seeking to rid itself of memories of Rome'.[52] Might the end of the sanctuary have been a mirror image of its beginnings?

---

[45] Cunliffe and Davenport 1985: 66–72.   [46] Cunliffe and Davenport 1985: 185.
[47] Gerrard 2007: 155–9.   [48] Cunliffe 1983: 72.   [49] Gerrard 2007.   [50] Petts 2016: 675–6.
[51] Gerrard 2005; Gerrard 2007: 155.   [52] Gerrard 2007: 160.

Thus began the Middle Ages. By the late seventh century, a convent had been founded at Bath,[53] and from the eighth century the monastery of St Peter was growing in importance: its abbey would be the site of the coronation of Edgar, king of all England, in 973.[54] I have now returned to where I started in Chapter 1: with the rise of Bath in the medieval period as a great cathedral city, commercial centre, and, soon, a place of healing.

I opened this book with the legendary story of Bladud and his pigs. I would like to close with *The Ruin*, the Old English poem almost certainly inspired by the ruins of the reservoir around the spring:[55]

> 'Splendid is this masonry – the fates destroyed it;
> the strong buildings crashed, the work of giants moulders away.
> The roofs have fallen, the towers are in ruins,
> the barred gate is broken …
>
> … .there were bright buildings, many bathing halls,
> plenty of tall pinnacles, a great noise of people,
> many a banqueting-hall full of revelry
> – until Fate the mighty changed everything …
>
> … There stood buildings of stone; the stream threw forth
> a broad surging of hot water. A wall received all of it
> within its bright bosom, where in the centre,
> were the hot baths: that was convenient.' (*The Ruin, lines* 1–4; 21–4; 38–41)[56]

We love to tell tales about the past. Even this unknown Anglo-Saxon poet long ago looked on the ruins of Aquae Sulis and imagined what it had been like when it was full of life. So ended Roman Bath, and so began posterity's quest to recover it.

---

[53] Sim-Williams 1975: 3. The grant of land for the convent by the Hwicce king Osric in 675 is recorded in a twelfth century copy of the foundation charter, currently held in the Parker Library at Corpus Christi College, Cambridge (CCCC MS 111).

[54] Cunliffe 1986: 51–4; Davis and Bonsall 2006: 33.

[55] Cunliffe 1983 has analysed the poem in light of the archaeological evidence for Bath in the eighth or ninth century, when the poem was most likely composed.

[56] Translation from Cunliffe 1983: 75–6, after Mackie 1934.

Bibliography

Adams, J. N. (1992). 'British Latin: the text, interpretation and language of the Bath curse tablets.' *Britannia* 23: 1–26.

Adams, G. W. (2009). *Power and Religious Acculturation in Romano-Celtic Society: An examination of archaeological sites in Gloucestershire. BAR British Series* 477. Oxford: Archaeopress.

Aldhouse-Green, M. (2004). *An Archaeology of Images: Iconology and Cosmology in Iron Age and Roman Europe.* London: Routledge.

Alcock, J. P. (1966). 'Celtic water cults in Roman Britain.' *Archaeological Journal* 122: 1–12.

Aldhouse-Green, M. (2006). 'Healing shrines in "Celtic" Europe: cult, ritual, and material culture.' *Archäologische Anzeiger* 2006.1: 259–74.

Aldhouse-Green, M. (2012). '"Singing Stones": contexting body-language in Romano-British iconography'. *Britannia* 43: 115–34.

Alexander, W. H. (1952). 'The enquête on Seneca's treason.' *Classical Philology* 47.1: 1–6.

Allason-Jones, L. and B. McKay. (1985). *Coventina's Well: A Shrine on Hadrian's Wall.* Hexham: Trustees of the Clayton Collection, Chesters Museum.

Allen, M. (2018). 'Coins and the church in medieval England: votive and economic functions of money in religious contexts.' In M. Burström and T. Ingvardson, eds., 160–173.

Alston, R. (2002). *Soldiers and Society in Roman Egypt: A Social History.* London: Routledge.

Álvarez Martínez, J. M. and T. Nogales Basarrate. (1990). 'Schema urbain de Augusta Emerita: Le portique du forum.' *Akten des XIII. internationalen Kongresses für klassische Archäologie, Berlin 1988*, 336–8. Mainz: von Zabern.

Ando, C. (2005). '*Interpretatio romana.*' *Classical Philology* 100.1: 41–51.

Ando, C. (2008). *The Matter of the Gods: Religion and the Roman Empire.* Berkeley: University of California Press.

Andrews, P., E. Biddulph, A. Hardy, and R. Brown. (2011). *Settling the Ebbsfleet Valley: High Speed I Excavations at Springhead and Northfleet, Kent. The Late Iron Age, Roman, Saxon, and Medieval Landscape. Volume I: The Sites.* Oxford: Oxford Wessex Archaeology.

Andrews, P., and A. Smith. (2011). 'The development of Springhead.' In P. Andrews, E. Biddulph, A. Hardy and R. Brown (2011), 189–213.

Arenas-Esteban, J. A., ed. (2010). *Celtic Religion Across Space and Time: IX Workshop F.E.R.C.AN*. Toledo: Molina de Aragón.

Aquilué, X., X. Dupré, J. Massó, and J. Ruis de Arbulo. (1991). *Tarraco: Guía Arqueológica*. Tarragona: El Mèdol.

Aquilué Abadías, X. (2004). 'Arquitectura oficial.' In X. Dupré Raventós, ed. *Las Capitales Provinciales de Hispania 3: Tarragona: Colonia Iulia Urbs Triumphalis Tarraco*, 41–53. Rome: "L'Erma" di Bretschneider.

Aubin G. and J. Meissonier. (1994). 'L'usage de la monnaie sur les sites de sanctuaires de l'ouest de la Gaule et de la Bourgogne.' In C. Goudineau, I. Fauduet and G. Coulon, eds. (1994), 143–52.

Audollent, A. (1904). *Defixionum Tabellae*. Paris: Fontemoing.

Aupert, P. (1991). 'Les thermes comme lieux de culte.' In *Les Thermes Romains: Actes de la Table Ronde Organisé par l'Ecole française de Rome*, 185–92. Rome: Ecole Française de Rome.

Barrett, A. A. (1979). 'The career of Tiberius Claudius Cogidubnus.' *Britannia* 10: 227–42.

Barrett, J. C. (1997). 'Romanization: a critical comment.' In D. Mattingly, ed. (1997), 51–66.

Bassani, M. (2014a). 'Per un carta distributiva degli spazi sacri alle fonti curative.' In M. Annibaletto, M. Bassani and F. Ghedini, eds., *Cura, Preghiera e Benessere. Le Stazioni Curative Termominerali nell'Italia Romana*, 143–60. Padua: Padova University Press.

Bassani, M. (2014b). 'I santuari e i luoghi di culto presso le sorgenti termominerali.' In M. Annibaletto, M. Bassani and F. Ghedini, eds., *Cura, Preghiera e Benessere. Le Stazioni Curative Termominerali nell'Italia Romana*, 161–88. Padua: Padova University Press.

Bauchhenß, G. (1981). 'Die Iupitergigantensäulen in der römischen Provinz Germania Superior.' In G. Bauchenß and P. Noelke (1981), 3–262.

Bauchhenß, G. (1984a). *Die Grosse Iupitersäule aus Mainz. CSIR Deutschland II, 2*. Mainz: Verlag des Römische-Germanischen Zentralmuseums.

Bauchhenß, G. (1984b). *Denkmäler des Iuppiterkultes aus Mainz und Umbegung. CSIR Deutschland II,3*. Mainz: Verlag des Römische-Germanischen Zentralmuseums.

Bauchhenß, G. (2013). 'Füllhörner und andere Nebenseitenmotive.' In Hofeneder, A., P. de Bernardo Stempel, M. Hainzmann, and N. Mathieu, eds., *Théonymie celtique, cultes, « interpretatio » = Keltische Theonymie, Kulte, « interpretatio »*, 145–55. Vienna: Verl. der Österreichischen Akademie der Wissenschaften.

Bauchhenß, G. and P. Noelke. (1981). *Die Iupitersäulen in den germanischen Provinzen*. Cologne: Rheinland-Verlag.

Bayard, D. and J.-L. Cadoux. (1982). 'Les thermes du sanctuaire gallo-romain de Ribemont-sur-Ancre (Somme).' *Gallia* 40: 83–106.

Beagrie, N. (1989). 'The Romano-British pewter industry.' *Britannia* 20: 169–91.

Beard, M. (1985). 'Writing and ritual: a study of diversity and expansion in the Arval Acta.' *Papers of the British School at Rome* 53: 114–62.

Beard, M. (1991). '*Ancient Literacy* and the function of the written word in Roman religion.' In M. Beard *et al. Literacy in the Roman World*, 35–58. *Journal of Roman Archaeology Supplementary Series* 3. Ann Arbor: Journal of Roman Archaeology.

Beard, M., J. North and S. Price. (1998). *Religions of Rome*. Cambridge: Cambridge University Press.

Bémont, C. (1960). 'Rosmerta.' *Etudes Celtiques* 9: 29–43.

Bémont, C. (1969). 'A propos d'un nouveau monument de Rosmerta.' *Gallia* 27.1: 23–44.

Betz, A. (1943). 'Zum Sicherheitsdienst in den Provinzen.' *Wiener Jahreshefte* 35: col. 137–8.

Biddulph, E., R. S. Smith, and J. Schuster. (2011). *Settling the Ebbsfleet Valley: High Speed I Excavations at Springhead and Northfleet, Kent. The Late Iron Age, Roman, Saxon, and Medieval Landscape. Volume II: Late Iron Age to Roman Finds Reports*. Oxford: Oxford Wessex Archaeology.

Bird, S. (1991). 'The Roman roads around Bath.' In P. Davenport, ed. (1991), 138–46.

Birley, A. and A. R. Birley. (2010). 'A Dolichenum at Vindolanda.' *Archaeologia Aeliana Series 5* 39: 25–51.

Birley, A. R. (2005). *The Roman Government of Britain*. Oxford: Oxford University Press.

Birley, A. R. (2008). 'Some Germanic deities and their worshipers in the British frontier zone.' In H. Börm, N. Erhardt and J. Wiesehöfer, eds. *Monumentum Et Instrumentum Inscriptum: Beschriftete Objekte aus Kaiserzeit und Spatantike als historische Zeugnisse. Festschrift Fur Peter Weiss Zum 65. Geburtstag*, 23–38. Stuttgart: Franz Steiner.

Birley, A. R. (2011). '*RIB* III in its historical context.' *JRA* 24: 679–96.

Birley, E. (1986). 'The deities of Roman Britain.' *Aufstieg und Niedergang der Römischen Welt* II.18.1: 3–112. Berlin: De Gruyter.

Bishop, M. C. (1988). 'Cavalry equipment of the Roman army in the first century A.D.' In J. C. Coulston, ed. *Military Equipment and the Identity of Roman Soldiers*, 67–195. *BAR International Series* 394. Oxford: British Archaeological Reports.

Blagg, T. F. C. (1979). 'The date of the temple at Bath.' *Britannia* 10: 101–7.

Blagg, T. F. C. (1990). 'The temple at Bath (Aquae Sulis) in the context of classical temples in the west European provinces.' *JRA* 3: 419–30.

Blagg, T. F. C. (1996). 'The external decoration of Romano-British buildings.' In P. Johnson with I. Haynes, eds. *Architecture in Roman Britain*, 9–18. *CBA Research Report* 94. York: CBA.

Blagg, T. F. C. (2002). *Roman Architectural Ornament in Britain. BAR British Series* 329. Oxford: Archaeopress.

Blänsdorf, J. (2010). 'The texts from the *Fons Annae Perennae*.' In R. L. Gordon and F. M. Simòn, eds. (2010), 215–44.

Boon, G. (1983). 'Potters, oculists and eye-troubles.' *Britannia* 14: 1–12.

Borsay, A. (2004). 'Oliver, William (1695–1764)'. *Oxford Dictionary of National Biography*. Oxford: Oxford University Press.

Bosanquet, R. C. *et al.* (1922). 'On an altar to the Alaisiagae'. *Archaeologia Aeliana, Series 3* 19: 185–97.

Bossert, M. (1998). *Die Figürlichen Reliefs von Aventicum. CSIR Schweiz I.1. Cahiers d'Archéologie Romande* 69. Lausanne: Association Pro Aventico.

Boucher, S. (1976). *Recherches sur les Bronzes Figurés de Gaule Pré-romaine et Romaine*. Rome: Ecole française de Rome.

Bourgeois, C. (1991). *Divona I: Divinités et Ex-voto du Culte Gallo-romain de l'Eau*. Paris: Boccard.

Bourgeois, C. (1992). *Divona II: Monuments et Sanctuaires du Culte Gallo-romain de l'Eau*. Paris: Boccard.

Bowman, M. (1998). 'Belief, legend and perceptions of the sacred in contemporary Bath.' *Folklore* 109: 25–31.

Bowman, A. K. and J. D. Thomas. (1983). *Vindolanda: The Latin Writing Tablets*. Britannia Monograph Series 4. London: British Museum Press.

Bowman, A. K. and J. D. Thomas. (1994). *The Vindolanda Writing Tablets (Tabulae Vindolandenses II)*. London: British Museum Press.

Bowman, A. K. and J. D. Thomas. (2003). *The Vindolanda Writing Tablets (Tabulae Vindolandenses III)*. London: British Museum Press.

Bradley, R. (1998). *The Passage of Arms: An Archaeological Analysis of Prehistoric Hoard and Votive Deposits*, 2nd ed. Oxford: Oxbow.

Bradley, R. (2017). *A Geography of Offerings: Deposits of Valuables in the Landscapes of Ancient Europe*. Oxford: Oxbow.

Bradley, R., J. Lewis, D. Mullin, and N. Branch. (2015). '"Where Water Wells up from the Earth": excavations at the findspot of the late Bronze Age hoard from Broadward, Shropshire.' *The Antiquaries Journal* 95: 21–64.

Breeze, D., ed. (2012). *The First Souvenirs: Enamelled Vessels from Hadrian's Wall. Cumberland and Westmorland Antiquarian and Archaeological Society Extra Series* 37. Kendal: Cumberland and Westmorland Antiquarian and Archaeological Society.

Brewer, R. J. (1986). *Wales. CSIR Great Britain: Volume I, Fascicule 5*. Oxford: Oxford University Press.

Brown, L. (2007). 'Prehistoric pottery.' In P. Davenport, C. Poole, and D. Jordan (2007), 22–3.

Burnham, B. C. and J. Wacher. (1990). *The 'Small Towns' of Roman Britain*. London: B. T. Batsford.

Calder, W. M. (1912). 'Colonia Caesareia Antiocheia.' *JRS* 2: 79–109.

Carneiro, S. (2016). 'The water supply and drainage system of the Roman healing spa of Chaves (Aquae Flaviae)'. In J. M. Faílde Garrido, A. Formella, J. A. Fraiz

Brea, M. Gómez Gesteira, F. Pérez Losada, and V. Rodríguez Vázquez, eds., *Libro de Actas del I Congreso Internacional del Agua :"Termalismo y Calidad de Vida": Ourense (España), 23–24 de Septiembre de 2015*. Ourense: Universidade de Vigo.

Casey, P. J. (1989). 'Review of Allason-Jones and McKay (1985) and N. Crummy (1987)'. *Numismatic Chronicle* 149: 260–2.

Casey, P. J. and B. Hoffmann. (1999). 'Excavations at the Roman temple in Lydney Park, Gloucestershire in 1980 and 1981.' *Antiquaries Journal* 79: 81–144.

Chapman, E. M. (2005). *A Catalogue of Roman Military Equipment in the National Museum of Wales*. BAR British Series 388. Oxford: Archaeopress.

Chenery, C., G. Müldner, J. Evans, H. Eckardt, and M. Lewis. (2010). 'Strontium and stable isotope evidence for diet and mobility in Roman Gloucester, UK.' *Journal of Archaeological Science* 37: 150–63.

Chevallier, R., ed. (1992). *Les Eaux Thermales et les Cultes des Eaux en Gaule et dans les Provinces Voisines: Actes du Colloque 28–30 Septembre 1990, Aix-les-Bains. Caesarodunum* 26. Tours: Centres de recherches A. Piganiol.

Clark, J. (1994). 'Bladud of Bath: The archaeology of a legend.' *Folklore* 105: 39–50.

Clarke, S. (1997). 'Abandonment, rubbish disposal and 'special' deposits at Newstead.' In K. Meadows, C. Lemke and J. Heron, eds. *TRAC 96: Proceedings of the Sixth Annual Theoretical Roman Archaeology Conference, Sheffield 96,* 73–81. Oxford: Oxbow.

Clauss, M. (1999). *Kaiser und Gott: Herrscherkult im Römischen Reich*. Stuttgart: Teubner.

Clayton, J. (1880). 'Description of Roman Remains discovered near to Procolitia, a Station on the Wall of Hadrian.' *Archaeologia Aeliana, New Series* 8: 1–49.

Cooke, N. and D. Holman. (2011). 'Coins.' In E. Biddulph, R. Seager Smith, and J. Schuster (2011), 159–89.

Cool, H. E. M. (2006). *Eating and Drinking in Roman Britain*. Cambridge: Cambridge University Press.

Coleman, S. (2002). 'Do you believe in pilgrimage?: communitas, contestation and beyond.' *Anthropological Theory* 2.3: 355–68.

Coleman, S. and J. Elsner. (1995). *Pilgrimage Past and Present: Sacred Travel and Sacred Space in the World Religions*. London: British Museum.

Collingwood, R. G. (1934). *Roman Britain,* 2nd edition revised. Oxford: Clarendon Press.

Collingwood, R. G. and J. N. L. Myres. (1937). *Roman Britain and the English Settlements*, 2nd ed. Oxford: Clarendon Press.

Collingwood, R. G. and R. P. Wright. (1965). *The Roman Inscriptions of Britain*. Oxford: Clarendon Press.

Collins, R. (2008). 'Identity in the frontier: theory and multiple community interfacing.' In Fenwick C., M. Wiggins and D. Wythe, eds., *TRAC 2007: Proceedings of the Seventeenth Annual Theoretical Roman Archaeology Conference*, 45–52. Oxford: Oxbow.

Constans, L. A. (1921). *Arles Antique*. Paris: E. de Boccard.

Corney, M. (2007). 'Roman coins'. In P. Davenport, C. Poole, and D. Jordan (2007), 149–51.

Corot, H. (1933). 'Les bronzes d'art des sources de la Seine.' *Mémoires de la Commission des Antiquités du Département de la Côte d'Or* 20.1: 107–20.

Corot, H. (1934). 'La quatrième champagne de fouilles au temple des sources de la Seine.' *Revue Archéologique, 6e Série* 3: 196–8.

Cottam, S., D. Dungworth, S. Scott, and J. Taylor, eds. (1994). *TRAC 94: Proceedings of the Fourth Annual Theoretical Archaeology Conference, Durham 1994*. Oxford.

Coulston, J. C. and E. J. Phillips. (1988). *Hadrian's Wall West of the North Tyne, and Carlisle. CSIR Great Britain: Volume I, Fascicule 6*. Oxford: Oxford University Press.

Courtney, W. P. (2004). 'Oliver, William (*bap.* 1658, *d.* 1716)'. Revised by S. Glaser. *Oxford Dictionary of National Biography*. Oxford: Oxford University Press.

Cousins, E. H. (2014). 'Votive objects and ritual practice at the King's Spring at Bath.' In H. Platts, J. Pearce, C. Barron, J. Lundock, and J. Yoo, eds., *TRAC 2013: Proceedings of the Twenty-Third Theoretical Roman Archaeology Conference, King's College, London 2013*, 52–64. Oxford: Oxbow.

Cousins, E. H. (2016). 'An imperial image: The Bath Gorgon in context'. *Britannia* 47: 99–118.

Cowen, J. D. and I. A. Richmond. (1935). 'The Rudge cup.' *Archaeologia Aeliana, Series 4* 12: 310–42.

Crawford, M. (1970). 'Money and exchange in the Roman World.' *JRS* 60: 40–8.

Crawford, M. H., C. R. Ligota, and J. B. Trapp, eds. (1990). *Medals and Coins from Budé to Mommsen*. London: Warburg Institute, University of London.

Creighton, J. (2006). *Britannia: The Creation of a Roman Province*. London: Routledge.

Crickmore, J. (1984). *Romano-British Urban Defences. BAR British Series* 126. Oxford: BAR.

Cripps, W. J. (1900). 'A Roman altar and other sculptured stones found at Cirencester in April, 1899.' *Proceedings of the Society of Antiquaries Series 2* 18: 177–84.

Cronina, T., L. Downey, C. Synnott, and P. McSweeney. (2007). 'Composition of ancient Irish bog butter.' *International Dairy Journal* 17.9: 1011–20.

Crummy, N. (1983). *Colchester Archaeological Report 2: The Roman Small Finds from Excavations in Colchester, 1971–9*. Colchester: Colchester Archaeological Trust.

Crummy, N. (2012). 'Characterising the small finds assemblage from Silchester's Insula IX (1997–2009).' In M. Fulford, ed. *Silchester and the Study of Romano-British Urbanism*, 105–25. *JRA Supplementary Series* 90. Portsmouth, RI: Journal of Roman Archaeology.

Cunliffe, B. (1966). 'The Temple of Sulis Minerva at Bath.' *Antiquity* 40: 199–204.

Cunliffe, B. (1969). *Roman Bath*. Oxford: Society of Antiquaries of London.

Cunliffe, B. (1971). *Roman Bath Discovered*, 1st ed. London: Routledge & Kegan Paul.

Cunliffe, B. (1976). 'The Roman Baths at Bath: the excavations 1969–75.' *Britannia* 7: 1–32.

Cunliffe, B. (1979). *Excavations in Bath: 1950–1975*. Bristol: Committee for Rescue Archaeology in Avon, Gloucestershire and Somerset.

Cunliffe, B. (1980). 'The excavation at the Roman spring at Bath 1979: a preliminary description.' *Antiquaries Journal* 60: 187–206.

Cunliffe, B. (1983). 'Earth's grip holds them.' In B. Hartley and J. Wacher, eds. *Rome and Her Northern Provinces: Papers Presented to Sheppard Frere in Honour of His Retirement from the Chair of the Archaeology of the Roman Empire, University of Oxford, 1983*, 67–83. Gloucester: Alan Sutton.

Cunliffe, B. (1986). *The City of Bath*. Gloucester: Alan Sutton.

Cunliffe, B., ed. (1988). *The Temple of Sulis Minerva at Bath. Volume 2: The Finds from the Sacred Spring*. Oxford: Oxford University Committee for Archaeology.

Cunliffe, B. (1989). 'The Roman tholos from the sanctuary of Sulis Minerva at Bath, England.' In R. I. Curtis, ed. *Studia Pompeiana et Classica: In Honor of Wilhelmina F. Jashemski: Volume II: Classica*, 59–86. New Rochelle, NY: Aristide D. Caratzas.

Cunliffe, B. (1995). *Roman Bath*. London: Batsford/English Heritage.

Cunliffe, B. (2000). *Roman Bath Discovered*, 4th edition. Stroud: Tempus.

Cunliffe, B. (2005). *Iron Age Communities in Britain: An Account of England, Scotland and Wales from the Seventh Century BC Until the Roman Conquest*, 4th ed. London: Routledge.

Cunliffe, B. (2011). 'In the fabulous Celtic twilight.' In L. Bonfante, ed. *The Barbarians of Ancient Europe*, 190–210. Cambridge: Cambridge University Press.

Cunliffe, B., and P. Davenport. (1985). *The Temple of Sulis Minerva at Bath: Volume 1(I) The Site*. Oxford: Oxford University Committee for Archaeology.

Cunliffe, B. and M. Fulford. (1982). *Bath and the Rest of Wessex. CSIR Great Britain: Volume I, Fascicule 2*. Oxford: Oxford University Press.

Curteis, M. (2005). 'Ritual coin deposition on Iron Age settlements in the south Midlands.' In C. Haselgrove and D. Wigg-Wolf (2005), 207–25.

Dark, K. (1993). 'Town or "temenos"? A reinterpretation of the walled area of "Aquae Sulis".' *Britannia* 24: 254–5.

Davenport, P., ed. (1991a). *Archaeology in Bath: 1976–1985*. Oxford: Archaeopress.

Davenport, P. (1991b). 'Evidence for ritual activity in the temple precinct of Sulis Minerva.' In P. Davenport, ed. (1991), 146.

Davenport, P. (1994). 'Town and country: Roman Bath and its hinterland.' *Bath History* 5: 7–23.

Davenport, P., ed. (1999). *Archaeology in Bath: Excavations 1984–1989. BAR British Series* 284. Oxford: Archaeopress.

Davenport, P. (2000). '*Aquae Sulis*. The origins and development of a Roman town.' *Bath History* 8: 6–26.

Davenport, P. (2007). '"How Dare they Leave all this Unexcavated!": continuing to discover Roman Bath.' In C. Gosden, H. Hamerow, P. de Jersey, and G. Lock, eds. (2007), 404–25.

Davenport, P., C. Poole, and D. Jordan. (2007). *Archaeology in Bath: Excavations at the New Royal Baths (the Spa), and Bellott's Hospital 1998–1999*. Oxford: Oxbow for Oxford Archaeology.

Davidson, H. E. (1999). 'Milk and the northern goddess.' In S. Billington and M. J. Green, eds. *The Concept of the Goddess*, 105–24. London: Routledge.

Davis, C. E. (1872). 'Letter to the secretary of the Society of Antiquaries, London.' *Proceedings of the Society of Antiquaries of London Series 2*: 5: 281–2.

Davis, G. and P. Bonsall. (2006). *A History of Bath: Image and Reality*. Lancaster: Carnegie.

de Bernardo Stempel, P. (2008). 'Continuity, *translatio*, and *identificatio* in Romano-Celtic Britain.' In R. Haeussler and A. King eds. (2008), 67–82.

d'Encarnação, J., ed. (2008). *Divindades Indígenas em Análise: Actas do VII workshop FERCAN*. Coimbra: Centro de Estudos Arqueològicos.

de Jersey, P. (2005). 'Deliberate defacement of British Iron Age coinage.' In C. Haselgrove and D. Wigg-Wolf (2005), 85–113.

de la Barrera, J. L. (2000). *La Decoración Arquitectónica de los Foros de* Augusta Emerita.' Rome: L'Erma di Bretschneider.

de Sury, B. (1994). 'L'ex-voto d'après l'épigraphie: contribution à l'étude des sanctuaires.' In C. Goudineau, I. Faudet and G. Coulon, eds. (1994), 169–73.

Dearne, M. J. and K. Branigan. (1995). 'The use of coal in Roman Britain.' *Antiquaries Journal* 75: 71–106.

Deonna, W. (1926). 'Les collections lapidaires au Musée d'art et d'histoire.' *Genava* 4: 218–322.

Derks, T. (1991). 'The perception of the Roman pantheon by a native elite: the example of votive inscriptions from Lower Germany.' In N. Roymans and F. Theuws, eds. *Images of the Past: Studies on Ancient Societies in Northwestern Europe*, 235–66. Amsterdam: Instituut voor Pre- en Protohistorische Archaeologie Albert Egges van Giffen.

Derks, T. (1995). 'The ritual of the vow in Gallo-Roman religion.' In J. Metzler, M. Millett, N. Roymans, and J. Slofstra, eds. (1995), 111–27.

Derks, T. (1998). *Gods, Temples and Ritual Practices: The Transformation of Religious Ideas and Values in Roman Gaul*. Amsterdam: Amsterdam University Press.

Deyts, S. (1966). *Ex-Voto de Bois, de Pierre et de Bronze du Sanctuaire des Sources de la Seine: Art Celte et Gallo-romain*. Dijon: Musée Archéologique de Dijon.

Deyts, S. (1983). *Les Bois Sculptés des Sources de la Seine. Supplément Gallia 42*. Paris: Editions du Centre national de la Recherche scientifique.

Dillon, M. (1997). *Pilgrims and Pilgrimage in Ancient Greece*. London: Routledge.

Downey, L., C. Synnott, E. A. Kelly, and C. Stanton. (2006). 'Bog butter: dating profile and location.' *Archaeology Ireland* 20.1: 32–4.

Drury, P. J. (1984). 'The Temple of Claudius at Colchester reconsidered.' *Britannia* 15: 7–50.

Dupré i Raventós, X. (1990). 'Un gran complejo provincial de época flavia en Tarragona: aspectos cronológicos.' In W. Trillmich and P. Zanker, eds. (1990), 319–25.

Eade, J. and M. J. Sallnow. (1991a). *Contesting the Sacred: The Anthropology of Christian Pilgrimage*. London: Routledge.

Eade, J. and M. J. Sallnow. (1991b). 'Introduction.' In J. Eade and M. J. Sallnow, eds. (1991), 1–29.

Eckardt, H., C. Chenery, P. Booth, J. A. Evans, A. Lamb, and G. Müldner. (2009). 'Oxygen and strontium isotope evidence for mobility in Roman Winchester.' *Journal of Archaeological Science* 36: 2816–25.

Elsner, J. (2007). *Roman Eyes: Visuality and Subjectivity in Art and Text*. Princeton: Princeton University Press.

Elsner, J. (2017). 'Excavating Pilgrimage.' In Kristensen and Friese, eds. (2017), 265–74.

Elsner, J. and I. Rutherford, eds. (2005). *Pilgrimage in Graeco-Roman and Early Christian Antiquity: Seeing the Gods*. Oxford: Oxford University Press.

Englefield, H. C. (1792). 'Account of Antiquities discovered at Bath 1790.' *Archaeologia* 10: 325–33.

Ensoli, S. (1997). 'Clipei figurati dei Fori di età imperiale a Roma e nelle province occidentali. Da sigla apotropaica a simbolo di divinizzazione imperiale.' In Arce, J., S. Ensoli and E. La Rocca, eds. *Hispania Romana: Da Terra di Conquisto a Provincia dell'Impero*, 161–169. Milan: Electa.

Espérandieu, E. (1907–1938). *Recueil Général des Bas-reliefs de la Gaule Romaine*. Paris: Imprimerie national.

Fagan, G. (1996). 'The reliability of Roman building inscriptions.' *Papers of the British School at Rome* 64: 81–93.

Faraone, C. A. (1991). 'The agonistic context of early Greek binding spells.' In C. A. Faraone and D. Obbink, eds. (1991), 3–32.

Faraone, C. A. and D. Obbink, eds. (1991). *Magika Hiera: Ancient Greek Magic and Religion*. Oxford: Oxford University Press.

Fear, A. (2005). 'A journey to the end of the world.' In J. Elsner and I. Rutherford, eds. (2005), 319–32.

Fears, J. R. (1981). 'The Cult of Virtues and Roman Imperial Ideology.' *Aufstieg und Niedergang der Römischen Welt* II.17.2: 827–948.

Feeney, D. (1998). *Literature and Religion at Rome: Culture, Contexts, and Beliefs*. Cambridge: Cambridge University Press.

Fentress, E. W. B. (1979). *Numidia and the Roman Army. BAR International Series* 53. Oxford: BAR.

Fielder M. and C. Höpken. (2013). 'Rituelle deponierungen im Domnus und Domna-Heiligtum von Sarmizegetusa (Dakien).' In A. Schäfer and M. Witteyer, eds. (2013) 199–213.

Fishwick, D. (1969). 'The imperial *numen* in Roman Britain.' *JRS* 59: 76–91.

Fishwick, D. (1987–2005). *The Imperial Cult in the Latin West: Studies in the Ruler Cult of the Western Provinces of the Roman Empire (ICLW)*. Leiden: Brill.

Fitzpatrick, A. P. and P. R. Scott. (1999). 'The Roman bridge at Piercebridge, North Yorkshire-County Durham.' *Britannia* 30: 113–32.

Formige, J. (1944). 'Le sanctuaire de Sanxay.' *Gallia* 3: 44–97.

Franks, A. W. (1864–7). 'Remarks.' *Proceedings of the Society of Antiquaries, Second Series* 3: 343–4.

Freeman, P. W. M. (2007). *The Best Training Ground for Archaeologists: Francis Haverfield and the Invention of Romano-British Archaeology*. Oxford: Oxbow.

Frere, S. S. and R. S. O. Tomlin, eds. (1992). *The Roman Inscriptions of Britain. Volume II: Instrumentum Domesticum (Personal Belongings and the like). Fascicule 4*. Stroud: Alan Sutton.

Fuhrmann, C. J. (2012). *Policing the Roman Empire: Soldiers, Administration, and Public Order*. Oxford: Oxford University Press.

Fulford, M. (2001). 'Links with the past: pervasive "ritual" behaviour in Roman Britain.' *Britannia* 32: 199–218.

Gager, J. G., ed. (1992). *Curse Tablets and Binding Spells from the Ancient World*. New York: Oxford University Press.

Gardner, A. (2013). 'Thinking about Roman imperialism: postcolonialism, globalisation and beyond?' *Britannia* 44: 1–25.

Gassner, V. (2013). 'Die Grube G11 im Heiligtum des Iuppiter Heliopolitanus in den Canabae von Carnuntum – Zeunis eines grossen Festes oder "sacred rubbish"?' In A. Schäfer and M. Witteyer, eds. (2013), 259–78.

Geertz, C. (1966). 'Religion as a cultural system.' In M. Banton, *Anthropological Approaches to the Study of Religion*, 1–46. London: Tavistock.

Gerrard, J. (2005). 'A possible Late Roman silver "hoard" from Bath.' *Britannia* 36: 371–3.

Gerrard, J. (2007). 'The Temple of Sulis Minerva at Bath and the end of Roman Britain.' *Antiquaries Journal* 87: 148–64.

Gerrard, J. (2009). '"The Drapers" Gardens Hoard: a preliminary account.' *Britannia* 40: 163–84.

Ghey, E. (2008). 'Empty spaces or meaningful places? A broader perspective on continuity.' In R. Haeussler and A. King, eds. (2008), 19–30.

Goffman, E. (1961). *Asylums: Essays on the Social Situation of Mental Patients and other Inmates*. Garden City, NY: Anchor Books.

Goldberg, D. M. (2006). 'Fertile imaginations: pastoralist production and a new interpretation of a Roman period relief sculpture from Bath.' In B. Croxford, H. Goodchild, J. Lucas, and N. Ray, eds. *TRAC 2005: Proceedings of the*

Fifteenth Annual Theoretical Roman Archaeological Conference, Birmingham 2005, 83–98. Oxford: Oxbow.

González Soutelo, S. (2011). *El valor del agua en el mundo antiguo. Sistemas hidráulicos y aguas mineromedicinales en el context de la Galicia romana*. A Coruña: Fundación Barrié.

González Soutelo, S. (2014). 'Medicines and spas in the Roman period: the role of doctors in establishments with mineral-medicinal waters.' In D. Michaelides, ed., *Medicine and Healing in the Ancient Mediterranean World*, 206–16. Oxford: Oxbow.

Gordon, R. L. and F. M. Simón, eds. (2010). *Magical Practice in the Latin West: Papers from the International Conference held at the University of Zaragoza, 30 Sept.–1 Oct. 2005*. Leiden: Brill.

Gorrochategui, J. and P. de Bernardo Stempel, eds. (2004). *Die Kelten und ihre Religion in <edg>Spiegel der epigraphischen Quellen: Akten des 3. F.E.R.C.AN.-Workshops*. Vitoria-Gasteiz: Servicio Editorial de la Universidad del País Vasco.

Gosden, C., H. Hamerow, P. de Jersey, and G. Lock, eds. (2007). *Communities and Connections: Essays in Honour of Barry Cunliffe*. Oxford: Oxford University Press.

Goudineau, C., I. Faudet, and G. Coulon, eds. (1994). *Les Sanctuaires de Tradition Indigène en Gaule Romaine*. Paris: Editions Errance: Musée d'Argentomagus.

Gould, E. H. (2004). 'Pownall, Thomas (1722–1805)'. *Oxford Dictionary of National Biography*. Oxford: Oxford University Press.

Gradel, I. (2002). *Emperor Worship and Roman Religion*. Oxford: Oxford University Press.

Granino Cecere, M. G. (2000). "Contributo dell''epigrafia per la storia del santuario nemorense.' In J. R. Brandt, A-M. L. Touati and J. Zahle, eds., *Nemi – Status Quo: Recent Research at Nemi and the Sanctuary of Diana*, 35–44. Occasional Papers of the Nordic Institutes in Rome 1. Rome: L'Erma' di Bretschneider.

Green, E. (1890). 'Thoughts on Bath as a Roman city.' *Proceedings of the Bath Natural History and Antiquarian Field Club* 7: 114–26.

Green, M. (1976). *The Religions of Civilian Roman Britain. BAR British Series* 24. Oxford: BAR.

Green, M. (1989). *Symbol and Image in Celtic Religious Art*. London: Routledge.

Green, M. (1995). *Celtic Goddesses: Warriors, Virgins and Mothers*. London: British Museum.

Green, M. (1996). *Celtic Art: Reading the Messages*. London: Weidenfeld & Nicolson.

Grenier, A. (1960). *Manuel d'Archéologie gallo-romaine: Quatrième partie: Les monuments des eaux*. Paris: Picard.

Groh, S. and H. Sedlmayer, eds. (2007). *Blut und Wein: Keltish-römische Kultpraktiken. Akten des Kolloquiums am Frauenberg bei Leibnitz (A) im Mai 2006. Protohistoire européenne* 10. Montagnac: M. Mergoil.

Gros, P. (1983). 'Le sanctuaire des eaux à Nîmes: l'édifice sud: deuxième partie.' *Revue Archéologique du Centre de la France* 22.3: 162–72.

Guidott, T. (1676). *A discourse of Bathe, and the hot waters there*. London: Henry Brome.

Gurval, R. A. (1997). 'Caesar's comet: the politics and poetics of an Augustan myth.' *Memoirs of the American Academy in Rome* 42: 39–71.

Haack, M.-L. (2003). *Les Haruspices dans le Monde Romain*. Pessac: Ausonius.

Haack, M.-L. (2006). *Prosopographie des Haruspices Romains*. Pisa: Istituti editoriali e poligrafici internazionali.

Haeussler, R. (2008). 'The dynamics and contradictions of religious change in *Gallia Narbonensis.*' In R. Haeussler and A. C. Kings, eds. (2008), 81–102.

Haeussler, R. and A. C. King. (2008a). 'Introduction: the formation of Romano-Celtic religions.' In R. Haeussler and A. C. Kings, eds. (2008), 7–12.

Haeussler, R. and A. C. King, eds. (2008b). *Continuity and Innovation in Religion in the Roman West. JRA Supplementary Series* 67. Portsmouth, RI: Journal of Roman Archaeology.

Hainzmann, M., ed. (2007). *Auf den Spuren keltischer Götterverehrung: Akten des 5. F.E.R.C.AN.-Workshop*. Vienna: Verlag der Österreichischen Akademie der Wissenschaften.

Hanson, C. A. (2009). *The English Virtuoso: Art, Medicine, and Antiquarianism in the Age of Empiricism*. Chicago: University of Chicago Press.

Haselgrove, C. and D. Wigg-Wolf, eds. (2005a). *Iron Age Coinage and Ritual Practices*. Mainz: P. von Zabern.

Haselgrove, C. and D. Wigg-Wolf. (2005b). 'Introduction: Iron Age coinage and ritual practices.' In C. Haselgrove and D. Wigg-Wolf, eds. (2005), 9–22.

Hassall, M. W. C. (1980). 'Altars, curses and other epigraphic activity.' In W. Rodwell, ed. *Temples, Churches and Religion: Recent Research in Roman Britain. Part I.*, 79–89. *BAR British Series* 77. Oxford: BAR.

Hassall, M. W. C. and R. S. O. Tomlin. (1982). 'Roman Britain in 1981. Inscriptions.' *Britannia* 13: 396–422.

Hassall, M. W. C. and R. S. O. Tomlin. (1984). 'Roman Britain in 1983. Inscriptions.' *Britannia* 15: 333–56.

Hassall, M. W. C. and R. S. O. Tomlin. (1986). 'Roman Britain in 1985. Inscriptions.' *Britannia* 17: 428–54.

Hassall, M. W. C. and R. S. O. Tomlin. (1987). 'Roman Britain in 1986. Inscriptions.' *Britannia* 18: 360–77.

Hassall, M. W. C and R. S. O. Tomlin. (1988). 'Roman Britain in 1987. Inscriptions.' *Britannia* 19: 485–508.

Hassall, M. W. C and R. S. O. Tomlin. (1989). 'Roman Britain in 1988. Inscriptions.' *Britannia* 20: 327–45.

Hassall, M. W. C and R. S. O. Tomlin. (1992). 'Roman Britain in 1991. Inscriptions.' *Britannia* 23: 309–23.

Hassall, M. W. C and R. S. O. Tomlin. (1993). 'Roman Britain in 1992. Inscriptions.' *Britannia* 23: 310–22.

Hassall, M. W. C and R. S. O. Tomlin. (1994). 'Roman Britain in 1993. Inscriptions.' *Britannia* 25: 293–314.

Hassall, M. W. C and R. S. O. Tomlin. (1995). 'Roman Britain in 1994. Inscriptions.' *Britannia* 26: 371–90.

Hassall, M. W. C and R. S. O. Tomlin. (1996). 'Roman Britain in 1995. Inscriptions.' *Britannia* 27: 439–57.

Hassall, M. W. C and R. S. O. Tomlin. (1998). 'Roman Britain in 1997. Inscriptions.' *Britannia* 29: 433–45.

Hassall, M. W. C and R. S. O. Tomlin. (1999). 'Roman Britain in 1998. Inscriptions.' *Britannia* 30: 375–86.

Hassall, M. W. C and R. S. O. Tomlin. (2003). 'Roman Britain in 2002. Inscriptions.' *Britannia* 34: 361–82.

Hassall, M. W. C and R. S. O. Tomlin. (2004). 'Roman Britain in 2003. Inscriptions.' *Britannia* 35: 335–49.

Hauschild, T. (1972). 'Römische Konstruktionen auf der oberen Stadtterrasse des antiken Tarraco.' *Archivo Español de Arqueologia* 45: 3–44.

Haverfield, F. (1905). 'Romano-British Derbyshire'. In W. Page, ed., *Victoria History of the County of Derbyshire, Volume I*, 191–263. London: Archibald Constable.

Haverfield, F. (1906). 'Romano-British Somerset.' In W. Page, ed., *Victoria History of the County of Somerset, Volume I*, 207–371. London: Archibald Constable.

Haverfield, F. (1915). *The Romanization of Roman Britan*, 3rd edition. Oxford: Clarendon Press.

Haverfield, F. (1920). 'Roman Cirencester.' *Archaeologia* 69: 161–209.

Haverfield, F. and H. Stuart Jones. (1912). 'Some representative examples of Romano-British sculpture.' *JRS* 2: 121–52.

Haynes, I. (1999). 'Introduction: the Roman army as a community.' In A. Goldsworthy and I. Haynes, eds., *The Roman Army as a Community*, 7–14. *JRA Supplementary Series* 34. Portsmouth, RI: Journal of Roman Archaeology.

Hembry, P. (1990). *The English Spa: 1560–1815*. London: Athlone.

Hembry, P. (1997). *British Spas from 1815 to the Present Day: A Social History*. London: Athlone.

Henig, M. (1969). 'The gemstones from the main drain.' In B. Cunliffe (1969), 71–88.

Henig, M. (1978). *A Corpus of Roman Engraved Gemstones from British Site. BAR British Series* 8. Oxford: BAR.

Henig, M. (1984). *Religion in Roman Britain*. London: Batsford.

Henig, M. (1985). 'Graeco-Roman art and Romano-British imagination.' *Journal of the British Archaeological Association* 138: 1–22.

Henig, M. (1988). 'The small objects.' In B. Cunliffe, ed. (1988), 5–35.

Henig, M. (1992). 'The Bath gem-workshop: further discoveries.' *Oxford Journal of Archaeology* 11.2: 241–3.

Henig, M. (1993). *Roman Sculpture from the Cotswold Region with Devon and Cornwall. CSIR. Great Britain: Volume I, Fascicule 7*. Oxford: Oxford University Press.

Henig, M. (1995). *The Art of Roman Britain*. London: Batsford.

Henig, M. (1999). 'A new star shining over Bath.' *Oxford Journal of Archaeology* 18.4: 419–25.

Henig, M. (2000). 'From Classical Greece to Roman Britain: some Hellenic themes in provincial art and glyptics.' In G. R. Tsetskhladze, A. J. N. W. Prag and A. M. Snodgrass, eds., *Periplous: Papers on Classical Art and Archaeology Presented to Sir John Boardman*, 124–35. London: Thames & Hudson.

Henig, M. (2002). *The Heirs of King Verica*. Stroud: Tempus.

Henig, M. (2004). *Roman Sculpture from the North West Midland. CSIR Great Britain: Volume I, Fascicule 9*. Oxford: Oxford University Press.

Herklotz, I. (2007). 'Arnaldo Momigliano's "Ancient History and the Antiquarian": a critical review'. In P. N. Miller, ed., *Momigliano and Antiquarianism: Foundations of the Modern Cultural Sciences*, 127–53. Toronto: University of Toronto Press.

Heurgon, J. (1951). 'The Amiens Patera'. *JRS* 41: 22–4.

Heurgon, J. (1952). 'La patère d'Amiens'. *Monuments Piot* 46: 93–115.

Heyward, A. (1991). 'Lead, gout and Bath Spa Therapy.' In G. Kellaway, ed. (1991), 77–88.

Hicks, M. (2004). 'Warner, Richard (1763–1857).' *Oxford Dictionary of National Biography*. Oxford: Oxford University Press.

Hill, C., M. Millett, and T. F. C. Blagg. (1980). *The Roman Riverside Wall and Monumental Arch in London: Excavations at Baynard's Castle, Upper Thames Street, London 1974–6. London and Middlesex Archaeological Society*: Special Paper No. 3. London: London and Middlesex Archaeological Society.

Hill, J. D. (1995). *Ritual and Rubbish in the Iron Age in Wessex: A study on the formation of a specific archaeological record. BAR British Series* 242. Oxford: Tempus Reparatum.

Hind, J. (1996). 'Whose head on the Bath temple-pediment?' *Britannia* 27: 358–60.

Hingley, R. (2005). 'Iron Age "currency bars" in Britain: items of exchange in liminal contexts?' In C. Haselgrove and D. Wigg-Wolf, eds. (2005), 183–206.

Hofeneder, A. (2008). 'C. Iulius Solinus als Quelle für die keltische Religion.' In Sartori, A., ed. (2008), 135–66.

Holder, P. (2012). 'The inscriptions on the vessels.' In D. Breeze, ed. (2012), 65–70.

Holman, D. (2005). 'Iron Age coinage from Worth, Kent and other possible evidence of ritual deposition in Kent.' In C. Haselgrove and D. Wigg-Wolf, eds. (2005), 265–86.

Hölscher, T. (1967). *Victoria Romana: Archäologische Untersuchungen zur Geschichte und Wesenart der römischen Siegesgöttin von den Anfängen bis zum Ende des 3. Jhs. n. Chr.* Mainz: P. von Zabern.

Horne, P. D. (1986). 'Roman or Celtic temples? A case study.' In M. Henig and A. King, eds. *Pagan Gods and Shrines of the Roman Empire*, 15–24. Oxford: Oxford University Committee for Archaeology.

Houlbrook, C. (2018). 'Why money does grow on trees: The British coin-tree custom.' In Myrberg Burström and Tarnow Ingvardson, eds. (2018), 87–108.

Hull, M. R. (1958). *Roman Colchester*. Oxford: Oxford University Press for the
   Society of Antiquaries, London.

Howgego, C. (1992). 'The supply and use of money in the Roman world 200 B.C. to
   A.D. 300.' *JRS* 82: 1–31.

Huskinson, J. (1994). *Roman Sculpture from Eastern England. CSIR Great Britain:
   Volume I, Fascicule 8*. London: British Museum Publications.

Hutton, R. (2011). 'Medieval Welsh literature and pre-Christian deities.' *Cambrian
   Medieval Celtic Studies* 61: 57–86.

Irvine, J. T. Irvine Papers: unpublished manuscript notes, letters, and plans. Owned
   by National Museums of Scotland, held in Bath Central Library.

Irvine, J. T. (1873). 'Notes on the remains of the Roman temple and entrance hall to
   Roman Baths Found at Bath in 1790.' *JBAA* 29: 379–94.

Jackson, P. (2004). 'Scharf, Sir George (1820–1895).' *Oxford Dictionary of National
   Biography*. Oxford: Oxford University Press.

Jackson, R. (1990). 'A New collyrium stamp from Cambridge and a corrected
   reading of the stamp from Caistor-by-Norwich.' *Britannia* 21: 275–83.

Jackson, R. (2012). 'The Ilam Pan.' In D. Breeze, ed. (2012), 41–60.

Jackson Williams, K. (2017). 'Antiquarianism: a reinterpretation.' *Erudition and the
   Republic of Letters* 2: 56–96.

James, S. (1999a). *The Atlantic Celts: Ancient People or Modern Invention?* London:
   British Museum.

James, S. (1999b). 'The community of the soldiers: a major identity and centre
   of power in the Roman empire.' In P. Baker, S. Jundi, and R. Witcher, (eds),
   *TRAC 98: Proceedings of the Eighth Annual Theoretical Roman Archaeology
   Conference, Leicester 1998*, 14–25. Oxford: Oxbow.

James, S. (2001). 'Soldiers and civilians: identity and interaction in Roman
   Britain'. In S. James and M. Millett, eds., *Britons and Romans: Advancing an
   Archaeological Agenda*, 187–209. *CBA Research Report* 125. York: CBA.

Johns, C. (1994). 'Romano-British precious metal hoards: some comments on
   Martin Millett's paper.' In S. Cottam, D. Dungworth, S. Scott, and J. Taylor, eds.
   (1994), 107–17.

Jones, W. H. S. (1963). *Pliny: Natural History. With an English Translation in Ten
   Volumes. Volume VIII: Libri XXVIII-XXXII. Loeb Classical Library*. Cambridge,
   MA: Harvard University Press.

Jordan, D. R. (1985). 'A survey of Greek defixiones not included in the Special
   Corpora.' *Greek, Roman, and Byzantine Studies* 26.2: 151–98.

Jordan, D. R. (1990). 'Curses from the waters of Sulis.' *JRA* 3: 437–41.

Kamash, Z. (2008). 'What lies beneath? Perceptions of the ontological paradox of
   water.' *World Archaeology* 40.2: 224–37.

Kellaway, G. A. (1985). 'The geomorphology of the Bath region.' In B. Cunliffe and
   P. Davenport (1985), 4–8.

Kellaway, G. A., ed. (1991a). *Hot Springs of Bath: Investigations of the Thermal
   Waters of the Avon Valley*. Bath: Bath City Council.

Kellaway, G. A. (1991b). 'Preface.' In Kellaway, ed. (1991), 13–22.

Kelleher, R. (2018). 'Pilgrims, pennies and the ploughzone: folded coins in medieval Britain.' In Myrberg Burström and Tarnow Ingvardson, eds. (2018), 68–86.

Kemmers, F. (2018). 'Worthless?: the practice of depositing counterfeit coins in Roman votive contexts.' In Myrberg Burström and Tarnow Ingvardson, eds. (2018), 192–208.

Kemmers, F. and N. Myrberg. (2011). 'Rethinking numismatics. The archaeology of coins.' *Archaeological Dialogues* 18.1: 87–108.

Keune, J. (1914). 'Rosmerta'. In G. Wissowa, W. Kroll and K. Witte, eds. *Paulys Real-Encyclopädie der classischen Altertumswissenschaft. Zweite Reihe (R-Z), Erster Halbband Ra-Ryton*, 1129–46. Stuttgart: J. B. Metzlersche Verlagsbuchhandlung.

Kiernan, P. (2001). 'The ritual mutilation of coins on Romano-British Sites.' *British Numismatic Journal* 71: 18–33.

Kindt, J. (2012). *Rethinking Greek Religion.* Cambridge: Cambridge University Press.

King, A. (2005). 'Animal remains from temples in Roman Britain.' *Britannia* 36: 329–69.

King, A. C. (2008). 'Coins and coin hoards from Romano-Celtic temples in Britain.' In R. Haeussler and A. C. King, eds. (2008), Volume 2, 25–42.

Knowles, W. H. (1926). 'The Roman Baths at Bath; with an account of the excavations conducted during 1923.' *Archaeologia* LXXV: 1–18.

Koch, J. T. (2007). 'Mapping celticity, mapping celticization.' In C. Gosden, H. Hamerow, P. de Jersey, and G. Lock, eds. (2007), 263–86. Oxford.

Koppel, E. M. (1990). 'Relieves arquitectonicos de Tarragona.' In W. Trillmich and P. Zanker, eds. (1990), 327–40.

Kristensen, T. M. and W. Friese, eds. (2017). *Excavating Pilgrimage: Archaeological Approaches to Sacred Travel and Movement in the Ancient World.* London: Routledge.

Kropp, A. (2008). Defixiones: *Ein aktuelles Corpus lateinischer Fluchtafeln.* Speyer: Kartoffeldruck-Verlag Kai Brodersen.

Künzl, E. (2012). 'Enamelled vessels of Roman Britain.' In Breeze, ed. (2012), 9–22.

La Trobe-Bateman, E. and R. Niblett. (2016). *Bath: A Study of Settlement Around the Sacred Hot Springs from the Mesolithic to the 17th Century AD: An Archaeological Assessment.* Oxford: Oxbow.

Lambert, P.-Y. (2002). *Recueil des Inscriptions Gauloises (R.I.G.). Volume II, fascicule 2. Textes gallo-latins sur* Instrumentum. Paris: CNRS Editions.

Leach, S., M. Lewis, C. Chenery, G. Müldner, and H. Eckardt. (2009). 'Migration and diversity in Roman Britain: a multidisciplinary approach to the identification of immigrants in Roman York, England.' *American Journal of Physical Anthropology* 140: 546–61.

Le Clert, L. (1898). *Bronzes: Catalogue Descriptif et Raisonné.* Troyes: Musée de Troyes.

Le Glay, M. (1982). 'Remarques sur la notion de *Salus* dans la religion romaine.' In U. Bianchi and M. J. Vermaseren, eds. *La Soteriologia dei Culti Orientali nell'Impero Romano*, 427–44. Leiden: Brill.

Lee, R. (2009). *The Production, Use and Disposal of Romano-British Pewter Tableware. BAR British Series* 478. Oxford: Archaeopress.

Leibundgut, A. (1976). *Die Römischen Bronzen der Schweiz. II. Avenches*. Mainz: P. von Zabern.

Lehner, H. (1930). 'Römische Steindenkmäler von der Bonner Münsterkirche.' *Bonner Jahrbücher* 135: 1–48.

Levine, P. (1986). *The Amateur and the Professional: Antiquarians, Historians and Archaeologists in Victorian England, 1838–1886*. Cambridge: Cambridge University Press.

Levitan, B. (1993). 'Vertebrate remains.' In A. Woodward and P. Leach (1993), 257–301.

Linders, T. (1987). 'Gods, gifts, society.' In T. Linders and G. Nordquist, eds. *Gifts to the Gods: Proceedings of the Uppsala Symposium 1985*, 115–22. *Uppsala Studies in Ancient Mediterranean and Near Eastern Civilizations* 15. Uppsala: University of Uppsala.

Lysons, S. (1813). *Reliquiae Britannico-Romanae*. London: T. Bensley.

Mackie, W. S., ed. (1934). *The Exeter Book: An Anthology of Anglo-Saxon Poetry*. London: Early English Text Society.

Mann, R. Mann Papers: unpublished manuscript plans with accompanying notes. Held in the Library of the Society of Antiquaries of London.

Margary, I. D. (1967). *Roman Roads in Britain,* Revised Edition. London: Baker.

Marwood, M. A. (1988). *The Roman Cult of Salus. BAR International Series* 465. Oxford: BAR.

Martin-Kilcher, S. (2013). 'Deponierungen in römischen Heiligtümern: Thun-Allmendingen und Loreto Aprutino.' In A. Schäfer and M. Witteyer, eds. (2013), 215–32.

Mateos Cruz, P., and F. Palma Garcià. (2004). 'Arquitectura oficial.' In X. Dupré Raventós, ed. *Las capitales proviniciales de* Hispania *2: Mérida: Colonia Augusta Emerita*. Rome: L'Erma' di Bretschneider.

Mattingly, D., ed. (1997). *Dialogues in Roman imperialism: Power, discourse, and discrepant experience in the Roman Empire. JRA Supplementary Series* 23. Portsmouth, RI: Journal of Roman Archaeology.

Mattingly, D. (2004). 'Being Roman: expressing identity in a provincial setting.' *JRA* 17: 5–25.

Mattingly, D. (2006). *An Imperial Possession: Britain in the Roman Empire*. London: Penguin.

Mattingly, D. (2011). *Imperialism, Power, and Identity: Experiencing the Roman Empire*. Princeton: Princeton University Press.

McGowen, S. (2007). 'The 'Altar' of Sulis Minerva at Bath: rethinking the choice of deities'. In M. Henig and T. J. Smith, eds., Collectanea Antiqua: *Essays in*

Memory of Sonia Chadwick Hawkes, 81–90. BAR International Series 1673. Oxford: Archaeopress.

McGowen, S. L. (2010). *Sacred and Civic Stone Monuments of the Northwest Roman Provinces*. BAR International Series 2109. Oxford: Archaeopress.

McIntyre, G. (2016). *A Family of Gods: The Worship of the Imperial Family in the Latin West*. Ann Arbor: Michigan University Press.

Merrifield, R. (1987). *The Archaeology of Ritual and Magic*. London: Batsford.

Metzler, J., M. Millett, N. Roymans, and J. Slofstra, eds. (1995). *Integration in the Early Roman West: The Role of Culture and Ideology*. Luxembourg: Musée national d'histoire et d'art.

Millett, M. (1990). *The Romanization of Britain*. Cambridge: Cambridge University Press.

Millett, M. (1994). 'Treasure: interpreting Roman hoards.' In S. Cottam, D. Dungworth, S. Scott, and J. Taylor, eds. (1994), 99–106.

Millett, M. and D. Graham. (1986). *Excavations on the Romano-British small town at Neatham, Hampshire, 1969–1979*. Winchester.

Mommsen, T., ed. (1864). *C. Iulii Solini collectanea rerum memorabilium*. Berlin: Weidmann.

Morinis, A. (1992). 'Introduction: The territory of the anthropology of pilgrimage'. In A. Morinis, ed., *Sacred Journeys: the Anthropology of Pilgrimage*, 1–28. Westport: Greenwood Press.

Mullen, A. (2007a). 'Evidence for written Celtic from Roman Britain: a linguistic analysis of *Tabellae Sulis* 14 and 18.' *Studia Celtica* 41: 31–46.

Mullen, A. (2007b). 'Linguistic evidence for "Romanization": continuity and change in Romano-British onomastics: a study of the epigraphic record with particular reference to Bath.' *Britannia* 38: 35–61.

Müller, F. (2002). *Götter, Gaben, Rituale: Religion in der Frühgeschicte Europas*. Mainz: P. von Zabern.

Müller, F. (2006). 'Sakrale Untiefen. Die Spuren vorgeschichtlichen Kultes in Gewässern.' In A. Hafner, U. Niffeler and U. Ruoff, eds., *Die Neue Sicht: Unterwasserarchäologie und Geschichtsbild*, 110–21. Antiqua 40. Basel: Archäologie Schweiz.

Myrberg Burström, N. (2018). 'Introduction: faith and ritual materialised: coin finds in religious contexts.' In Myrberg Burström and Tarnow Ingvardson, eds. (2018), 1–10.

Myrberg Burström, N. and G. Tarnow Ingvardson, eds. (2018). *Divina Moneta: Coins in Religion and Ritual*. London: Routledge.

Naumann, R. (1937). *Der Quellbezirk von Nîmes*. Berlin: de Gruyter.

Neale, R. S. (1981). *Bath 1680–1850: A Social History, or, a Valley of Pleasure yet a Sink of Iniquity*. London: Routledge & Kegan Paul.

Noelke, P. (1981). 'Die Iupitersäulen und –pfeiler in der römischen Provinz Germania inferior.' In G. Bauchhenß and P. Noelke (1981), 267–515.

Nurse, B. (2004). 'Englefield, Sir Henry Charles, Seventh Baronet (*c*.1752–1822).' *Oxford Dictionary of National Biography*. Oxford: Oxford University Press.

O'Hare, J. P., A. Heywood, N. D. Millar, J. M. Evans, R. J. M. Corrall, and P. Dieppe. (1991). 'Physiology of immersion in thermal waters.' In Kellaway, ed. (1991), 71–6.

Oestigaard, T. (2011). 'Water.' In T. Insoll, ed., *The Oxford Handbook of the Archaeology of Ritual and Religion*, 38–50. Oxford: Oxford University Press.

Ogden, D. (2008). *Perseus*. London: Routledge.

Orme, B. (1974). 'Governor Pownall'. *Antiquity* 48: 116–24.

Piboule, A. and M. Piboule. 'Le culte des sources rurales en Bourbonnais.' In A. Pelletier, ed. (1985). *La Medicine en Gaule: Villes d'Eaux, Sanctuaires des Eaux*. Paris: Picard.

Pollard, S. (1985). 'Conservation of pewter objects from the Roman reservoir at Bath.' In G. Miles and S. Pollard, eds., *Lead and Tin: Studies in Conservation and Technology* 3, 57–63. London: United Kingdom Institute for Conservation.

Petsalis-Diomidis, A. (2010). *Truly Beyond Wonders: Aelius Aristides and the Cult of Asklepios*. Oxford: Oxford University Press.

Petts, D. (2016). 'Christianity in Roman Britain.' In M. Millett, L. Revell and A. Moore, eds., *The Oxford Handbook of Roman Britain*. Oxford: Oxford University Press.

Petsalis-Diomidis, A. (2010). *Truly Beyond Wonders: Aelius Aristides and the Cult of Asklepios*. Oxford: Oxford University Press.

Phillips, E. J. (1977). *Corbridge, Hadrian's Wall East of the North Tyne. CSIR Great Britain: Volume I, Fascicule 1*. Oxford: Oxford University Press.

Picard, G. (1974). 'Informations archéologiques: circonscription du centre.' *Gallia* 32.2: 299–317.

Piranomote, M. (2010). 'Religion and magic at Rome: the Fountain of Anna Perenna.' In R. L. Gordon and F. L. Simòn, eds. (2010), 191–213.

Piranomonte, M. (2013). 'Rome. The Anna Perenna Fountain, religious and magical rituals connected with water.' In A. Schäfer and M. Witteyer, eds. (2013), 151–66.

Piso, I. and G. Cupcea. (2014). 'Ein *centurio regionarius* aus der *legio X Fretensis* in Dakien.' *Tyche* 29: 115–23.

Potter, T. W. (1985). 'A Republican healing-sanctuary at Ponte di Nona near Rome and the classical tradition of votive medicine.' *Journal of the British Archaeological Association* 138: 23–47.

Poulton, R., and E. Scott. (1993). 'The hoarding, deposition and use of pewter in Roman Britain.' In E. Scott, ed. *Theoretical Roman Archaeology: First Conference Proceedings*. Aldershot: Avebury.

Pownall, T. (1795). *Descriptions and Explanations of Some Remains of Roman Antiquities Dug Up in the City of Bath, in the year MDCCXC*. Bath: Cruttwell.

Price, S. (1984). *Rituals and Power: The Roman Imperial Cult in Asia Minor.* Cambridge: Cambridge University Press.

Radnotí, A. (1941). 'Le camp romain et les monuments épigraphiques de Környe.' In *Laureae Aquincenses: Memoriae Valentini Kuzsinszky Dicatae, Volume I,* 91–105. Leipzig: O. Harrassovitz.

Rea, J. (1972) 'A lead tablet from Wanborough, Wilts.' In R. P. Wright and M. W. C. Hassall. 'Roman Britain in 1971. Inscriptions.' *Britannia* 3: 352–70.

Recke, M. (2013). 'Science as art: Etruscan anatomical votives.' In J. M. Turfa, ed. *The Etruscan World,* 1068–85. London: Routledge.

Reece, R. (1993). 'The coins.' In A. Woodward and P. Leach (1993), 80–7.

Reece, R. (2002). *The Coinage of Roman Britain.* Stroud.

Reinach, S. (1884). 'Les chiens dans le culte d'Esculape et les kelabim des stèles peintes de Citium'. *Revue Archéologique Troisième Série* 4: 129–35.

Revell, L. (2007). 'Religion and ritual in the western provinces.' *Greece & Rome* 54.2: 210–28.

Revell, L. (2009). *Roman Imperialism and Local Identities.* Cambridge: Cambridge University Press.

Richmond, I. A. (1945). 'The Sarmatae, *Bremetannacum Veteranorum* and the *Regio Bremetennacensis.*' *JRS* 35: 15–29.

Richmond, I. A. and J. P. Gillam. (1951). 'The Temple of Mithras at Carrawburgh.' *Archaeologia Aeliana, Series 4* 29: 1–92.

Richmond, I. A. and J. M. C. Toynbee. (1955). 'The Temple of Sulis-Minerva at Bath.' *JRS* 45: 97–105.

Ritchie. A. (2011). *A Shetland Antiquarian: James Thomas Irvine of Yell.* Lerwick: Shetland Amenity Trust.

Rives, J. (2007). *Religion in the Roman Empire.* Oxford: Oxford University Press.

Rivet, A. L. F. and C. Smith. (1979). *The Place-Names of Roman Britain.* London: Batsford.

Rolls, R. (1991). 'Quest for the quintessence.' In Kellaway, ed. (1991), 57–63.

Romeuf, A.-M. (2000). *Les Ex-voto Gallo-romains de Chamalières (Puy-de-Dôme): Bois Sculptés de la Source des Roches.* Paris: Editions de la Maison des sciences de l'homme.

Rooke, H. (1789). 'Account of a Roman Building and Camp lately discovered at Buxton, in the County of Derby.' *Archaeologia* 9: 137–40.

Root, J. (1994). 'Thomas Baldwin: his public career in Bath, 1775-1793'. *Bath History* 5: 80–103.

Ross, A. (1967). *Pagan Celtic Britain: Studies in Iconography and Tradition.* London: Routledge & Kegan Paul.

Roth-Congès, A. and P. Gros. (1983). 'Le sanctuaire des eaux à Nîmes. Le nymphée – Chapitre IV.' *Revue Archéologique du Centre de la France* 22.2: 131–46.

Rouquette, J.-M. and C. Sintès. (1989). *Arles Antique: Monuments et Sites.* Guides Archéologiques de la France. Paris: Ministère de la Culture, de la Communication, des Grans Travaux et du Bicentenaire.

Roymans, N. and J. Aarts. (2005). 'Coins, soldiers and the Batavian Hercules cult. Coin deposition at the sanctuary of Empel in the Lower Rhine region.' In C. Haselgrove and D. Wigg-Wolf, eds. (2005), 337–60.

Rüpke, J. (2007). *Religion of the Romans*. Gordon, R., trans. Cambridge: Cambridge University Press.

Rüpke, J. (2016). *On Roman Religion: Lived Religion and the Individual in Ancient Rome*. Ithaca: Cornell University Press.

Sallnow, M. J. (1987). *Pilgrims of the Andes: Regional Cults in Cuzco*. Washington, DC: Smithsonian Institution Press.

Sallnow, M. J. (1991). 'Pilgrimage and cultural fracture in the Andes.' In J. Eade and M. J. Sallnow, eds. (1991), 137–53.

Salway, P. (1981). *Roman Britain*. Oxford: Oxford University Press.

Sartori, A., ed. (2008). *Dedicanti e* Cultores *nelle Religioni Celtiche: VII Workshop F.E.R.C.AN., Gargnano del Garda (9–12 maggio 2007)*. Milan: Cisalpino.

Sauer, E. (1996). 'An Inscription from northern Italy, the Roman temple complex in Bath and Minerva as a healing goddess in Gallo-Roman religion.' *Oxford Journal of Archaeology* 15.1: 63–93.

Sauer, E. (2005). *Coins, Cult and Cultural Identity: Augustan Coins, Hot Springs and the Early Roman Baths at Bourbonne-les-Bains. Leicester Archaeology Monographs* 10. Leicester: University of Leicester, School of Archaeology and Ancient History.

Scarth, H. N. (1857). 'On Roman Remains at Bath.' *JBAA* 13: 257–73.

Scarth, H. N. (1862). 'On Roman Remains at Bath (Continued from Journal, March 1861, vol. xvii, p. 18).' *JBAA* 18: 289–305.

Scarth, H. N. (1864). *Aquae Solis*. London: Simpkin, Marshall.

Schäfer, A. (2013). 'Gruben als rituelle Räume: Das Fallbeispiel eines bakchischen Versammlungslokals in der *Colonia Aurelia Apulensis*'. In A. Schäfer and M. Witteyer, eds. (2013), 183–98.

Schäfer, A. and M. Witteyer, eds. (2013). *Rituelle Deponierungen in Heiligtümern der Hellenistisch-römischen Welt: Internationale Tagung Mainz. 28–30 April 2008. Mainzer Archäologischer Shriften* 10. Mainz: Generaldirektion Kulturelles Erbe, Direktion Landesarchäologie.

Scharf, G. (1855). 'Notes upon the Sculptures of a Temple discovered at Bath.' *Archaeologia* 36: 187–99.

Scheid, J. (1991). 'Sanctuaires et thermes sous l'Empire.' In *Les Thermes Romains: Actes de la table ronde organise par l'Ecole française de Rome*, 205–16. Rome: Ecole française de Rome.

Scheid, J. (1992). 'Épigraphie et sanctuaires guérisseurs en Gaule.' *Mélanges de l'École française de Rome 104*.1: 25–40.'

Schörner G. (2013). 'Stelenfelder und Deponierungen in Saturnheiligtümern NordAfrikas.' In A. Schäfer and M. Witteyer, eds. (2013), 171–82.

Schuster, J. (2011). 'Springhead Metalwork.' In In E. Biddulph, R. Seager Smith, and J. Schuster (2011), 189–291.

Sellwood, L. (1988). 'The Celtic coins.' In Cunliffe, ed. (1988), 279–80.

Shaw, B. (1983). 'Soldiers and society: the army in Numidia.' *OPUS* 2: 133–57.

Sims-Williams, P. (1975). 'Continental influence at Bath monastery in the seventh century.' *Anglo-Saxon England* 4: 1–10.

Smith, A. H. V. (1996). 'Provenance of coals from Roman sites in U.K. counties bordering River Severn and its estuary and including Wiltshire.' *Journal of Archaeological Science* 23: 373–89.

Smith, D. J. (1962). 'The shrine of the nymphs and the *genius loci* at Carrawburgh.' *Archaeologia Aeliana, Series 4* 40: 59–81.

Smith, R. S., K. M. Brown, and J. M. Mills. (2011). 'The pottery from Springhead.' In E. Biddulph, R. S. Smith and J. Schuster, eds. (2011), 1–133.

Speidel, M. P. (1984). 'Regionarii in Lower Moesia.' *ZPE* 57: 185–8.

Spickermann, W. and R. Wiegels, eds. (2005). *Keltische Götter in Römischen Reich: Akten des 4. Internationalen Workshops "Fontes Epigraphici Religionis Celticae Antiquae" (F.E.R.C.AN.)*. Möhnesee: Bibliopolis.

Stanton, W. I. (1991). 'Hydrogeology of the hot springs of Bath.' In Kellaway, ed. (1991), 127–42.

Strang, V. (2004). *The Meaning of Water*. Oxford: Berg.

Sunter, N. and D. Brown. (1988). 'Metal vessels.' In B. Cunliffe, ed. (1988), 9–21.

Sweet, R. (2004). *Antiquaries: The Discovery of the Past in Eighteenth-Century Britain*. London: Hambledon and London.

TED'A (Taller Escola d'Arqueologia de Tarragona). (1989). 'El foro provincial de Tarraco, un complejo arquitectónico de época flavia.' *Archivo Español de Arqueologia* 62: 141–91.

Thomas, E. and C. Witschel. (1992). 'Constructing reconstruction: claim and reality of Roman rebuilding inscriptions from the Latin West.' *Papers of the British School at Rome* 60: 135–77.

Todd, M. (2007). *Roman Mining in Somerset: Excavations at Charterhouse on Mendip 1993–1995*. Exeter: Mint Press.

Tolkien, J. R. R. (1932). 'The name 'Nodens''.' In R. E. M. Wheeler and T. V. Wheeler. (1932), 132–7.

Tomlin, R. S. O. (1988a). 'Inscriptions on metal vessels.' In B. Cunliffe, ed. (1988), 55–7.

Tomlin, R. S. O. (1988b). 'The curse tablets.' In B. Cunliffe, ed. (1988), 59–280.

Tomlin, R. S. O. (1991). 'Roman Britain in 1990. Inscriptions.' *Britannia* 22: 293–315.

Tomlin, R. S. O. (1992). 'Voices from the Sacred Spring.' *Bath History* 4: 7–24.

Tomlin, R. S. O. (1993). 'The inscribed lead tablets: an interim report.' In A. Woodward and P. Leach (1993), 113–30.

Tomlin, R. S. O. (1997). 'Roman Britain in 1996. Inscriptions.' *Britannia* 28: 455–72.

Tomlin, R. S. O. (2002). 'Writing to the gods in Britain.' In A. Cooley, ed. *Becoming Roman, Writing Latin?: Literacy and Epigraphy in the Roman West*, 165–79. *JRA Supplementary Series* 48. Portsmouth, RI: Journal of Roman Archaeology.

Tomlin, R. S. O. (2009). 'Roman Britain in 2008. Inscriptions'. *Britannia* 40: 313–63.

Tomlin, R. S. O. (2010). 'Cursing a Thief in Iberia and Britain.' In R. L. Gordon and F. M. Simón, eds. (2010), 245–73.

Tomlin, R. S. O., R. P. Wright, and M. W. C. Hassall. (2009). *The Roman Inscriptions of Britain, Volume 3*. Oxford: Oxford University Press.

Toynbee, J. M. C. (1964). *Art in Britain Under the Romans*. Oxford: Clarendon Press.

Travis, J. R. (2008). *Coal in Roman Britain. BAR British Series* 468. Oxford: Archaeopress.

Trigger, B. G. (2006). *A History of Archaeological Thought*, 2nd edition. Cambridge: Cambridge University Press.

Trillmich, W., Th. Hauschild, M. Blech, H. G. Niemeyer, A. Nünnerich-Asmus, and U. Kreilinger, eds. (1993). *Hispania Antiqua: Denkmäler der Römerzeit*. Mainz: P. von Zabern.

Trillmich, W. (1990). 'Colonia Augusta Emerita, die Haupstadt von Lusitanien.' In W. Trillmich and P. Zanker, eds. (1990), 299–318.

Trillmich, W. and P. Zanker, eds. (1990). *Stadtbild und Ideologie: Die Monumentalisierung hispanischer Städte zwischen Republik und Kaiserzeit*. Munich: Verlag der Bayerischen Akademie der Wissenschaften.

Tuffreau-Libre, M. (1994). 'La céramique dans les sanctuaires gallo-romains.' In C. Goudineau, I. Faudet and G. Coulon, eds. (1994), 128–37.

Turcan, R. (1996). 'La Promotion du sujet par le culte du souverain'. In A. Small, ed. *Subject and Ruler: The Cult of the Ruling Power in Classical Antiquity*, 51–62. *Journal of Roman Archaeology Supplementary Series* 17. Ann Arbor: Journal of Roman Archaeology.

Turner, E. G. (1963). 'A curse tablet from Nottinghamshire.' *JRS* 53: 122–4.

Turner, V. and E. Turner. (1978). *Image and Pilgrimage in Christian Culture: Anthropological Perspectives*. New York: Columbia University Press.

Van Andringa, W. (2002). *La Religion en Gaule Romaine: Piété et Politique (Ier – IIIe siècle apr. J.C.)*. Paris: Editions Errance.

Versnel, H. S. (1991). 'Beyond cursing: the appeal to justice in judicial prayers.' In C. A. Faraone and D. Obbink, eds. (1991), 60–106.

Versnel, H. S. (2004). 'Defixio.' In H. Cancik and H. Schneider, eds. *Brill's New Pauly: Antiquity*. Leiden: Brill.

Versnel, H. S. (2010). 'Prayers for justice, east and west: new finds and publications since 1990.' In R. L. Gordon and F. M. Simón, eds. (2010), 275–354. Leiden.

Verzàr, M. (1977). *Aventicum II: Un Temple du Culte Impérial*. Cahiers d'archéologie romande 12. Avenches: Association pro Aventico.

Vetters, H. (1952). 'Ein neues Denkmal des Sicherheitsdienstes in den Provinzen?' *Wiener Jahreshefte* 39: col. 105–6.

Veyrac, A. and J.-M. Pène. (1994–95). 'L'*Augusteum* de la fontaine de Nîmes: étude archéologique du bassin de la source et de la canalisation souterraine ouest.' *Revue Archéologique Narbonnaise* 27–28: 121–63.

Walker, D. (1988). 'The Roman coins.' In Cunliffe, ed. (1988), 281–358.

Walton, P. J. (2008). 'The finds from the river.' In H. E. M. Cool and D. J. P. Mason, eds. *Roman Piercebridge: Excavations by D. W. Harding and P. Scott 1969– 1981*, 286–293. *The Architectural and Archaeological Society of Durham and Northumberland Research Report* 7. Durham: Architectural and Archaeological Society of Durham and Northumberland.

Walton, P. J. (2012). *Rethinking Roman Britain: Coinage and Archaeology. Collection Moneta* 137. Wetteren: Moneta.

Walton, P. J. (2016). 'Was the Piercebridge assemblage a military assemblage?' *Journal of Roman Military Equipment Studies* 17: 191–4.

Ward, J. (1753–1754). 'An attempt to explain an antient roman inscription, cut upon a stone lately found at Bath.' *Philosophical Transactions* 48: 332–46.

Warner, R. (1797). *An Illustration of the Roman Antiquities Discovered at Bath*. Bath: W. Meyler.

Watson, A. (2007). *Religious Acculturation and Assimilation in* Belgic Gaul *and Aquitania from the Roman Conquest Until the End of the Second Century CE. BAR International Series* 1624. Oxford: Archaeopress.

Webster, J. (1995a). '*Interpretatio*: Roman word power and the Celtic gods.' *Britannia* 26: 153–61.

Webster, J. (1995b). 'Translation and subjection: interpretation and the Celtic gods.' In J. D. Hill and C. G. Cumberpatch, eds. *Different Iron Ages: Studies on the Iron Age in Temperate Europe*, 175–84. *BAR International Series* 602. Oxford: Tempus Reparatum.

Webster, J. (1997a). 'A negotiated syncretism: readings on the development of Romano-Celtic religion.' In D. Mattingly, ed. (1997), 165–85.

Webster, J. (1997b). 'Necessary comparisons: A post-colonial approach to religious syncretism in the Roman provinces.' *World Archaeology* 28.3: 324–38.

Wedlake, W. J. (1966). 'The City Walls of Bath, the Church of St James, South Gate, and the area to the east of the Church of St James.' *Proceedings of the Somersetshire Archaeological and Natural History Society* 110: 85–107.

Wedlake, W. J. (1979). 'Arlington Court, 1959-1960'. In B. Cunliffe, ed. (1979), 78–83.

Wedlake, W. J. (1982). *The Excavation of the Shrine of Apollo at Nettleton, Wiltshire, 1956–1971*. London: Society of Antiquaries of London.

Weinstock, S. (1971). *Divus Julius*. Oxford: Clarendon Press.

Wellington, I. (2005). 'Placing coinage and ritual sites in their archaeological contexts: the example of northern France.' In C. Haselgrove and D. Wigg-Wolf (2005), 227–45.

Wheeler, R. E. M. and T. V. Wheeler. (1932). *Report on the Excavation of the Prehistoric, Roman, and Post-Roman Site in Lydney Park, Gloucestershire. Reports of the Research Committee of the Society of Antiquaries of London* IX. Oxford: Society of Antiquaries of London.

Wiblé, F. (2013). 'Offrandes rituelles et dépôts de consécration en *Vallis Poenina* (Grand Saint-Bernard, Martigny, Leytron, Massongex)'. In A. Schäfer and M. Witteyer, eds. (2013), 233–58.

Wigg-Wolf, D. (2018). 'Death by deposition? Coins and ritual in the late Iron Age and early Roman transition in northern Gaul.' In Myrberg Burström and Tarnow Ingvardson, eds. (2018), 13–29.

Winkler, L. (1995). *Salus: vom Staatskult zur Politischen Idee*. Heidelberg: Verlag Archäologie und Geschichte.

Winwood, H. H. (1886). 'Upon some sculpture recently discovered at the Cross Bath.' *Proceedings of the Bath Field Club* 6: 79–84.

Wissowa, G. (1916–19). 'Interpretatio Romana: Römische Götter im Barbarenlande.' *Archiv für Religionswissenschaft* 19: 1–49.

Wood, J. (1765). *A Description of Bath*. London: W. Bathoe.

Woodward, A. and P. Leach. (1993). *The Uley Shrines: Excavation of a ritual complex on West Hill, Uley, Gloucestershire: 1977–9*. London: English Heritage.

Woolf, G. (1998). *Becoming Roman: The Origins of Provincial Civilization in Gaul*. Cambridge: Cambridge University Press.

Woolf, G. (2001). 'Representation as cult: the case of the Jupiter columns.' In W. Spickermann, H. Cancik and J. Rüpke, eds. *Religion in den germanischen Provinzen Roms*, 117–34. Tübingen: Mohr Siebeck.

Woolf, G. (2013). 'Ethnography and the Gods in Tacitus' *Germania*.' In E. Almagor and J. Skinner, eds. *Ancient Ethnography: New Approaches*, 133–52. London.

Wright, R. P. (1958). 'Roman Britain in 1957 – Inscriptions.' *JRS* 48: 130–55.

Wright, R. P. (1969). 'Roman Britain in 1968 – Inscriptions.' *JRS* 59: 198–246.

Wright, R. P. and M. W. C. Hassall. (1973). 'Roman Britain in 1972: Inscriptions.' *Britannia* 4: 324–45.

Wythe, D. (2008). 'Coin finds from 75 Roman temple sites in Britain.' In R. Haeussler and A. King, eds. (2008), 43–65.

Zanker, P. (1968). *Forum Augustum: das Bildprogramm*. Tübingen: Wasmuth.

Zanker, P. (1988). *The Power of Images in the Age of Augustus*. A. Shapiro, trans. Ann Arbor: University of Michigan Press.

Zienkiewicz, J. D. (1986). *The Legionary Fortress Baths at Caerleon: II. The Finds*. Cardiff: National Museum of Wales.

Zoll, A. (1994). 'Patterns of worship in Roman Britain: double-named deities in context.' In S. Cottam, D. Dungworth, S. Scott, and J. Taylor, eds. (1994), 33–44.

Zoll, A. (1995). 'A view through inscriptions: the epigraphic evidence for religion at Hadrian's Wall.' In J. Metzler, Millett, M., Roymans, N., and Slofstra, J., eds. (1995), 129–37.

Zuchtriegel, G. (2013). 'Eine begehbare Votivegrube mittelrepublikanischer Zeit in Gabii.' In A. Schäfer and M. Witteyer, eds. (2013), 167–70.

Index